MILLION DOLLAR BABY

MILLION DOLLAR BABY

An Intimate Portrait of Barbara Hutton

by
Philip Van Rensselaer

G. P. PUTNAM'S SONS
NEW YORK

Library of Congress Cataloging in Publication Data

Van Rensselaer, Philip.
  Million dollar baby.

  1. Hutton, Barbara. 2. Millionaires—United States—Biography. .I. Title.
CT275.H796V36   1979   973.9′092′4 [B]   79-18546
ISBN 0-399-12366-0

PRINTED IN THE UNITED STATES OF AMERICA

I would like to acknowledge several sources which helped me verify my memory of the facts of Barbara Hutton's life:

London Was Yesterday by Janet Flanner
The Million Dollar Studs by Alice-Leone Moats
How to Marry the Super Rich by Sheila Graham
The Very Rich, A History of Wealth by Joseph Thorndike, Jr.
Merman—An Autobiography by Ethel Merman
I Married the World by Elsa Maxwell
The Golden Studs by Alice-Leone Moats
The Power and the Glory by William Manchester
Who Killed Society? by Cleveland Amory
No Bed of Roses by Joan Fontaine
Life Is a Banquet by Rosalind Russell
Heiress by William Wright
The Daily News
The New York Times
Vogue
And Hartley Ramsay, who helped get all my
Hutton diaries in order.

Time magazine wrote in 1932: "To millions of U.S. newspaper readers, Barbara is a serial study, exciting, enviable, absurd, romantic, unreal."

And here it is.

PREFACE

Behind the stately columned facade of the Ritz, Barbara's history continued. I sat by the bedside, the newest prince consort in attendance.

"Grandpa Woolworth used to say, 'Barbara, you're going to be able to buy the whole world.' And Father always told me if I wanted anything to buy it and never count the cost."

"And did you?" I asked.

"I'm afraid I was the reverse of the American Dream. Both my father and grandfather were businessmen who reached the top of the money pyramid. But have you ever wondered what happened to their children? The inheritors?" She gave a mocking laugh, then reached for a gold box, took a pill, and swallowed it with some water. "My dear," she continued with irony, "you're looking at America's Dollar Princess—yes, that's what the press always called me, or the poor little rich girl. In any case, I was the backwash after a great ocean liner sank to the bottom of the sea; I was the flotsam that came to the surface, a drowning man if

9

you like, a desperate drowning man struggling to survive in a raging sea.''

''Did you survive?'' I asked.

''I don't know,'' she laughed. ''That's for you to decide,'' she replied with a resentful expression.

So began Barbara Hutton's story on those rainy autumn days in her splendid apartment at the Ritz Hôtel. Her tall windows overlooked the traffic at the Place Vendôme, but the stone walls were so thick that we never heard a sound. The weird and discordant strains of Japanese music played in the background. Exotic incense reminiscent of jasmine nights in Tangier burned behind a lacquered screen. Adding to the luxuriousness of the setting, Barbara's amazing collection of jewelry was spread out over the ivory lace coverlet on her enormous bed. These emeralds, sapphires, rubies, and pearls were gemstones with historical backgrounds. Barbara was particularly fond of running Marie Antoinette's pearls through her fingers.

Now on the dim rainy afternoon she was playing with these pearls while the incense burned and the Japanese chant droned. ''Well, my dear,'' she continued, ''I inherited everything but love, I've always been searching for it because I didn't know what it was. Have you ever had it?''

''I'm still searching,'' I replied.

Her extraordinarily large blue eyes gazed at me wistfully from under her heavy black brows. I felt we'd connected, took her hand.

''After my mother died, Grandpa Woolworth took me in,'' Barbara continued in her gentle voice. ''By then he was a little loony but he was sweet to me; his houses on Fifth Avenue and in Glen Cove were horrors—the country house modeled after Versailles, all white marble and gloom, and the Fifth Avenue one all stained glass and medieval tapestries—both pure Robber Baron although I must confess grandpa was not a Robber Baron. He was a country boy who had strong genes and vigor which I have inherited, thank God. But I was glutted with privilege, softened by luxury, weakened by indulgent nannies, and made to feel special by all my governesses and chauffeurs and personal maids. When you inherit as much money as I did, it destroys whatever incentive or goal you might have.''

"Didn't you want anything?''

"No," she replied. "I just wanted to get even with my father.''

"So you self-destructed?'' I asked.

"Did I ever!''

She shot me an angry glance, so angry that I felt disturbed. Her fine red lips drooped savagely at the corners. Uneasily, I moved in my Louis Quinze chair by her bedside.

"I'm not boring you, am I, Philip dear?''

"No, the story of your life is far more exciting than any movie, play, or novel. And what an escape for me!''

This rather pleased the frail woman lying in the immense French bed. "So you like to escape, too?''

"Escape is the story of my life,'' I said.

"Well, we have a lot in common,'' she said. "It seems as if I've known you forever.'' She gave me her lovely smile.

"You've always been a favorite of mine,'' I told her. "I thought you were so beautiful when you were married to Cary Grant.''

"I'm not beautiful anymore,'' she smiled. "But you are.''

"Of course you are,'' I said enthusiastically.

"My jewels are a great comfort to me,'' she said. "Sometimes I lie here for weeks at a time and just have these boxes of jewelry brought up from the safe downstairs. My friends say that I'm retreating too much; Ticki my old governess says that it's very unhealthful to withdraw from the current of life as I do. But being solitary is the only way that I protect my sanity. Do you know what I mean?''

"Yes, I do,'' I said, nodding grimly.

We smiled at each other and felt comforted.

Presently she said, "Let's have a drink. Yes, we'll toast Grandpa Woolworth. It will help to dispel the rain and the phantoms. Oh Philip, I am so overjoyed we met in Venice, aren't you? I mean, I don't feel I'm drowning anymore, do you? Oh I hope you can save me.''

"From what?''

"From myself. Aren't we our own worst enemies? . . .''

"Indeed we are!'' Another warm current passed between us.

Barbara Hutton and I had been drawn to each other when we met in Venice in late August 1957. As Barbara said, we were like two drowning people desperately grabbing at any rope that someone might throw us. In that period together we both hoped to be each other's savior.

It had been raining without stop in Paris that fall and Barbara's vast apartment was melancholy in the half light. She did not want to get out of bed. She felt if she did she would get into more trouble. And trouble was one thing she'd had plenty of. Trouble with men, that is. When I knew her she was unhappily married to her sixth husband, a German tennis ace called Baron Gottfried von Cramm, and newspapers would soon call me Lucky Seven. Be that as it may, I was fond of her and growing more fond of her each passing day. There was something strange and disturbing about such a beautiful and charming woman suffering in incredible luxury as she was. She always said to me that she was born to suffer. Well, the bed was a safe place from the demons around her.

How I looked forward to coming into the glittering lobby of the Ritz every day at lunch time and running down the long corridor that led to the double doors of her drawing room. Here were the enormous Louis Vuitton wardrobe and steamer trunks; some were stamped Mrs. Cary Grant, some were stamped Princess Mdivani or Princess Troubetzkoy with an elaborate coronet on top; others were stamped Countess Haugwitz-Reventlow, and still others were stamped Madame Rubirosa or bore her latest name and title, Baroness von Cramm.

When I was a teenager at boarding school, Churchill and de Gaulle were heroes and Vivien Leigh, Greta Garbo, and Barbara Hutton were my favorite heroines. Barbara was radiant in those long-ago days. Now it took a great deal of love and attention on my part to restore that look of radiance.

"People have always said I had everything," Barbara continued, lighting a cigarette and inhaling deeply. "I was beautiful and I was rich, although both of these things are only temporary. The thing that matters is that I've survived, God knows *why* I've survived," she went on. "Sometimes I like to think there must be a reason for my existence. Perhaps my story will help you not to make the same mistakes I've made. For I've made many mistakes and in the world's eyes I am a failure."

"No, you're not," I said tenderly, moved by her look of tragedy.

"Don't be polite, Philip dear. We've all been brought up to be too polite, and politeness just masks our real feelings. Certainly, my dear, you don't have to stand on ceremony with me."

I liked her for saying that and took her hand and kissed it.

She stared thoughtfully at my face. "The cards were stacked against me from the very beginning, I'm afraid."

"How so?" I asked, my eyes never leaving hers.

"From the very beginning I was a pawn, never allowed to be comforted by any reality; great wealth is dehumanizing, you know—or you'll soon know. In any case, my debut in 1930 was a terrible slap in everybody's face. My father never should have thrown such an elaborate party for me during the Depression, for the press picked up on it and made me a sitting duck. Very definitely my life began on the wrong foot like so many young people with no values or standards. Perhaps when people know the details of my life they won't judge me so harshly. I'm really quite like a heroine of Tennessee Williams, lonely, vulnerable, overly sensitive, and my history is one of damages, loss, and corruption. Long ago, if you can believe it, I was an open, imitative child; I merely formed my ideas from what I saw around me. Doesn't every child?"

"I certainly did. I copied my mother completely."

"If I was incapable of love," said Barbara, gazing at me in a melancholy way, "it was because I saw no love around me.

Mother died when I was four and father was merely bored by my presence and pushed me at an early age into boarding school to get rid of me. As I've said, he never gave me any love or attention, but he dumped a lot of money in my lap when I was twenty-one, and the thing that's motivated me all these years is spending all this money, this root of all evil, to get even with him. Of course getting even with someone only hurts you. But how was I to know that when I was eighteen? Eighteen! Sometimes I can't believe that I was so young and wide-eyed—although of course I was tainted and corrupt even then and sick in spirit, too. But a young pretty face covers up all that very nicely. Well, to make a long story short, Rudy Vallee sang at my debut, he was the Frank Sinatra of my day, and as the three orchestras played at my party for over a thousand people, and scrambled eggs, champagne and caviar were served at eight in the morning, there were bread lines and soup kitchens just around the corner. You can imagine how very popular I was with the American people—''

MILLION DOLLAR BABY

CHAPTER 1

Four million people were out of work in 1930, forty percent of the nation's farms were mortgaged. Tabloids all over America had a field day with the event of Barbara Hutton's New York debut in December 1930. A month before her sensational debut Miss Hutton had celebrated her eighteenth birthday. At the height of the Depression, the news was out that she was soon to inherit $45,000,000 tax-free. Her extravagant coming-out party started the career of an American phenomenon.

MISS BARBARA HUTTON WILL BOW TO SOCIETY
AT $60,000 PARTY AT THE HOTEL RITZ

blazed the *New York Sun.*

RICHEST GIRL IN THE WORLD COMES OUT
TONIGHT AT FABULOUS RITZ DINNER DANCE!

the *New York Mirror* clamored.

17

MILLION DOLLAR BABY FROM THE FIVE & TEN CENT
STORES INTRODUCED TO 'STUFFED SHIRTS' TONIGHT
AT $100,000 BASH. RUDY VALLEE WILL SING AND AR-
GENTINE DANCERS WILL PERFORM AMIDST BOWER OF
ORCHIDS AND GARDENIAS

headlined the *New York Evening Post*.

Outside the french windows of the Ritz Hotel festive yellow
lights fell on the snowy streets. Jazz music drifted out and Rudy
Vallee's voice was seductive, sugary. Opulent black town cars
drew up before the hotel. One thousand people had been invited
to this much-talked-about party. Half the guests were debutantes
and college boys, the other half were parents of the above-mentioned youths, the aristocracy of Boston, Philadelphia, and
Washington, not to mention a sprinkling of good titles from London, Paris, and Rome.

Several thousand people were held back by police lines at the
awning of the Ritz on 46th Street and Madison Avenue. Through
this freezing cold night, the Depression crowds would endure any
torment to see the plump and pretty ''Dollar Princess''—Miss
Barbara Hutton. In these dreary times she had captured the imagination of the American public. She symbolized freedom and un-
limited extravagance. What wouldn't they give to have her inherited money! Oh, to be free from rent evictions and slavery to a
hateful job! Miss Hutton was above all the sordid problems of ev-
eryday folk. Freedom she had, blessed freedom—to do what she
wanted; she had choices; they didn't.

Now at eight o'clock these hungry, poorly dressed people were
watching the limousines unload the dazzling Hutton guests. How
weary, cynical, and unconcerned were these faces of rich people.
The Harvard, Yale, and Princeton boys strode arrogantly out in
white tie and tails while fresh-faced girls from Brearley, Farmington, and Hewitts in their fresh white dresses and ermine coats
stepped gingerly through the slush in their fragile satin shoes.
One observer noted that it was a pity to think the young kids
would grow up to be as snobbish as their mothers and fathers.

The New York *Sun* observed:

Even the decks of that great new ocean liner, the *Titanic*, didn't blaze as brilliantly as the french windows of the Hotel Ritz on the occasion of Barbara Hutton's debut.

And prophetically they added:

The *Titanic* raced carelessly over the wintery seas while ahead lay the iceberg that was to rip a great slash in the liner's hull and cause it to sink to the bottom of the ocean some twelve thousand feet below. The debutante herself made quite a brilliant spectacle in her white satin and pearls. Miss Hutton, along with her aunt and uncle, Mr. and Mrs. Edward F. Hutton, were the first to arrive. Mrs. Hutton was the former Marjorie Merriweather Post.

Miss Barbara Hutton is the only child of Mr. Franklyn Laws Hutton. Miss Hutton's mother was Edna Woolworth, one of the three daughters of Mr. Frank Winfield Woolworth. Mr. Woolworth was the founder of the chain of five-and-ten-cent stores that bear his name all over the United States. There are some stores even in Great Britain. Miss Hutton's fortune is said to be somewhere between forty and fifty million dollars, which puts her in the league with another debutante of the season, Miss Doris Duke. The only other debutante that might rival Miss Hutton and Miss Duke is Miss Alisa Mellon. In any case, let's hope Miss Hutton fares better than the *S.S. Titanic* on her maiden voyage.

The conservative *Herald Tribune* reported that:

The Ritz Ballroom has been transformed into a costly bower of flowers and trees. Silver birches and pink and white roses had been planted in the corners of the cream and gold pillared room. Bowls of gardenias and roses were at all the supper tables. Mrs. Edward Hutton was a great admirer of white lilac and American Beauty roses, so there were many lavish bouquets at the older people's tables. Miss Hutton herself favored the silver birches; she said she greatly admired their beauty. Three orchestras played until daybreak and many famous performers sang and danced.

At nine in the morning the guests began to depart; the long line of Packards, Cadillacs, and Rolls-Royces carried their load back to apartments on Fifth and Park avenues.

The soft pink light of day was beginning to streak through the gray, wintery sky. Miss Hutton, her father, and stepmother stepped into the cold morning air and shivered. The glowing debutante was smiling. "The Man I Love" was going through her mind, but she stopped humming the Gershwin tune when she saw the waiting crowds. There were still some bedraggled people standing by the revolving door. The pinched faces of these poor people were gray and tired. Dark circles were under their eyes that told of their despair. Barbara Hutton smiled encouragingly at these people but they didn't smile back at her. They continued staring at her; she moved ahead with a frown and drew her ermine coat more tightly around her.

Barbara was haunted by these despairing faces as her stately black Rolls-Royce carried her back to 1020 Fifth Avenue.

"Those poor people," Barbara sighed, staring sadly out into the wintry streets.

"Don't think of them," snapped Frank Hutton.

"Nobody thinks of poor people today!" cried Frank's wife, Irene. "You of all people, Barbara Hutton, shouldn't think of the poor."

"Why?"

"Because you're above their sordid problems."

Barbara winced. The vulgarity of her father and stepmother disturbed her.

Later that morning in her oyster damask and walnut-paneled bedroom overlooking Central Park, Barbara stared thoughtfully into the glowing coals of her pink marble fireplace. The room was staggeringly luxurious, softly gleaming with silk-shaded wall lights that were made of gilded bronze. On her inlaid tulip-wood dressing table with spindly legs, the fourteen-carat gold toilet set shone as brightly as the fire. Her father had given the set to her today; now she stared at it with hatred. It was vile that she should have these useless things, when millions of people outside in the cold didn't know where their next meal was coming from. "What should I do?" thought Barbara. "Oh, if only I could do something." At eighteen Barbara had integrity and compassion, and the social injustice of these times kept her awake many nights.

She took up her pen and began to write. She was a romantic girl and liked to escape her troubled thoughts by composing poetry. Now as the diamond numerals of her rock crystal boudoir clock rested on 8:00 she scribbled in her pretty, large, generous hand:

Why?
Why should some have all
And others be without?
Why should men pretend
And women have to doubt?

The melancholy words of "The Man I Love" started to go through her head again. Her party had been lovely. So many handsome boys had danced with her. A husky Princeton football player had pressed himself against her and told her that he was mad for her. Could he meet her at the Plaza's Palm Court at five today? He was awfully attractive with tender blue eyes, but she didn't like his voice and she definitely didn't like his crude amorous advances on the dance floor. All of her schoolmates at Farmington were hungry to have a flirtation with this paragon, but Barbara didn't take to him at all. What was the matter with her? Why did she always have this awareness that set her apart from other people. She always seemed to see through the facade of people and this increased her sense of loneliness.

Outside the windows sleet began to patter against the glass. There was something about the rhythm of the rain that made her mind wander back to solitary days at boarding school when she used to lie awake and listen to the trains passing through the night. "Why am I so alone?" Barbara thought, burying her face in the pile of silk and lace pillows. "Other girls have love and a home. Why shouldn't I?" Lying there in the half light, the rain seemed to trigger a whole chain of past associations, and suddenly, as it always did in moments of reflection, her mind wandered back to her childhood days. "Oh, Mother," she cried, "please don't leave me, please come back. Please. . . ."

Barbara often said this to me and I felt the same.

CHAPTER 2

Frank Winfield Woolworth, a rugged, handsome, and driven farm boy from upstate New York, founded the first chain of five-and-ten-cent stores. His initial store was opened in 1879, but by 1929 there were 2,100 red-fronted stores all over America; even in Germany, France, and England. When he was twenty-four he married his childhood sweetheart, Jennie Creighton. She was from the same simple background and their marriage was a long and happy one—until she began to lose her mind.

Like Marshall Field, John Wanamaker, and George Huntington Hartford, Woolworth became one of the great merchant princes in American history—a true Horatio Alger story. Like the Vanderbilts, Astors, and Goulds he hungered to own a palace on Fifth Avenue. In 1899 Cass Gilbert designed a spectacular Gothic mansion for him at 990 Fifth Avenue, at 80th Street, with three similar houses for his three plump daughters.

Frank's father was a farmer, a good, solid, industrious man. Now he gazed at the opulent limestone mansion. "This must

23

have cost a lot of money, son. I hope it doesn't give you a swelled head.''

"It won't, Pa," replied the forty-seven-year-old Frank, bursting with pride. "Why, it's just as grand as Otto Kahn's and Felix Warburg's and soon I'll own the whole block like the Vanderbilts down at Fifty-seventh and Fifty-eighth streets.''

"Competition is healthy," replied old Woolworth. "But don't get sucked into that High Society void; those lightweights are destructive to the likes of you and me.''

"I know," chuckled Frank.

"Why, all those Astors and Vanderbilts do is give parties and build grand houses and marry their daughters off to phony titled foreigners," continued the old man. "I hope you're not getting frivolous, son.''

"I'm not," said Frank Woolworth emphatically and then voiced aloud one of his favorite credos: "No one ever built a business on thoughts of having a good time.''

"Well," chuckled the old man, "let's hope your daughters don't get pulled into that High Society business. Those social people are fools.''

Of course, the three daughters did want to make social marriages and were determined to have a good time above all else. Helena Woolworth married "social" Charles McCann and had a grand English country life in the Locust Valley set. Jessie married good-looking playboy James Paul Donahue from humble Irish origins and showered him with presents. Edna, the prettiest and most talented, was swept off her feet by the numerous charms of good-looking, well-built stockbroker Franklyn Laws Hutton, a Yale graduate from a middle-class family. Both Hutton brothers, Frank and Ed, were handsome as well as ambitious and were determined to make brilliant alliances to establish themselves in New York society and the business world. Ed, who was more handsome, landed the most prominent heiress of the time, Marjorie Post of the cereal fortune. Frank Hutton courted and married Edna Woolworth—a beautiful, sensitive, though at times morbid, girl. Her father's favorite, she was gifted with a singing voice of almost concert caliber.

On November 14, 1912 little Barbara Hutton was born in New York City. She came to be known as the world's most famous heiress and the original "poor little rich girl." Her early life certainly prepared her for this title.

Early in her marriage, Edna Woolworth Hutton learned with horror that her husband was a great womanizer. When she discovered a certain love affair of his, her mind snapped. The Huttons were living at the Plaza Hotel at the time. With her husband's incriminating letter to his mistress in her hand, Edna paced up and down her plush drawing room for hours. The gray weather, the gray despair inside her was something she wanted to end. Finally, she summoned the courage to do something which had been on her mind for some time. Swiftly she took out a vial of poison from her pocketbook, poured some into a glass, and swallowed it. With horror she looked at herself in a gilt-framed mirror, a queer smile flickering across her lips. Her eyes looked demented—as demented as her mother's, her poor mother who was so disenchanted with her life. Barbara told me the dramatic account of her mother's suicide with great feeling.

Outside on the Grand Army Plaza in front of the hotel, a motorcar had hit a horse and carriage; the noise of the horns and angry cries drifted up to her. She sank into a tufted damask sofa bordered with a red fringe. The heavy bronze wall lights and chandeliers seemed enveloped in the same gray mist that was outside. Edna tried to stand up and, gasping for breath, fell to the floor. It was in this position that Barbara found her thirty-five-year-old mother a few hours later. Many years later Barbara could still remember her mother lying on the Turkey-red carpet. The poor woman was wearing a white lace dress and the pink enamel and gold parasol she carried was broken in two as if there had been a terrible struggle.

Barbara was to say many times to me, "I've missed my mother all my life. I never really had a father, either. Thank heavens there were Grandpa and Grandma Woolworth. After mother died at the Plaza, I went to live with them at that gloomy house on Fifth Avenue. In one way or another we are all shaped by the situations and circumstances in our early years, and Grandpa's isolated life hardly prepared me for a normal existence. By then Grandma had lost her mind. She rocked all day on the terrace of the Glen Cove house and Grandpa's family tragedies began to affect his sense of reality. . . .''

A certain grandiosity overcame Woolworth in his later life. His passion for organ music led him to install immense organs in his great mansions on Fifth Avenue and Glen Cove. The white marble mansion still stands on Long Island, as vulgar and monstrous as any of the Vanderbilt palaces in Newport, Rhode Island. Frank Woolworth also loved the drama of flashing colored lights, so when he played the organ, thunder and lighting sounded in a psychotic storm. Little Barbara, alone upstairs in her nursery with its stained-glass windows, dark oak linenfold paneling, and Renaissance tapestries, was terrified. Being a companion for an old man and old woman who was not in her right mind, in an isolated and gloomy house, was not a good beginning for a sensitive, imitative child. Barbara's lunch and dinner companions consisted of the Woolworths and nurses in attendance, with a bust of Beethoven appearing in the dim light.

These were Barbara's earliest memories, although she also recalled the little white ermine coat and hat her father gave her, the walks she took down Fifth Avenue by his side, and the policemen who tipped their hats as they passed by.

"Good morning, Miss Barbara," they used to say.

And Barbara would reply, "Good morning, and say hello to my doll Edna."

At an early age Barbara was catered to and treated as a queen. All of the servants in this household knew of her immense inheritance and acted accordingly. Her every wish was instantly gratified. At an early age she felt a sense of power.

The memory that always haunted Barbara was of the terrible dream she had of her mother. She was running into an empty drawing room and there was her mother's figure in a white lace dress lying on a Turkey-red carpet. "Mother, Mother," Barbara would cry, "wake up, wake up!" But the figure in her arms would not move. "Mother, don't leave me. You *mustn't* leave me!"

Years later, her cousin Jimmy Donahue told me of the terrifying blank look in Barbara's blue eyes. Whenever her mother was mentioned, "her eyes would dilate and she looked crazed," Jimmy added.

After Grandpa Woolworth's death in 1919, which was soon followed by Jennie Woolworth's in 1922, Barbara inherited some $25,000,000 at the age of ten. That sum would be equal to $600,000,000 today, what with inflation and the shrinking dollar. Her father, a stockbroker of no mean talent, took hold of the fortune and in the frantic gambling days of the crazy twenties managed to work up the money into the huge sum of $50,000,000. He had vision enough to sell out early in 1929 so that when the great crash came in October of that year he was sitting pretty. The richest man in the world at that time, Harrison Williams, the public utilities king, didn't sell out and he lost a billion.

Frank Woolworth's obituary recorded one of the most remarkable incidents in his life. The gray-haired, blue-eyed, and handsomely mustached Frank Woolworth had consummated his building mania when he spent $13,500,000 of his own money to finance the Woolworth Building, the skyscraper wonder of the world completed in 1913. This spectacular Gothic building boasted twelve miles of marble wainscoting. The tower itself rose to a record 792 feet. At the great gala opening President Woodrow Wilson pressed a button in the White House and 80,000 light bulbs flashed in the completed Woolworth Building, that was called "The Cathedral of Commerce."

How happy the obituary would have made Frank Winfield Woolworth. He wanted the world to remember him. Since he left no male heir, he left behind the great phallic tower of the Woolworth Building; what other mortal could do that? And if people didn't remember the ambitious farm boy and his dreams of glory, they would certainly remember his favorite granddaughter, "the poor little rich girl," Miss Barbara Hutton, who would soon make splashier headlines than he ever did. But the tragic tale of the Donahues and the even more tragic one of Barbara Hutton would surely have made him wonder about his achievement of the Great American Dream.

CHAPTER 3

There is nothing more snobbish and cruel than little girls and boys at fancy boarding schools and their horrid behavior to outsiders. Barbara Hutton was always made to feel an outsider by the spiteful girls at Hewitts, and Farmington in Connecticut. A school friend of Barbara's from that time recalls a pretty girl of sixteen, with large dreamy eyes, always reading romantic novels. "We all felt sorry for her because when holiday time came Barbara was left there in the care of the headmistress at Christmas or Easter. And I remember so well one snowy Christmas vacation, driving away from school and looking up and seeing Barbara standing there wistfully looking out the window as all of us left for home. . . ."

Barbara's schoolmates did everything they could to let her know that they considered her father a cheap and common operator. They laughed at the vulgar display of all those Hutton Rolls-Royces and Barbara's private railroad car. Her extravagant and notorious aunt, Jessie Donahue, provoked their taunting even more.

29

Aware of the mockery she inspired, Barbara was miserable. Fortunately, there was her Aunt Marjorie and her handsome and vigorous uncle, Edward Hutton, who often took the little girl on school vacations to their triplex on Fifth Avenue, sometimes to the camp in the Adirondacks, or the great villa on the sea in Palm Beach called Mar-a-Lago. On the other hand, Barbara's Aunt Jessie, famous for her jewelry collection and Russian sables, was married to James Donahue, an effeminate dandy "who swished around the dance floors" of Southampton and Palm Beach. They were definitely wrong in the eyes of the Farmington girls and their parents. Hearst society columnist Cholly Knickerbocker wrote that the Donahues were "rowdy and raucous." In 1931 Mr. Donahue killed himself by taking poison. There were many sinister and mysterious accounts revolving around his death. Jessie Donahue closed the house at 6 East Eightieth Street and bought another one downtown, where she lived with her son, Jimmy. Both Barbara and Jimmy Donahue were familiar with lack of acceptance and approval at an early age. Both of them certainly understood the word "rejection." And both were motivated by a desire for vengeance and a tendency for self-destruction. The bond between them was a strong one, which lasted until Jimmy's tragic, untimely death.

Barbara wanted desperately to be accepted at school, but her two aunts, Jessie Donahue and Helena McCann, didn't help her cause by motoring up to school, conspicuously dripping in jewels and furs, in enormous Rolls-Royces. All the other little girls had mothers and fathers who were low-keyed in voice, manners, and clothes. Even Rockefeller and Du Pont mothers dressed like governesses. Barbara yearned to be a member of the elite, to be accepted by aristocratic people.

Barbara never understood the Old Guard in America: Saltonstalls and Lodges from Boston; Byrds and Randolphs from Virginia; Biddles from Philadelphia, who were not only rich but distinguished. They did not show their money. A mink coat and a diamond bracelet worn in the daytime was considered vulgar by these people. Though she longed for acceptance, Barbara herself was never attracted to these puritan and rather provincial people.

Her belief was If you had money, why not show it?—which was certainly true in the rowdy Donahue set.

Like so many other children, Barbara was strongly influenced by Hollywood stars and the films she saw. Pola Negri, Mae Murray, and Gloria Swanson were her idols, and all three of these ladies had made titled marriages to glamorous foreign noblemen. Pola Negri had married Serge Mdivani and Mae Murray had married David Mdivani. Both these men were handsome Russian princes, polo players, and playboys. As for Gloria Swanson, she had married the Marquis de la Falaise and was known as Madame la Marquise.

Barbara's aunt, Marjorie Post Hutton, was as beautiful and alluring as the cinema queens. She was a great spender and was attractive to men. Barbara, who was imitative by nature, took on the colors of this vivid woman. Barbara's vacations in Palm Beach opened fabulous vistas to the teenaged girl. Mar-a-Lago, the Palm Beach home, cost $8,000,000 ($80,000,000 today) and was staffed by eighty servants. Marjorie had a fleet of Rolls-Royces, an astonishing jewel collection, palatial houses all over America, a queenly retinue of personal maids, chauffeurs, footmen, gardeners. She had the grand manner—and that was what Barbara wanted. She also wanted to give parties as fabulous as Aunt Marjorie's, which were like something out of the Arabian Nights.

Mar-a-Lago had begun to take shape in 1923. Nothing was spared to build this great Palm Beach hacienda. It was to be the biggest and grandest showplace in that famous resort. The seventeen-and-a-half acres ran from the beachfront all the way back to Lake Worth. Like most of the Palm Beach mansions, it was a fantasy Spanish creation, part Moorish and part *Ziegfeld Follies*. Like Grandpa Woolworth, Aunt Marjorie had a building compulsion. It was awesome to watch her creation take shape. Three shiploads of Italian stone, marble, and tile had gone into this amazing villa. There was a great tower rising seventy-five feet. With 122 rooms, baronial drawing rooms that were a hundred feet long with fireplaces big enough to stand in, and an antique collection that would have made William Randolph Hearst envious, Mar-a-Lago was definitely Palm Beach's most impressive home. "My God," cried Harry K. Thaw, who shot Stanford White, the great architect, around the turn of the century, "My God—I killed the wrong architect!"

Acting out her building compulsion even more, Aunt Marjorie had her Fifth Avenue mansion torn down and erected an apartment building on its site so that she could have the top three floors, where her seventy rooms put her a slight distance from the noise and soot of Fifth Avenue. Aunt Marjorie also had one of the world's most stupendous sailing yachts, *The Sea Cloud* with four masts and an overall length of 350 feet. All the cabins were decorated like bedrooms in a private home, with canopied beds and chintz curtains. There was also a movie projection room, a barber shop, antique furniture and, below, four diesel engines kept going when the wind failed. In full sail this yacht looked like something out of a pirate movie.

When Mar-a-Lago was completed in January 1927, Aunt Marjorie gave a party that would long linger in Palm Beach's memory. The event also shaped the thoughts of fifteen-year-old Barbara Hutton. Barbara ordered a Rolls-Royce just like Aunt Marjorie's. She was attended by a French personal maid, footmen, and chauffeur wherever she traveled. Aunt Marjorie had a private railroad car that whisked her down from New York to Palm Beach in glittering style; soon Barbara would have one herself. It cost $150,000 a year to maintain—but what fun to have a drawing room on wheels!

Barbara would long remember her initial visit to Mar-a-Lago at Christmas 1928. A blue-and-white Hutton Rolls-Royce had met her at the private railroad car. She and Jimmy Donahue were driven down South Ocean Boulevard. The turquoise sea sparkled brightly in the December morning. The smell of saltwater and oleanders excited the teenage girl and she leaned forward eagerly and rolled down the window.

"My God," said Jimmy Donahue, "look at Aunt Marjorie's house! It's bigger than mother's!"

"I want something just like it," cried Barbara brightly.

The limousine passed through the fanciful main gates and pro-

ceeded up a long drive lined with coconut palms. The sweeping
green lawn was like a golf course, and the flowering red hibiscus
put on a dazzling display.

Two footmen ushered the cousins into the spacious hall. The
walls were covered with antique Spanish tiles. There was a hood-
ed fireplace with a bust of Homer on one side and Hadrian on the
other.

"Mrs. Hutton will receive you in the drawing room," said a
pompous English butler.

And what a drawing room! It was bigger than any movie palace they had ever seen, and the enormous ceiling of finely carved
gold leaf was a copy of the famous Thousand Winged Ceiling in
Venice's Accademia. The room was incredibly luxurious in feeling and was proportioned to accommodate seven tapestries from
a Venetian palace. The décor was pure *Sunset Boulevard.* There
were huge tables filled with silver-framed pictures of grand people, heavy crystal chandeliers, priceless Persian rugs, and arch-
ways and gloom similar to a Spanish church. Aunt Marjorie was
sitting on an enormous velvet sofa. Behind her towered a great
arrangement of white and red roses mixed with orange blossoms,
white tuberoses, and pink oleander. Her thick hair was beautifully waved and on her finger was an extraordinary diamond ring. A
fragrant sea breeze drifted through the oppressive splendor.

"What do you think?" asked Aunt Marjorie, swinging forward to meet them in her energetic way.

"How much did it cost?" said Jimmy.

"More than I dare say," said Aunt Marjorie, a charming slender figure in her French dress.

"Don't ever mention money," said Frank Hutton, sitting in a
Renaissance armchair.

"Why not?" cried Jimmy Donahue, a provocative thirteen-
year-old boy.

"If you want something," said Frank Hutton, "just buy it and
never count the cost."

"Then why can't I have a house like this, Father?" drawled
Barbara.

"If the market gets any better, you will," said Frank Hutton, "and the way the market is going these days, you'll still be one of the richest girls in the world. Why every stock I buy today turns to gold the next."

Another formal butler stepped into the room and announced Mrs. Phipps, Mrs. William Randolph Hearst, and Mrs. Evelyn Walsh McLean had arrived for lunch.

Presently the richly dressed ladies were sipping their tomato juice—Aunt Marjorie never served cocktails in her house—and Barbara was bug-eyed seeing the famous Hope diamond resting on Mrs. McLean's bosom. It had once belonged to Marie Antoinette, was reported to be the largest diamond in the world, and was said to bring bad luck to its owner. That it was an ill-fated gemstone further appealed to Barbara's romantic imagination. On the spot, Barbara resolved that she would buy such a gem when she came of age.

"Well, dear children, you're having lunch at the Bath and Tennis Club across the way," said Aunt Marjorie in her most winning fashion to Barbara and Jimmy.

"Why can't we lunch with you, Aunt Marjorie?" said Barbara eagerly.

"You can dine with me tonight," said Marjorie, kissing the pretty plump girl warmly. "I'm having a little party for Grand Duke Alexander. Sixty will join us for dinner and eighty are coming in for dancing after."

As the Woolworth cousins stepped out of the huge cypress doors of the drawing room, they almost bumped into His Royal Highness Cyril of Bulgaria. He bowed low before Barbara and kissed her hand. "What a delicious girl and what lovely eyes," he said.

As the heavy Rolls-Royce carried the Woolworth cousins out of the imposing wrought-iron gates of Mar-a-Lago, Jimmy said, "That was royalty, Barbara. Mother can't even get him to her house, although she's trying. Aunt Marjorie's really making it."

Barbara stared wistfully out at the endless horizon of turquoise sea. Birds were singing brightly in the pink and white oleander bushes. Far away she could see a steam yacht like J. P. Morgan's moving imperiously across the ocean. She brought her hand to her face. Cyril of Bulgaria's Russian Leather cologne still lingered on her fingers and echoes of his courtly old-fashioned manners rang in her ears. If only the parents of those nasty little girls at Farmington treated her like this!

Aloud she voiced her discontent to her favorite cousin. "Jimmy—do you think I'm a lady?"

"I don't know. I guess so," said Jimmy.

"Well, Aunt Marjorie and your mother are great ladies, aren't they?" asked Barbara thoughtfully.

"They have the most money, anyway."

"But I read that Cyril of Bulgaria doesn't have any money," said Barbara gravely. "Nor does Grand Duke Alexander."

"They're royal and historic titles," said Jimmy.

"That's what I want," said Barbara, surveying her sensitive fingers critically. "Perhaps I'm not a lady by birth but I will be through marriage."

"I thought you were going to marry John Gilbert?"

"I've decided those film people are vulgar," said Barbara.

"La-di-dah," sang Jimmy.

"I'd like to be the Duchess de Vendôme," replied Barbara. "Or the Princess Mdivani."

"Anything's possible in the world we live in," said Jimmy. "Why Nanny said if you have money like we do, you can do anything. And your father said to buy anything you want and not count the cost."

"That's true," said Barbara, gnawing insecurely on her finely shaped oval nail. She was immensely proud of her beautiful nails and tiny, beautifully shaped feet.

Lunch was an anticlimax for Barbara and Jimmy. There was no one interesting or spectacular in the Bath and Tennis Club. Being with royalty was far more stimulating.

"What'll we do now?" whined Jimmy after they finished their meringue glacé.

"Go to the movies. What else?" said Barbara.

As soon as the lights went out in the movie theater and the

characters began to perform on the screen, Barbara felt happy. All of her loneliness and sense of awkwardness faded. She identified with the characters in the film, lost herself completely in what was going on before her. Sometimes it seemed the incidents on the screen were far more real than her own life. Often she had dreams where she was a Princess in ermine coats and diamond bracelets, like Pola Negri or Mae Murray, who in actuality were Princesses Mdivanis. Oh yes, Barbara Hutton hungered above all to be a Duchess or a Princess, and have a husband with a historic name and background. That would make those nasty little girls sit up and take notice.

"I hate Farmington, and those snobbish schoolmates," said Barbara as the chauffeur carried them back to the splendid isolation of Mar-a-Lago.

"When you've got your money, you can show the world," said Jimmy, giggling delightedly.

"Yes, I'll show the world," said Barbara with a determined expression.

"Who's the first person you're going to tell to go to hell?" said Jimmy.

"My father," said Barbara, her eyes narrowing. "He'll be sorry he didn't pay attention to me."

"Well, what about your debut?" asked Jimmy. "That'll really show people, won't it?"

"Yes, Aunt Marjorie promised me the most beautiful debut ever! And after I'm twenty-one I can be a Princess and tell everyone to go to hell."

"And back."

Her maid helped her get dressed for the dinner party that evening. Aunt Marjorie had promised to seat her next to Charles Lindbergh or at least handsome Jimmy Cromwell. Jimmy was so good-looking, had such delightful manners, and danced divinely. Later as the strains of the orchestra played the latest Jerome Kern and Oscar Hammerstein music from *Show Boat,* Barbara drifted down the stairs in canary yellow chiffon and diamonds. Her aunt was receiving in the drawing room in a Louis XV gown of blue taffeta trimmed with rare old lace and silver. Her collection of sapphires and diamonds blazed at her throat, wrists, and ears.

"The cast of *Show Boat* will perform after dinner," said Aunt Marjorie, "and there'll be fireworks, too, from the yacht."

"Lovely," said Barbara.

At dinner Barbara had a talk with Lady Wavetree, who wore a diamond tiara. This gracious woman invited her to stay in London and said she would introduce her to all the English nobility at the Royal Enclosure at Ascot. Grand Duke Alexander, stunning in white tie and tails, informed her that she had the most exquisite blue eyes and fresh Fragonard coloring he had ever seen, and he'd be so pleased if she came to Paris next spring.

Yes, things were looking up for Barbara Hutton. That night in her balconied chamber overlooking the perfumed gardens and the sea, Barbara dreamed of being married to Grand Duke Alexander. Everyone was kissing her hand and bowing low before her. At nine o'clock the next morning when she was having coffee on the loggia with fresh gardenias on her breakfast tray, the dream lingered seductively in Barbara's mind. Oh yes, she'd soon show those vipers at school. Barbara Hutton would soon make them eat crow! . . . And wouldn't they be sorry when they read of her goings on. She'd even outdo Aunt Marjorie. Definitely outdo Mae Murray and Pola Negri. Her father had told her that cinema people spent every dollar to keep up a front, but Barbara, he said, could live off the income of her enormous capital and always be on top.

And on top she always wanted to be.

CHAPTER 4

There are many pictures of Barbara Hutton at her sensational New York debut on December 21, 1930. At eighteen, Barbara resembled her grandfather, Frank Winfield Woolworth. She had the same thick eyebrows, splendid healthy skin, enormous blue eyes, and a fine straight nose. She also had his vitality and determined, almost willful disposition. Her debut pictures reveal a round fleshy face with heavily rouged cheeks. For all the world she looked like a candy-box cover, pretty, but with none of the aristocratic distinction she later achieved. As the famous columnist and party-giver Elsa Maxwell remarked: "Barbara's figure was rather lumpy and shapeless at this point with no waistline and rather heavy, pendulous breasts. However, her voice was soft and pleasing, she had gentle manners, but the most charming thing of all was her lovely smile. When she smiled at you, all you wanted to do was please her. She had the power of winning you over immediately."

After the furor of her much publicized debut had died down,

Barbara's father and stepmother thought it prudent to introduce her to London society. Irene Hutton was socially ambitious, just like Aunt Jessie and Aunt Marjorie, but she lacked the charm and beauty of the two heiresses. Irene, however, was no slouch in the climbing department. She quickly realized young Barbara could help her open doors in London. It didn't take much work to get Barbara included in the event that all high society considered imperative in 1931: to be presented at the Court of St. James to Queen Mary and King George V. Barbara's friend, Miss Doris Duke, the American tobacco heiress, who was also an only child, had just made her curtsy before the monarchs. Barbara wanted to have what Doris had; there was a strong sense of competition between the two girls.

Barbara's suite at the Hotel Ritz was in a state of great excitement the morning of her presentation.

"Oh, Miss Barbara," cried her personal maid, "I hope the handsome Prince of Wales is there."

"Do you think he'll dance with me?" Barbara said, anxiously regarding her plump image in the mirror.

"He should *marry* you," cried Irene Hutton fiercely. "Why, that royal fellow is as rich as you are, Barbara. He has ten million a year, I read."

"Gracious," said Barbara vaguely.

"Wouldn't a royal marriage tickle your father pink?" said Irene.

"Yes," replied Barbara dreamily. She was distinctly apprehensive about meeting old Queen Mary. Aloud she said, "Perhaps my dress isn't right, Irene?"

"Right!" cried Irene angrily. "Why, it's the best money can buy. Not even Pola Negri has a dress and feathers like yours. Stop biting your nails, you'll be a hit with all those swells. No doubt about it."

Barbara winced under these vulgarities and exchanged a woeful look with her companion, Ticki.

At the garden party Barbara felt distraught. "What if she didn't curtsy properly? What if she tripped over her long train?"

A debutante friend watched Barbara and said, "Have a glass of champagne, darling, and then nothing will matter; in fact it will make you feel like a new girl."

"That's the way I want to feel," said Barbara.

Nervously Barbara took a glass of champagne and downed it. Almost immediately a sweet buzzing went up to her head and all her fears faded. After another champagne she even managed to feel high spirited and almost reckless. Why hadn't she ever discovered champagne before? She smiled gratefully at her friend.

Barbara made a good impression on old Queen Mary. The old woman thought Barbara's eyes were rather like a doe's, so wounded, so vulnerable. She thought it was a pity her son was so taken by that other American woman.

In her heavy shimmering white satin dress Barbara curtsied gracefully before the monarchs. A diadem of diamonds held some ostrich feathers in her hair. She was in an agony of suspense about whether these feathers would fall over her eyes.

"You look smashing, Barbara," said her new friend, admiringly. "Now we'll see what handsome boys will dance with us."

After the presentation there was a dance under a large awninged tent. The band was playing "Tea For Two" and debutantes were being chosen by eligible sons of Dukes, Earls, and Ambassadors. What if nobody danced with her? She quickly had a vision of herself running in panic back to the Ritz and of her father gloating over her failure.

"Would you care for this dance?" said the small and handsome Prince of Wales.

"Delighted," said Barbara, with a timid smile.

All eyes seemed to be upon them and Barbara prayed she wouldn't step on his toes. Desperately she racked her mind to think of something clever to say, but she couldn't. Thank heavens the Prince was most sympathetic.

"I saw you in Biarritz two years ago," the Prince was saying.

"Yes," said Barbara, shyly meeting his eyes. "Elsa Maxwell took me to a wonderful party there two years ago."

"Old battering-ram Elsa gives the best parties in the world," grinned the Prince.

"Oh, yes!"

"Are you going to her party in Biarritz next month?" he asked.

"Alas no," said Barbara, her heart sinking.

"In that case," said the Prince, "come as my guest."

Barbara smiled radiantly.

"Oh, your Royal Highness—you're so kind."

Everybody Barbara met in London was always saying "You're so kind" and she hoped it wasn't a cliché. Such worries a debutante had!

When Barbara returned to her father's cluttered suite at the Ritz, Irene Hutton was surrounded by dressmakers, antique dealers, and jewelers who had brought her their best wares. Irene had been told that a lady didn't go to shops.

"Barbara, how do you like this?" asked Irene, sporting a showy silver lamé trimmed with sable.

"It's lovely," lied Barbara.

"Well," said Frank Hutton, coming into the drawing room, "well, dear chubby daughter, I hope when you slim down you'll be able to get into some of these expensive gladrags. Aren't you going to give your old father a kiss?"

Barbara ran toward him and stumbled over a low footstool, blushed furiously at her awkwardness.

"What a clumsy girl I have," chuckled Frank Hutton disagreeably.

The Huttons looked at each other and laughed. Barbara hated it when people laughed at her.

Irene glanced at Barbara with a bored expression.

"Drop that long face, Babs. We're all invited to a lot of good parties in Paris and you're going to marry somebody from the crème-de-la-crème, isn't she, Frank?"

"Uh huh," said Frank Hutton, sitting in a velvet lounge chair and picking up the *Wall Street Journal*. "G.M.'s dropped," he added seriously.

Business, business, business—that's all her father cared about. And she detested people who called her Babs! "Goodness, how can I give them the slip in Paris?" she wondered.

Two days later, the Huttons were all lunching at the dining room in the Hôtel Ritz in Paris. Irene was peering around with a diamond-studded lorgnette, waving and hoping to be noticed. Barbara gritted her teeth at her stepmother's lack of social knowledge.

At this time, Elsa Maxwell came into Barbara's life. Elsa was a con artist extraordinaire. She saw great potential in Barbara and knew that she could use her. Right away she cleverly caught the situation among Barbara, her father, and stepmother. Bull-like Elsa plumped herself down in a fragile chair between the Huttons and amused them all with all the latest gossip. A Philadelphia couple in Cannes were her new undertaking, but they were difficult to put across on the social scene.

"You see, he likes big Hungarian soldiers and she likes Spanish matadors and they insist on dragging them about. What can I do?" chortled Elsa.

"Drop them," said Frank Hutton.

"They're very lucrative," said Elsa, "and a girl alone has to earn her money somehow. Why, I put Monte Carlo on the map and I hardly made anything out of it."

Frank Hutton was entertained by masculine Elsa's "being a girl alone" and chuckled appreciatively.

"I'd like to try Monte Carlo," said Irene.

"Don't," boomed Elsa. "Come to Biarritz instead. I'm giving a big party there the day after tomorrow. Everybody will be there, from the Astors to Zog of Albania."

"Who's paying?" asked Frank Hutton.

"My Philadelphia couple!"

"Can we, Frank?" said Irene hopefully.

"Let the girl go," said Frank, who detested resorts and felt like a fish out of water among idlers with no purpose.

"Heavenly," cried Barbara.

Elsa patted Barbara's hand and beamed at her. "Darling, I'll introduce you to my whole gay, fun group."

"Will they like me?" asked Barbara.

Elsa chuckled to herself. She was always amused by the inferiority complexes of the very rich. Like her? Why, all the great houses in Europe were hungry for fresh money like Barbara Hutton's. Every penniless Count, Viscount, Earl, Marquis, Prince, and Duke would take to this girl like a bee to honey. Barbara might get stung, but so what? Elsa would be sure to get her commission for arranging the match. Elsa rarely drank hard liquor at midday but she was so excited at the prospect of a new victim that she ordered a Napoleon brandy, downed it in one gulp, and then belched. Just that morning she had been going through a terrifying moral inventory and she didn't like what she saw at all. She was getting old and had no security and she'd let a lot of golden chances go by. Now this pretty little pigeon was dropped right into her lap. And right away Elsa said her prayers and gave her thanks for her incredible opportunity. No opportunist in the world had an opportunity like this.

Elsa put her arm around Barbara's waist, whispering that they were going to have one hell of a good time in Biarritz together.

Barbara was thrilled to be made such a fuss over by Elsa Maxwell.

"Do you have a Rolls, Barbara?" asked Elsa.

"Oh, yes, many—many! Shall we take the yellow one or the robin's-egg-blue?"

"Well," said Elsa, "tell your chauffeur and footmen to be ready to drive us down tomorrow afternoon. Do you know the Duke and Duchess De Nemours? We'll drop in on them on the way. They're so divinely attractive. You'll love them and they'll love you. She's American and sweee-eeet and rich. My dear child, I don't mind telling you that I've lost my heart completely to you, and everybody else will feel the same."

Barbara drank in the words and felt a nice warmth go through her. She had a feeling that a whole new life was going to open up for her now that Elsa had taken such a shine to her.

"Dear Elsa, you make me feel so lovely."

"That's why I'm popular, my girl, and you'll be beloved soon yourself and belong in the right group that will appreciate you! Leave everything in my capable hands."

"I will. Definitely."

Both women had happy dreams that evening. Biarritz!

CHAPTER 5

The polo field at Biarritz was a scene from a Raoul Dufy with some of the decadence of a Bérard, who sketched all the fashionables in *Vogue* in the 1930s. Spanish flamenco music was playing, flags were flying, the arrogant drawl of the bored rich indulging in flirtations drifted like their expensive Guerlain perfume through the Basque air. There was nothing more seductive to Barbara than listening to the polo mallet hitting the ball. Seductive, too, was athletic and good-looking Alexis Mdivani astride his polo pony. The polo match itself was fraught with excitement, but the graceful way Prince Mdivani swung the mallet from his steed was something to see. Barbara felt his love of life, his sense of adventure, and wanted to be a part of it. To think that his brothers were married to Pola Negri and Mae Murray!

"Alexis is scrumptiously attractive, isn't he?" said Elsa Maxwell, her small eyes watching Barbara shrewdly.

"He's the most attractive man I've ever seen," said Barbara. "Goodness, I hope he wins."

"Mdivanis always win," said Elsa meaningfully.

Barbara turned her head and gazed at Elsa, struck by the significant tone of the older woman. "I feel you're dying to tell me something, Elsa," she laughed.

"The Mdivani brothers are absolutely wicked and corrupt," cried Elsa emphatically. "And—"

"And what?" asked Barbara, breathlessly waiting for Elsa's next words.

"They're very dangerous to young impressionable girls," said Elsa in exaggerated tones.

"How perfect," thought Barbara.

The two women were sitting in the wooden grandstand among hundreds of exquisitely dressed members of the International Set, who were enjoying idle resort life for the July season. They had just flirted in London and Paris and soon would wander off to more intrigues in Monte Carlo and Venice. All these fashionables were Night People. For the first time Barbara was initiated into the Lost Midnight Brigade who rarely went to bed before dawn. Easy to talk to, they struck up casual acquaintances with Barbara. They made her feel at home and welcomed her as one of their own "special group." The nine-to-five syndrome was to be avoided at all costs, and there was always someone to pick up the tab. Frank Hutton called them "careless, irresponsible children," but Barbara thought them fascinating. Both the men and women were glamorous in appearance, elegant in their ways, and had titled names which lingered long in Barbara's mind. She wanted very much to belong to this world. They seemed to trail from one beautiful resort scene to the next with no worries or cares. What better way to live? Besides, they seemed far more elegant than the people she met at Aunt Marjorie's or Aunt Jessie's. No doubt about it, Europeans did have style, they all lived grandly, and no one criticized them. It seemed this aristocracy had lived like this forever, Depression or no Depression. They took all the good times as if they were their due. At the same time, Biarritz itself was atmospheric and full of Old World charm. Nearby St. Jean de Luz and Lourdes held a mystery to her that America did not possess.

Barbara's reflections were shattered by a wave of applause that rippled through the crowd. Fat Elsa sprang to her feet and cried joyfully, "Alexis has made another goal!"

Barbara directed her field glasses to the green turf below and the horses galloping about. Now she trained her binoculars on the muscular figure of Alexis Mdivani. She took in every detail of his costume—no man wore his clothes with such flair. His white clinging polo shirt was open at the throat, revealing his powerful chest, heavy arms and shoulders. He was laughing triumphantly. Barbara noticed with an odd little feeling at the pit of her stomach the thick veins in his tanned muscular arms. Curiously breathless, she had never felt such a physical attraction for a man before.

Elsa watched Barbara's face with amusement. "We're going to Jean Patou's party and everyone you want to know will be there, my little Juliet."

"Will Prince Mdivani be there?" asked Barbara.

"I've given you marks for being more subtle, my dear. You're really quite an innocent."

"Yes, I am innocent," confessed Barbara softly.

"It's a pity he's married," said Elsa.

"Isn't it," said Barbara faintly, her binoculars still glued on the manly form of Mdivani.

"Louise Mdivani is an heiress, but a minor one," Elsa put in and her optimistic tone made Barbara stare at her.

"You mean? . . . ."

"I mean there's a chance for you . . ." soothed Elsa, devilishly.

Barbara frowned. "Elsa, I forbid you to talk to me in this fashion."

"But isn't it what you wanted to hear?"

Lord Warwick, at Barbara's side, suddenly uttered words that Barbara was longing to hear. "*Eh bien*, Barbara, let's go down and pay our respects to that wicked Mdivani. We were at Eton together, you know . . . with Jimmy Van Alen, Louise's brother."

Barbara could hardly remember what happened during the next

five minutes, but all of a sudden there she was talking to the triumphant and vigorous Alexis Mdivani. Lady Ribblesdale and other famous beauties were hanging on the winner's every word, uttering feminine cries of admiration, hoping to be singled out by his eyes. But, strange to say, he only noticed Barbara Hutton herself! "Well, Barbara," he said, giving her a warm look, "what are you going to give the winner?"

Barbara was a novice at flirtation and didn't know how to respond. Under his warm gaze she felt her knees would give way and she couldn't utter a sound. She was painfully aware of the drops of sweat on his forehead and the wet shirt clinging to his athletic torso.

"Cat got your tongue?" he asked playfully.

"Yes," she nodded dumbly.

"Whew, I am hot!" cried Alexis. Impulsively, he took off his shirt and flung it at Barbara. He had the thick dark skin of a Mediterranean man, smooth and supple. Again she felt tongue-tied and gulped at his steady gaze.

To further the romance and intrigue, Elsa said, "What a charmer you are, Alexis; you'll be pleased to hear my little lamb here will grace Jean Patou's party tonight."

"Then will you talk to me, Barbara?" asked Alexis Mdivani in his intriguing foreign accent. The timbre of his voice seemed to make all of her nerve ends quiver, but she responded with a simple, "Yes."

Back in the Hôtel de Palais, formerly the villa of Empress Eugénie, overlooking the whitecapped sea, Elsa and Barbara calmed their nerves with some tea and cakes in the grand lounge. A three-piece orchestra was playing tea music, a sprightly piece from Offenbach, and the potted palms waved in the sea breeze coming through the french windows. Count de la Rochefoucauld and his party and the Duchess of Rutland and her party joined the Rothschilds at a table nearby.

"Well, my pretty puss, you made quite an impression on that naughty Alexis Mdivani this afternoon," said Elsa, munching on her chocolate éclair.

"Is he so naughty?" inquired Barbara, hoping to hear more and swallowing a rum cake.

"No one is naughtier than Alexis Mdivani," said Elsa significantly.

After some amusing oiling and licking of the Rothschilds, Elsa put her hand on Barbara's knee. "Now darling, let's go upstairs and have a massage and then I'll pick out the dress you'll wear tonight. I suppose you don't have a revealing and alluring Patou, do you?"

"Father would have a fit," laughed Barbara.

Barbara was staggered by the midnight entrance of Louise and Alexis Mdivani into dressmaker Patou's Art Deco silver-and-white house. Barbara was standing on the balustraded terrace watching the moon shimmering on the water when she heard a car crunching up the gravel drive. Turning her gaze she noticed a huge imperial Rolls-Royce with an elaborate coat of arms emblazoned on the doors. Liveried footmen with knee britches, stockings, and powdered wigs stood on the running board. They reminded Barbara of the footmen she had just seen in Buckingham Palace. Who could own such a splendid car, she wondered? Presently the chauffeur opened the door and out stepped Louise Van Alen and her recent bridegroom, Prince Alexis Mdivani. Louise was fortunate to have an Astor as her grandmother and a mother who was old Fred Vanderbilt's heir. Watching her, Barbara felt a terrible envy. Louise Van Alen was chic and social. She remembered with panic those snobbish Farmington girls. She was convinced that Louise would not even give her the time of day. As for Alexis, she knew she'd better forget him completely.

Her heart was filled with a masochistic pleasure that was entirely new to her. She liked the fact that she had to work to get him and that other girls wanted him. He was a prize.

Things turned out very differently from what Barbara had imagined. Louise was friendly and polite with her. Alexis danced with her and then waltzed her out onto the moonlit terrace. They watched the sea a moment and were struck by the beauty of the night. The smell of the fertile fields and flowering trees came to them. Far away a solitary dog was barking. The stars were incredibly brilliant.

Barbara was seated on the marble balustrade gazing adoringly up at Alexis' handsome face. He was even more seductive-looking in the evening, especially in his white-pleated shirtfront and white dinner jacket. She noticed his hands were incredibly strong with thick, well-shaped fingers. The same veins that throbbed in his muscular arms were visible on his large hands. On his shirt she noted ruby studs circled with diamonds. Oh, she would give him bigger and better ones.

"I hope you're returning to Paris this fall," Alexis was saying.

"You'll be there?" asked Barbara, shyly.

"Yes, I'll be there," purred Alexis, throatily.

"Then so will I," chimed Barbara.

"Darling," he said, and kissed her deeply. No man had ever kissed her in such a fashion and she felt weak in his arms.

Presently they drew apart and he said tenderly, "To Paris, then."

Paris! My God! What of Louise? What an intrigue! Now she was living! And how angry it would make her father, who loathed international idlers! *How sweet revenge would be!*

CHAPTER 6

That fall the *Herald Tribune* and *Paris Match* were full of the grand entertainments of Prince and Princess Mdivani. *Paris Match* compared their parties to the Rothschilds'. A gossip columnist in the *Herald Tribune* wrote that Louise's mother, Mrs. Van Alen, a tiny slender empress with blue hair and a collar of pearls, had tried to stop her daughter's extravagance. However, there was no stopping Alexis Mdivani. The little Russian boy was acting out all of his dreams of glory, although, if the truth were known, there was not enough Van Alen money to suit him. Alexis wanted the Prize, as Barbara was known to all the Mdivanis.

Lying there in her luxurious suite at the Ritz, Barbara read of these parties and fantasies about Alexis flowered in her mind.

The Mdivanis rented a magnificent limestone townhouse on the Place des États Unis that fall. When Barbara arrived in Paris at the end of September, the leaves were falling in the Tuileries Gardens and a melancholy rain began to pour. The Donahues and the Huttons were rushing here and there to various dinner parties

51

and luncheons, indulging in wild shopping orgies that kept them manic. Finding the people loud and aggressive, Barbara begged her aunt and stepmother not to go to any more of these affairs. She felt ill at ease with the crass American businessmen who talked only of their stocks and bonds and loathed their overbejeweled wives who talked only of their shopping sprees and social triumphs with dubious Dukes and Duchesses. Many evenings in her room at the Ritz, Barbara lay on her bed and tearfully waited for the phone to ring, hoping that Alexis would call.

Barbara's fantasies somehow had a way of becoming real. One rainy November day, she was hurrying through the corridors of the hotel and out the gilded revolving doors on her way to an English bookshop on Rue de Rivoli. Suddenly she was astonished to see the husky figure of Alexis Mdivani stepping gracefully out of his maroon-and-silver Rolls-Royce. On this gray day he was a dazzling sight with tight riding breeches that clung to his muscular thighs, a cashmere turtleneck, and a Harris tweed jacket with suede elbow patches. She nearly swooned when she saw him striding toward her and was filled with dismay at her drab flannel suit and little cloche hat. After the women she had seen Alexis with, she felt as if she looked like a governess. She would have given her soul to look like some of those worldly Duchesses and Princesses she had seen in the Ritz lobby with their taut red lips and porcelain complexions, and that alluring air of experience—sexual experience.

"Barbara, my dear, I didn't know you were in town," came the throaty voice of the handsome Russian Prince. "Why don't you give Louise and me a call?" He spoke so sincerely and with such feeling, as if they were long-time friends and had chatted intimately.

"I've been leading a very quiet life," she said, her cheeks blushing under his gaze. "Father keeps sending me off to museums and I spend a lot of time perfecting my conversational French."

"Let me hear you speak," he said. And she obliged him.

"You're fabulous, Barbara!" he said with such enthusiasm that she smiled delightedly.

"Really?" she whispered.

"Really!"

Without a word he escorted her back into the glittering hallways of the hotel. People never could resist Alexis. They just went along with what he wanted to do. Barbara was soon to learn that he could be very sweet indeed, providing he had his own way.

"I want you to have a champagne cocktail with me," he grinned, "to celebrate."

"To celebrate what?" she asked, her knees wobbly.

"To celebrate our friendship!" he cried in that engaging manner, his incredible amber eyes watching her speculatively.

She wondered what he was thinking, but he was being nice to her. At that moment her father stepped out of the elevator. She felt her blood turning to water. Her father repeatedly told her that she was stupid, that she had to protect herself from people interested only in her money.

Alexis, like all great con men, was sensitive to other people's feelings. Sensing her discomfort, he brushed her cheek with his warm lips and whispered, "Louise and I are having a little dinner tomorrow night. Just sixty of our nearest and dearest friends. Although I wonder if any of them are really friends! I hope you'll join us." He gave such a merry-sounding laugh that she had to smile, too. This morning she had felt depressed, as she looked out her window at the rain, but now she felt full of joy and anticipation. "I think maybe you are the only friend I have in Paris," he added with a playful wink.

She was absolutely tongue-tied by his presence and his engaging and manly air. Abruptly, without a word, he left, taking long strides in his heavy leather riding boots.

Mr. Hutton walked over to his daughter and his cold blue eyes watched her from behind his pince-nez. "Wasn't that that cheap fortune-hunting Russian guy?" grunted Hutton.

"Yes, Father," she said meekly, fluttering her lashes in panic.
"He's got a bad reputation!"

"Has he?" she said brightly. "Well, I adore his wife, Louise,
and they have invited me to a party tomorrow night."

"To which you are NOT going," said Frank Hutton in his
tough voice.

"But Father, I'm perfectly safe with a married man."

"You were looking at him as if he were a meringue glacé and
he looked like the Big Bad Wolf watching Little Red Riding
Hood. If you were older, Barbara, my imbecile, I'd tell you what
that four-flusher had in mind."

Irene Hutton breezed up wearing a silver-fox coat and hat and
some large cabochon ruby bracelets and matching clips. "Well,
what are you two looking so serious about?" she said good-
naturedly, putting her arm around Barbara in a motherly way.
Irene Hutton knew which side her bread was buttered on. She and
her husband spent many hours a day wondering how grateful Barbara would be to her father for doubling her fortune.

"Daddy's being old-fashioned and silly," said Barbara, tossing her head petulantly.

"That cheap Mdivani character asked Barbara for a big dinner
party tomorrow night, and I told her she couldn't go!" Hutton angrily informed his wife.

"But Louise Van Alen is a dear, very proper girl, and everyone tells me that she and Alexis are happily married. So why not,
Frank?" Irene patted Frank Hutton's jowls in an affectionate gesture.

"Absolutely not!" shouted Hutton, his thin lips drooping sourly.

"Well, Ticki will go with her," said Irene, "and everything
will be perfectly respectable."

Frank Hutton shrugged helplessly. He wanted to go to his
brokerage office around the corner and check on closing prices at
the New York Stock Exchange. Listening to women's petty problems really annoyed him, and he loathed the idle wastrels that
polluted the fashionable resorts that his wife and daughter loved.

The one thing that really interested him was business and all the wheeling and dealing that went with it.

"Oh, all right, Barbara," he grunted, pulling out a cigar.

A little later Barbara was poring through the new romantic novels at Smith's bookshop, situated in the damp arcade on the Rue de Rivoli. She was flipping through the pages of a new Edna Ferber book, but she couldn't keep her attention on the pages. She kept seeing the athletic figure of Mdivani striding by in his riding clothes.

"Barbara!" said Ticki her chaperone, "I think it's time for lunch. We'll go to the Meurice. It's right next door and we'll gorge ourselves on Coquille St.-Jacques and chocolate éclairs."

Barbara clapped her hands childishly.

"Heavenly! Heavenly! And can we go and see Jeanette Mac-Donald in that divine new movie on the Champs Élysées?"

There was nothing that Barbara liked better than spending long rainy autumn afternoons at the movies. Sitting in the darkened theaters she could indulge her blessed daydreams. At four o'clock she was sitting in a turn-of-the-century theater, all red plush and gilt columns, on the Champs Élysées. Jeanette Mac-Donald was singing "Dream Lover" from a moonlit balcony as suave Maurice Chevalier drank in her words. Barbara nestled down into her seat and in the darkness she gave free vent to her happy feelings.

CHAPTER 7

The air of gaiety and romance from *The Love Parade* was swimming through Barbara's head that misty November evening when Mr. Hutton's Rolls-Royce carried her up the wide lanes of the Champs Élysées. At the Rond-Point the fountains sent up silvery sprays. As the great automobile, with the inevitable chauffeur and footman in the open front, turned left and headed down the tree-lined Avenue Montaigne, Barbara's eyes lingered on the stately buildings, with balustraded balconies and french windows. Really, Paris was the only place to live. New York was too modern, too obsessed with business and getting ahead, and there was no glamorous air of the past. Every corner of Paris seemed like something from Monet or Pissarro, and one sensed leisure and joy here. By the Plaza Athénée Hôtel a horse and carriage clip-clopped by, bringing to Barbara's mind scenes from her beloved Zola, Flaubert, or Guy de Maupassant. She particularly identified with the handsome de Maupassant because he loved a good time and died young. She hoped she would be dead and gone by the age of forty. She didn't want to get dreary and old. She had resolved to spend her entire fortune by that time!

The gray, stone eighteenth-century house of the Mdivanis was a dignified monument and Barbara took in every detail of the grandeur. She already had a lively appreciation of splendor. As the liveried footman escorted her up the marble steps of the vestibule and then up a beautiful staircase, her eyes lingered on the blue and green Louis XV tapestries and the bronze mountings on the antique inlaid parquetry commodes. Another footman appeared at the top of the stairs and led her toward tall and impressive double doors, where a frigid butler inquired her name and then led her into a palatial chamber with celadon and gilt paneling and a marvelous set of eighteenth-century furniture. The magnificence of the room made her think only beautiful words should be said in such a place. Indeed, all the aristocratic people in the room looked slim and elegantly dressed. The conversation was hushed and low, a piano and violin were playing the melodies from the *Merry Widow* by Franz Lehar—a far cry from the raucous parties of the Huttons where jazz bands blared and saxophones wailed.

The honeymooners, Louise and Alec Mdivani, moved graciously toward Barbara to welcome her. Barbara envied Louise's social ease and the way she made everyone feel at home. Barbara still felt an outsider, a leftover from those Farmington days when those snobbish waspy girls made her feel inferior. Now Louise embraced her warmly and Alec smiled at her like a big brother.

Alexis squeezed Barbara's arm playfully. "I don't know why the orchestra is playing the *Merry Widow*. You know, my brother, David, was married to Mae Murray, but she wasn't rich enough, so David gave her the gate." He winked roguishly and Barbara couldn't help smiling. She loved to listen to this careless chatter of rich and glamorous people. She was convinced this was the way Marie Antoinette and her court must have carried on.

A slim energetic woman with the good looks of the Mdivani family made her way through the guests and joined the trio.

Roussie Mdivani Sert had cleverly stolen the millionaire artist J. M. Sert away from his wife and now was managing her brothers' careers. She knew every bit of information about Barbara Hutton. As her eyes went up and down Barbara's figure, she was thinking "the velvet dress is the wrong model for her, her figure is dumpy, her face is pretty but unremarkable, but, my God, what potential!" Roussie knew she could make Barbara into the most beautiful woman in Europe, with real distinction and style. She turned her hypnotic eyes on Barbara and said in her haunting Russian voice, "Alec is my favorite brother; he is dearer to me than anything in the world, but is also the naughtiest, so you mustn't believe a word he says. I'm Roussie Sert, by the way, and I've heard so many *wonderful* things about you. I hear you write poetry, too, and I'm dying to read some!"

Barbara smiled at her gratefully. Since her father and stepmother expressed no interest in her poetry, it was heartwarming to have anybody be so attentive to her. Barbara felt that Madame Sert genuinely liked her and she felt the same warmth coming from her that she felt from Roussie's fascinating brother. However, she didn't feel good vibrations from Louise, who was regarding her in the same way that those Farmington girls had looked at her with their tight smiles that amounted to sneers. Actually, Louise had no hostile feeling toward Barbara, but now with the appearance of Roussie, who was always manipulating her brothers, and pulling the strings behind the scenes, she felt a wave of fear. She was not going to have the common Woolworth heiress steal Alec away from her.

Barbara felt a rush of affection toward Roussie Sert. "My Father always laughs at my literary efforts," explained Barbara in her shy manner.

"Forget your critics," cried Roussie exuberantly, very much "onstage," in full control of the situation. "In art you have to forget about your past and think only of the people who understand you and your needs."

Barbara nodded, falling into the kind of hypnotic trance that everyone experienced under Roussie's powerful personality. "You're right," she said. "Father has no comprehension of my needs. He only understands business and money."

The brother and sister exchanged quick looks at the mention of money; a look that was lost to the two innocent heiresses, and Roussie took Barbara's arm and cried, "Darling, I've lost my heart to you! You're one of us—young and brave and rebellious! Youth must be rebellious and we all must go forward. Come, chérie, and I will introduce you to some people who will stimulate your ideas. The world that you come from must be so cold and static. Ah, New York frightens me so, with all its materialism. . . ."

Roussie and Barbara were talking on a luxurious French sofa, covered in rich amber velvet. Roussie was giving a great performance, talking with much vitality, smoking with a long jade cigarette holder, punctuating her dramatic sentences with waves of her heavily perfumed chiffon handkerchief that was stitched with her name and the usual coronet. Barbara hung on her every word and drank in every detail from this worldly woman. Roussie's rock crystal and diamond bracelets and her fragile sandals were works of art.

"Ah, my little poet," Roussie was saying, "Alec told me of your meeting at the Ritz yesterday. It was fate that brought you here tonight. When I saw you coming into the room, looking so forlorn and vulnerable, my heart went out to you. We Russians are capable of deep, deep feelings, my dear. And of course like all sensitive people, we, too, are terribly vulnerable."

She paused a moment to see what reaction her victim would have. Seeing that Barbara was in a sort of trance of joy, she carried on her act.

Barbara loved all the attention of this intriguing woman and she made a mental note to go to Cartier tomorrow and buy a gold and jade cigarette holder, just like Roussie's.

Suddenly the band began to play the score from *The Love Parade* and Barbara glanced up to see the young couples spinning by in the graceful waltz. Louise looked exotic in her fluttering chiffon and again Barbara wondered why she had worn the heavy and sumptuous velvet.

"Oh, Madame Sert, they're playing the music from a movie I saw yesterday afternoon!"

"Do you like going to the movies, my dear?" asked Roussie, leaning closer over the rich downy pillows of the ancient sofa.

"Movies are my only escape from my loneliness."

"Of course I can tell that your vulnerability stems from terrible loneliness and untold misery in your home. You don't have a home, my darling? But you must feel that you have a home with the Mdivanis. Why, we are the original wayfarers!"

"Oh!" said Barbara, almost in ecstasy, "I often think of myself as a wayfarer; a sort of vagabond."

"Well," said Roussie, patting her arm affectionately, making full use of her hypnotic eyes, "Alec and my brothers will be like big brothers to you now. Of course, Alec is a very manly and vigorous boy and he will try to flirt with you."

"Really?" said Barbara, gulping. "Movies and novels are my favorite pastimes," whispered Barbara. "And, of course, my daydreams . . ."

"And what do you daydream about, Barbara?"

"A companion, a loved one. A master—a husband," cried Barbara, her huge eyes fixed on Alex's waltzing figure.

They were talking in such an intimate way when Alexis came up and with a playful flourish bowed low and kissed Barbara's hand. "A waltz, Lady Barbara?" he asked seductively, his eyes resting on her lips.

"Enchanted!" cried Barbara, standing up. "And how did you know that there is nothing I'd love in the world more than having a title!"

Again, brother and sister exchanged a quick, meaningful look and Roussie's expression seemed to tell her brother to go full steam ahead and not spare the horses!

Like all people who love life a great deal and strongly feel the zest of living every day, Alexis Mdivani was an expert dancer and he loved to improvise. In the beginning he whirled Barbara around expertly in a waltz, holding her politely and uttering casual gentlemanly phrases. But then he flung himself into the steps of a tango, even put his arms around her waist, leaning her far back in a most erotic fashion.

"Oh, Alexis, you mustn't!" cried Barbara.

"Why not?"

"Louise will kill me!"

"And do you care about Louise?" His handsome tanned face twisted into a devilish but boyish expression.

Suddenly they both began to laugh and when they did, Barbara felt incredibly close to him.

The sixty guests were served a sumptuous dinner and the eight courses would have delighted the most discriminating epicure. There was the inevitable cream turtle soup, followed by striped bass, followed by squabs in champagne sauce.

Barbara sat between a young Count with an historical name and a young American stockbroker, who was working at Morgans and had been a childhood friend of Louise's at Newport. The French Count asked what she had seen in Paris and told her of some more special places to visit. "I'd be glad to motor you down to Chartres to see the cathedral," he said to her. "We can have lunch at my château, nearby."

The American next to her asked her if she was going to ski at Saint-Moritz at Christmas time. When she replied that she wasn't sure where she was going, he remarked that everyone at the table tonight was going to be there.

"Then, I must go," said Barbara, sipping her champagne.

"We'll have a good time," he promised.

For the first time in her life Barbara really felt popular and sought after.

After dinner there was entertainment of Russians playing balalaikas and two men and Alexis did a flaming saber dance. At one o'clock Alexis suggested they all go to a sinister nightclub in Montmartre.

"We must go home, Barbara," said her chaperone, Ticki.

"Oh, must we?" moaned Barbara.

"You don't want your father to punish you, do you? And you know how mean he can be. . . ."

"All right, Ticki. . . ."

Barbara sighed and stood up obediently. She made her farewell to the fascinating Mdivanis and floated downstairs and into her great car.

They moved smoothly down the boulevards into the Place de la Concorde. Gazing at the illuminated statues and fountains, Barbara realized that this was the best evening she had ever spent in her whole life. She wanted it to go on and on forever. She consoled herself by thinking that in two short years she would be master of her own destiny. Then she could join the Mdivanis and their enchanting friends in their wonderful revels until daybreak.

Nine A.M. found her fully conscious, unable to sleep after the splendid evening. She stared at the array of the little buzzers at the bedside table. Finally, she could no longer stand lying in bed. She flung back the linen sheets and put on her pink satin and lace dressing gown.

She was having breakfast when her stepmother knocked and entered. "Tell me all about your evening, darling!" cried Irene Hutton.

"It was the happiest evening of my life," said Barbara, her whole face lighting up with the emotion she felt.

"How so?" said Irene, her eyes narrowing suspiciously.

"I feel like the Mdivanis are my family," confessed Barbara naïvely.

Irene paled. What she had feared worst of all was coming to pass. She was going to lose her little pigeon to those fiendish Mdivanis.

"Well," said Irene, drawing up a gilt-legged armchair next to her stepdaughter, "whatever you're doing seems to agree with you, my sweet."

"Roussie Sert is the most intriguing woman!" bubbled Barbara. "And I want to rush off to Cartier today and buy a cigarette holder just like hers."

"You're going to smoke, then?" cried Irene.

"I *am* grown up, aren't I?"

"Almost," smiled Irene. "Now, I hope you haven't forgotten that we are going to have lunch today?"

"Roussie Sert *did* ask me," said Barbara. Then seeing her stepmother's furious expression, she stopped.

"Would you rather go to Madame Sert's for lunch?"

"Oh, no," lied Barbara. "You and I will go shopping after lunch and have a lovely, lovely time, buying whatever captures your fancy." Barbara was a great people-pleaser and more than anything she wanted the people around her to love her. That day she felt that Irene did love her, especially after the Cartier splurge, although she was wretched thinking that she could not lunch with Roussie Sert. In any case, she sent Roussie four dozen long-stemmed yellow roses and four dozen long-stemmed white peonies. Peonies were Barbara's favorite flower. She always had masses of them wherever she landed.

CHAPTER 8

Barbara was often invited to the Mdivanis splendid parties, which, of course, were all written about in the Paris newspapers. Barbara was beside herself reading descriptions of her furs, dresses, and jewelry, and what clever thing she had said to this Prince or this Count. Invariably her visits resulted in savage remarks from her father and martyred scenes from Irene Hutton.

"You prefer the company of those Russians to your Father and me!" cried Irene Hutton, playing a tragic queen and rolling her eyes like Greta Garbo.

"You see," explained Barbara, "they're young—my age, and most of the people I see are almost in their graves. . . ." Then right away she realized she had said the wrong thing.

Frank Hutton imagined he was superman and would live forever. You could not mention age or death to him. "What have I done to have a daughter like this?" he shouted. "And after all I have done for you!" His words were so biting that Barbara felt faint. She never could cope with anger and didn't dare to express any of her own.

"You just don't know who your real friends are!" cried Irene Hutton in a fury. "Your Father and I are the only ones who really care for you."

Frank Hutton snarled his usual "Good Jesus Christ, you're stupid! Repeatedly Irene and I have warned you about those third-rate Mdivanis—as have your aunts Jessie and Marjorie. But you *stubbornly* refuse to pay any attention to us. That Roussie Sert would kill her mother for a dollar. And those Mdivani brothers have sucked the blood out of Mae Murray and Pola Negri. Those poor girls don't even have any flesh left on their bones because your vulture friends picked them clean."

Barbara put her hands to her ears. "Please," she sobbed, "I don't want to hear such ugly things about my friends."

"Fine friends they are," sneered Hutton, "getting you all that terrible publicity, day after day, week after week, in these Depression times when nobody has a dime to spend. And it's only because of *me* that you are written about at all. Where would you be without my clever business brain?" He began to tap his temple significantly.

Irene saw a good chance to get rid of all her pent-up hostilities and hysterical jealousy. "Your Father and I have been so good to you, Barbara, looking out for your best interests. And now you avoid us and our friends because you're getting such a swelled head, palling around with all that international nobility. Titles, titles, titles! They're just trash—trash—trash! And that's all you talk about, morning, noon, and night. Fine values you have, and what gratitude after your very own Father slaved and doubled your fortune!" Barbara's blood froze.

"To think that my own daughter would turn out to be such a snob," shouted Frank Hutton. "To have your head turned by those idle aristocrats that don't amount to a hill of beans. I suppose you're going to throw us over today for a luncheon engagement with Madame Sert and her brothers and all those phony nobles?"

Barbara gnawed her nail and frowned. The Huttons' words had the desired effect on her. They knew their victim well. Barbara was a people-pleaser of the first order. And now she winced and paled as Irene and her father glared at her. The awful thing was that her father's words did have a bit of truth in them. Her head was turned by the glamour of the Mdivanis and their entourage. Indeed, Barbara admitted to herself she had never been so impressed in her life. She knew well the little thrills she felt when a Count or Prince courted her. It was twice as exciting as the attentions of a mere mortal. However, cringing under the Huttons' hard looks, Barbara felt a heavy sense of guilt fall over her, and it increased her depression.

Hoping that she could alter their opinion of her and make them love her, Barbara meekly crossed over the large sitting room and kissed her stepmother. She had every intention of lunching with the Mdivanis today, but she said with a pretty smile, "Of course, I'm lunching with you today, you sillies. And then, Irene, you and I will go to Cartier and I want you to have those pendant diamond and emerald earrings."

Irene's thin eyes narrowed greedily. Barbara's presents were essential to Irene's happiness. If she didn't receive these costly gifts every week she would give Barbara the silent treatment for a day.

As for Frank Hutton, he had always resented his daughter. And now his resentment would give him no peace. The thought that this stupid little girl had all that money dumped into her lap burned through his mind every day. And he, Frank, had earned all the money—had slaved seven days a week and sometimes didn't even take a vacation in the summer so he could stay near Wall Street. And now she was going to behave just like one of those ludicrous Gould or Vanderbilt heiresses and be seduced by one of those pompous titled people who acted so grand. And what had these European aristocrats ever done to act so grand? They had had an ancestor who had done something terrific 200 years ago and they had been living off that reputation ever since. Oh yes, wily Frank Hutton saw through the whole structure of international society. But his romantic daydreaming daughter seemed to thrive on all that attention of those corrupt nobles. Watching his daughter sharply, he suddenly wondered if he should change his philosophy of dealing with her. Perhaps he should court her like the others? . . .

As she gave him a little kiss on his cheek, he attempted a smile and some gentle words but instead a snarl came out. Jesus, he hated and resented this kid. He just couldn't help himself. He had already made ten million from handling her forty million. It had taken a lot of clever and almost criminal maneuvering to pocket that amount. He was determined to end up with more money than his daughter! As he was trying to force his lips into a pleasant smile, he hated himself for making up to her. It really irritated him that this girl had all the trump cards in her hand. It infuriated him to read the gossip columns about "the pretty heiress, Miss Hutton, surrounded by gilded youths and the raciest and most fashionable set in Europe." Even that fat vulture, Elsa Maxwell, was getting on the bandwagon and writing glowing things about his daughter. Then suddenly he was seized by one of his brilliant ideas. "Listen, Barbara," he said in honeyed tones, "I've got to get back to New York to do a lot of business related to your estate . . ." He spoke with impressive sincerity and depth of feeling, great showman that he was. "And I'd really like it if you came back to America with us."

Barbara fluttered her long dark lashes at her father. She couldn't resist him when he talked so kindly to her. She had made plans to go to Saint-Moritz with Roussie and the Mdivanis, but now she knew she must return to New York with her father.

Later, when she telephoned Roussie to give her the news of her departure, Roussie gave an agonizing sigh and said, "I'll pray for you, my little lamb. New York is such a crass and vulgar place. A place where no sensitive artist can flourish and grow. How can one be nourished in all that steel and cement?"

"I'll write every day," Barbara said.

"I will, too," replied Roussie. "We won't lose touch."

So, reluctantly, Barbara tore herself from her brilliant and stimulating activities with the Mdivanis to return to 1020 Fifth Avenue, to that cold duplex filled with expensive objects that were bought merely because they were costly. Somehow it had none of the grace and charm of the Mdivanis' way of life.

Years later, Barbara's favorite cousin, Jimmy Donahue, told me that Barbara used to read her love letters from Alexis Mdivani to him and cry, telling how hopeless the whole love affair was. Jimmy went on to tell me how he used to try to cheer Barbara up by inviting her on the town with his new friends Libby Holman and Ethel Merman. These two high-powered ladies made Barbara almost forget the Mdivanis, though drinking in speakeasies wasn't exactly her style. Of course, pretty Jimmy with his bee-stung lips and effeminate airs adored playing stage-door Johnny to Libby because she introduced him to all the pretty chorus boys. Libby was known as the torch singer, and Barbara had never known anyone who could drink the way she did. Libby also had a highly destructive group of misfits around her. Since Barbara didn't really enjoy getting drunk or picking up every Tom, Dick, and Harry, she steered away from these raucous Broadway outings.

When Barbara and Jimmy went backstage to see Miss Merman, Barbara's presence proved to be such a sensation that even Ethel herself was quite tongue-tied. Once Libby remarked, "Gee, kid, I wish you'd leave me your pearls." Once again Barbara's fortune made her deeply aware of her separateness. The morning papers were full of vicious attacks.

"Why do people hate me so?" Barbara used to ask her father and stepmother.

"Your Rolls-Royce is just too big," replied Frank Hutton, in the walnut-paneled living room with the large windows opening on a sweeping vista of Central Park.

"Perhaps your ermine coats are too showy, honey," chirped Irene, happy with her inevitable martini.

"Well," said Barbara, bewildered, "I read that Kay Francis

turned her old ermine coats into bathmats. And look how grandly Doris Duke lives in her house on Fifth Avenue and at Newport. Why should I get the brunt of all the criticism?''

It was in this period in the spring of 1932 when unemployment was unusually high and the business picture was particularly gloomy that Barbara began to feel this terrifying wave of hostility directed at her. A salesgirl at Bergdorf Goodman was openly rude to her and one young doorman at 1020 Fifth Avenue ignored her completely. She began to get ugly letters in the mail, criticizing her behavior and filling her with a sense of persecution that was quite justified.

Jimmy Donahue said that Barbara's father hired two body-guards to look after her and claimed they were needed to protect Barbara because of the dangerous Depression crowds. Poor people hated Barbara all right, but it was mostly due to the bad publicity that old Frank was giving out to the newspapers himself. In any case, Jimmy said it was a terrible thing for Barbara to wake up in the morning and feel that there were people who hated her, right out there in the streets. Naturally, Barbara was angry about all this, but she was brought up not to express any rage. She brooded all alone and her depression grew. You can't blame her for wanting to get out of New York and return to the Mdivanis, whom she felt really understood and loved her.

Finally after more rudeness from her doormen and the dreaded silent treatment from Irene, not to mention acid criticism from her father, she told Ticki, "Order the royal suite on the Île de France tomorrow evening. Don't pay any attention to Father," she added willfully. "From now on, I'm doing exactly as I please!"

"You're becoming just like Miss Becky Sharp," said Ticki, "so headstrong—ooh, la, la."

"It's my life, isn't it?" cried Barbara defiantly. "I'm tired of all this criticism and being treated like an imbecile." She stamped her foot and flung a Chinese porcelain vase against the paneling.

Maternal Ticki crossed over to her and put her arms around

her. She loved Barbara as her own daughter, tried not to spoil her, but the girl was so headstrong. Who could tell Barbara Hutton anything, when she was about to come into such an enormous fortune? The old Frenchwoman felt waves of futility settle over her. No matter how she handled Barbara it seemed to be wrong somehow.

"You're high-strung, chérie," soothed Ticki. "Ever since your mother's death your nervous system hasn't been strong."

Barbara glared at her.

"Are you insinuating that I'm going to end up insane like Grandma Woolworth?"

"Of course not, darling Barbara," Ticki replied gently. "But you must have some discipline over your emotions. Will you try, darling?"

"I'll try, dear Ticki," smiled Barbara, her flare-up fading.

"An ocean voyage will do you a world of good," said Ticki.

"It certainly will," cried Barbara, willful again. "I'm sick to death of all these horrors that the newspapers print about me here."

"Calm yourself, dear," said Ticki. "A great love awaits you in Paris, and remember, I'll always be with you to look after you."

"Promise?"

"Promise."

The two women embraced and Barbara thanked God for Ticki. "I never knew what I'd do without Ticki," Barbara often confessed to me years later. "I was always lost but I would have been completely lost without her."

CHAPTER 9

With a heady sense of anticipation, Barbara returned to her beloved Paris in the summer of 1932. Roussie had been in constant contact with Barbara. Although some of her letters were opened by the Huttons, Roussie cleverly sent messages via Jimmy Donahue. A flood of amber tea roses greeted Barbara in her suite at the Hôtel Ritz with a message signed, "Yours forever, Alexis." There was a book of Tagore's poetry from Roussie, signed "To beloved Barbara, in hopes that she will spend the summer with me in Spain." Barbara's personal maid and the hotel maids had barely unpacked her thirty wardrobe trunks when the phone began ringing shrilly. Ticki announced that Mme. Sert was on the wire. As soon as Barbara heard her vigorous, throaty voice, she felt a sense of well-being and her New York depression faded. People on the boat train to Paris and at the dock were so friendly to her. The concierge and the bellboy downstairs greeted her like a long-lost friend.

"If you're not too tired, my darling," said Roussie, "will you join José and me for dinner tonight at Maxim's?'' Then she mentioned some thrilling titled and movie people who were going to be in the party whom Barbara had been dying to meet. Barbara hung up and suddenly felt so happy that she poured the whole bottle of Mary Chess gardenia bath oil into the tub. She chose to wear a low-cut, flesh-colored satin dress with *diamante* embroidery that Ticki was most disapproving of. "You look like Mlle. Jean Harlow," observed Ticki, appalled.

"Would that I did!"

Colossally rich people have choices. Barbara had a passion for trains, especially night trains and blue sleeping cars, so she decided to take a wagon-lit to Biarritz. She'd met two wonderfully attractive couples at Maxim's, a young English Duke and Duchess and a naughty Italian Prince and Princess. Impulsively, Barbara invited them to go to Biarritz with her on the night train, and of course they accepted the invitation of the celebrated heiress. On a sunny morning they arrived in the lobby of the sumptuous Hôtel Palais and were greeted by the concierge and bellboys like royalty. Her Rolls-Royce arrived that afternoon.

Barbara had always loved the Basque country, surrounded by fertile farmlands and the haunting fragrance of damp hay and the briny sea. San Sebastián, across the border in Spain, was also a beautiful resort by the ocean with splendid hotels and villas and a cosmopolitan group of good-looking, idle aristocrats. A few years before, Hemingway had written his brilliant novel *The Sun Also Rises*. Barbara very strongly identified with his self-destructive heroine, Lady Brett Ashley, a sophisticated creature of thirty-four who ran off with a young bullfighter. Barbara herself had absolutely no intention of running off with a bullfighter because she didn't even like the bullfight itself. However, she did enjoy the excitement of the arena and the noisy Spanish crowd cheering the matadors and toreadors. And of course she enjoyed the presence of Alexis Mdivani, who suddenly joined Roussie's house party. His handsome face, tanned brown by the Basque sun, had never appeared more dazzling.

By the ocean one day, Barbara noticed again how powerful

and well-developed his chest, arms, and legs were and she wondered what it would be like to be kissed by his thick, well-shaped lips. The couple often held hands at the bullfights, and sometimes at dinner he pressed his warm knee against hers. And once at a party in Madrid at a great ducal palace, Alexis danced with her and held her unusually close. She felt him pressing erotically against her. Boys had often done this to her, dancing in New York, but she had not encouraged any further advances; now, however, she quite enjoyed the sensation of Alexis wanting her. It gave her a sense of power that she had never felt before. Louise watched him like a hawk, but being a Van Alen, she was far too polite to make any open criticism. She never indulged in scenes or showed any emotion. So the summer went tensely by, with visits to people in their villas and castles in Spain, Portugal, and France, with Alexis growing ever more ardent with every passing day.

"Do you care for him?" Roussie asked one evening in San Sebastián.

"Yes," said Barbara. "Terribly, terribly. What shall I do?"

"Louise does not understand him," purred Roussie.

"Yes?"

"You understand him and he understands you," said Roussie.

"I'm afraid Louise is going to make a scene any minute," sighed Barbara, playing with the gardenia entwined in her rock-crystal-and-diamond bracelet—the exact replica of Roussie's.

The inevitable scene occurred. It was so shattering that Barbara remembered it for a long time afterwards. It became part of the permanent repertoire that she told to her courtiers years later. They were all staying at Roussie's villa near Barcelona and the men had been put in one cottage and the women in another. Alexis and Louise were in the main house with the Serts. Things had definitely begun to get sticky between Louise and Barbara, creating a feeling of friction between the two of them. Barbara took every opportunity of taking her car and chauffeur and running off to other places nearby. She sensed that the blowup was near.

Feeling too tired to get out of bed one day, Barbara decided to spend the whole day in her room. Things were pressing around her and she had to be alone to gather her thoughts and plan her escape—for she knew she must leave. After her maid had brought her customary breakfast of tea, toast, and scrambled eggs, Barbara lay back on the coroneted pink linen pillows and sighed. Last night at a great tango party Alex had pressed her close and whispered divinely erotic things in her ear. Again she felt Louise's eyes glaring at her. She was yearning to surrender to sweet Alex but her idealistic sense held her back. When Roussie came in an hour later she found her young friend sobbing uncontrollably.

"What's the matter, Barbara?" she said softly, sitting on the edge of the bed and putting her arm around the young girl.

"I was just thinking about Alex and our dance last night," confessed Barbara, "and he was doing terrible things to me."

"I'm sure they weren't so terrible," said Roussie with a cynical smile.

"Oh yes," said Barbara, "he was kissing me and he even proposed to me. Naturally, such a thing is out of the question."

"Why?" purred Roussie.

"Because Alex is married to Louise," burst out Barbara with fresh sobs.

"He's miserable with her," said Roussie. "I can arrange an amicable divorce if you'd like."

Barbara and Roussie stared at each other in a tense moment. Barbara's throat felt dry.

A little later Roussie left her, saying that she would have a little talk with Louise and then send Alex down to comfort her. Barbara lay waiting breathlessly in her bed in an agony of terror. An hour went by and then when the little diamond numerals of her Cartier clock hit noon, she could bear the suspense no longer and rang for her maid.

"Pack everything!" cried Barbara. "Tell the chauffeur to have the car ready to take us back to Paris!"

Barbara's mouth felt dry and she was almost panting. It was an unusually hot day, steaming and moist, and the crickets were making a maddeningly loud noise. The fragrance of jasmine and mimosa wafted through the open french windows and mixed with the heady perfume from the bowl of gardenias on her writing table. Nearby she heard the sound of the waves falling on the sand. The rhythm of the sea was seductive and strangely disturbing. Breaking her reverie, the butler announced Prince Mdivani. She quickly buttoned up her beige silk traveling dress.

"You shouldn't be here, Alex," she said, nervously screwing on her pearl-and-diamond earrings at the dressing table, afraid to look him in the eyes.

"This is the *only* place I should be," he said, crossing the large room to stand behind her. He was dressed all in white and the short sleeves and the open collar of his polo shirt gave her a curious shiver of desire. His large warm hands rested on her shoulders. She felt so breathless she could hardly speak.

"Please, you must leave," she said, still not daring to look up at him.

His reply was to bend down and give her a long, full kiss. She caught the smell of his sweat, mixed with Russian Leather cologne, closed her eyes, and gave herself up to complete abandonment. She put her arms around his neck and kissed him longingly. They were kissing thus when some of the guests entered the room and found them.

Barbara sprang to her feet and Alex had presence of mind to say that Barbara had suddenly decided to return to Paris and he was saying goodbye to her. Always eager to please, Barbara smiled at the young aristocrats.

"Never explain," said the Italian Princess with a knowing smile that made Barbara want to vanish through the floor. In any case, Barbara quickly pulled herself together, told Alex to leave again, but he refused.

"I have other things to say to you," he said, kissing her even more ardently.

"Please," said Barbara, "you've done enough damage already. And I have too many enemies without making fresh ones."

"Why do you care what other people think of you?" said Alex. "What really matters is that one person adores you. And I love you deeply, with all my heart. You've known that from the very beginning."

Barbara kept thinking of Louise and all her friends who would surely take her side against Barbara. She just wanted to bow out of the whole thing gracefully, flee to Paris, and be alone. For a moment her feeling of passion turned to downright hatred and she said coldly, "I must go to Paris immediately. I can't cope with a scandal."

"Can you cope with me?" Alex said passionately. "Can you cope with the responsibility of having me love you? Are you mature enough to make the commitment of love?"

Barbara ran away from him in confusion. "Yes, yes, perhaps . . . I don't know."

"Go, then," said Alex, watching her with solemn eyes. "Go then, but remember that I love you and I want to marry you."

"That's all my father needs to hear," said Barbara with a bitter laugh.

"Who cares about your father?" cried Alex. "What are your needs? Don't you love me? Besides, soon you won't have to give a damn what your father says or does."

Their eyes met in a long meaningful moment. Then, without a word, Alex turned on his heels and went out the door.

A few minutes later Barbara, followed by her retinue, went to the main house to say goodbye. She awkwardly made her exit from the villa and the summer with Roussie came to an end.

Alex's question echoed in her mind. Could she cope with love? She really had no idea what it was.

In October she returned to the ponderous gloom of the Fifth Avenue duplex. The usual New York depression settled over her.

CHAPTER 10

By December 1, 1932 Louise Mdivani got her divorce in The Hague and Alex began bombarding Barbara with marriage proposals and gifts. The fateful year of 1933 dawned—the year that Barbara was to come into her enormous inheritance. The world press suddenly went wild with speculations. In New York she was afraid even to cross the street alone. The only time she wasn't afraid was when she was walking with her beloved Jimmy Donahue, whose strength and self-confidence brushed all her fears away. One evening her limousine was circled by a hostile mob on West 44th Street and Broadway. When she came out of the theater, several young people cried terrifying things at her and one woman said she was going to fix her face with acid.

The next morning found Barbara in a frenzied state. "Pack everything," she sobbed. "Oh Ticki, I hate New York, and I refuse to stay here another minute."

"Cry on my shoulder," said Ticki, taking the girl in her arms. It took all morning long for the middle-aged Frenchwoman to calm Barbara down.

The morning mail held all sorts of fresh horrors; from even far-

away Montana and Oregon and Kentucky came letters burning
with soul-searing abuse. "Who did she think she was?—behaving like that. She was worse than any cheap floozy and deserved
the worst that God gave her." Religious freaks implored her to
pray for her salvation and a Catholic priest wrote her to convert
and give her money to the Church.

Even parents of girls she had gone to school with tried to ex-
ploit her. Barbara was pleased when they wanted her on their
committees, but then she was invariably disillusioned when they
asked for a large donation. Money was the only thing that anybody wanted from her.

"You've got to face it, Barbara," said Jimmy many times.
"People are just out to take us and that's that. People only like us
for our money."

"You mean Billy doesn't like you?" she said, mentioning a
young dancer Jimmy had been going around with.

"Billy wouldn't give me the time of day if some greenbacks
didn't change hands."

"What about that handsome actor?" asked Barbara. "He
seemed so fond of you. I'm going to have him decorate my apartment as soon as I get my own home."

"Tom only bothers with me because I take him to parties and
introduce him to people."

"So there's no hope for us?" said Barbara.

"No hope," said Jimmy.

"Doomed?"

"Doomed."

More and more it seemed to Barbara that the only person who
loved and cared for her was Jimmy Donahue. She shared all her
problems with him, telling him about Alex and how she had not
wanted to hurt Louise at all. "But," she always concluded, "I
just can't live without Alex and Roussie."

She revealed all her self-doubts to him, especially her confusion about who she really was.

"You'll know who you are when you get your lovely avalanche of stocks and bonds," Jimmy would say. "Gee, I wish I
didn't have to suck around the old lady to get handouts."

"Didn't your father leave you anything?" asked Barbara.

"No. The old man was just like me—an irresponsible drunk who would do anything to avoid the nine-to-five syndrome. And he liked the boys, too, Barbara."

"Oh, Jimmy!" cried Barbara, shocked. "How could you say such a thing about your father?"

"Well, it's the truth, isn't it?" cried Jimmy with an ugly expression on his weak but pretty face.

"I don't want to hear the truth," cried Barbara. "I just want to escape from all the ugliness in the world."

"Well," said Jimmy, raising his Brandy Alexander, "we can afford to escape." He kissed the glass and gave a grateful wink. "What's your escape, Barbara?"

"Daydreams," she said. "Daydreams . . ."

Jimmy was the only person other than Roussie to whom she dared confess her rapturous feelings about Alexis, but she couldn't even reveal to Jimmy how her fantasies were growing more and more sexual. Of course her daydreams were still tinged with a romantic coloring; the idea of consummating her passion was rather frightening to her. She yearned most for gentle words, tender kisses, bouquets of flowers, books, and long walks in the countryside. She read romantic novels voraciously; she also became addicted to biographies of great Queens of history: Catherine of Russia, Christina of Sweden, Elizabeth of England. All these monarchs had handsome men in attendance. Barbara naïvely believed that a husband would be a companion and would devote all his waking hours to making her happy. She in turn would honor him with money and presents. From the very beginning, her values were rather distorted.

Alexis arrived in New York in early 1933 and stayed at the Savoy Plaza Hotel. The very day of his arrival he presented himself at six o'clock at the lavish Hutton duplex. Alexis must have been overjoyed to be in this temple of money. After the butler left him in the drawing room, he waited there for what seemed like hours and became angrier by the minute. He could not believe that Barbara would treat him with such discourtesy. Even Mrs. Van Alen, who detested him, had always been on time for her appointments. In any case, Alex had the good sense to turn a bad situation into a good one. He examined the furniture, paintings, and rugs with the knowing eye of a man from Christie's Auctioneers. So when Mr. Hutton finally did appear in the splendid room, Alex made an appreciative and intelligent comment on the Hutton home.

Years later Alex told his brothers and sister that Hutton interrupted him rudely and said, "What do you want?"

"Your daughter," came the honest answer.

Barbara said it was the only honest thing Alex ever said.

As for Barbara, she had spent the whole afternoon daydreaming, having her hair done, and searching her closets for the suitable dress. Alex always noticed women's clothes and was highly critical. She wanted so much to please him.

So a little after six thirty she came down the curving marble staircase in an anxious state. In her fantasies she had seen Alex as a warm and gentle consort, vulnerable as she was, but full of self-confidence, nevertheless. However, when the butler opened the door and she saw the subject of her daydreams in reality, Alex appeared so different in the flesh that she looked at him with bewildered eyes. He looked glum and tired. His debonair smile, careless chatter, and wonderful *joie de vivre* were missing. Their meeting was a disaster and further confused her. When he walked out the door, he gave her a hurt look and said that he would telephone her in the morning.

The next morning Aunt Marjorie Post Hutton telephoned from her nearby Fifth Avenue triplex of seventy rooms. After some polite fencing about, the beautiful and outspoken Marjorie said, "Barbara, you must forget this cheap Russian. All the Mdivani brothers are bad news. You don't want to be taken and made a fool of, do you?"

Barbara whispered, "No." But in her heart she felt she deserved to be taken. She even blurted this out to Jimmy Donahue at lunchtime.

"Barbara, you're going to be the greatest sucker in history in a few short months," Jimmy laughed hysterically over his brandy-and-cream cocktail.

"Then you don't think it's wrong that I marry Alex?"

"Baby, I hear he's hung like a horse so treat yourself to the best. If Pola and Mae paid for those great Russian battering rams, why can't you?"

"Jimmy!" said Barbara coldly, "I forbid you to use such language!" In silence they ate their creamy meringue rolls smothered with rich chocolate sauce. Jimmy was so sulky and glum that Barbara was sorry that she had scolded him. When she told him that she was sorry, he burst into tears. And she couldn't stop his sobbing. He was only eighteen and such a baby! A gentle maternal feeling went over her.

"Come, Jimmy, we'll go to Cartier's and I'll buy you some new cufflinks and a new watch."

He sat up and dried his tears. "Will you buy me the ribbed gold cigarette case? With the *pavéed* sapphires?"

"Anything your heart desires, sweetheart."

He smiled his boyish, deceptively innocent smile at her. Giving expensive things was the only way that Barbara knew how to please people. The two of them went mad in Cartier's, having a real orgy of spending. There was a jade necklace, a rock-crystal-and-diamond boudoir clock (for herself), and she gave Jimmy his cigarette case and black pearl-and-diamond cufflinks, with matching studs for his shirtfront. She purchased two other cigarette cases for his boyfriends, and a solid gold horse for Alex, made by the sculptor Marshall Hazletine. The total bill was $98,000. She often spent her afternoons shopping, though the total was a little higher than *usual*.

"Gee, Barbara," said Jimmy. "Do you think your father will pay this bill?"

"He'll have to," she laughed. "Won't he?"

Jimmy giggled. "The ogre wouldn't want to see you behind bars, Barbara. And think what publicity you would get in Sing Sing! Oh, Barbara," he added wickedly, "let's buy more! Before we're behind bars."

And they did.

Half-a-dozen beaming salesmen ushered them out of Cartier's and into the Rolls-Royce. In the pearl-gray interior, Barbara took

Jimmy's arm. "You're a terrible influence on me, Jimmy," she said.

"But don't you love me the best?"

"Yes, I do," said Barbara.

"I guess we bring out the worst in each other," said Jimmy.

"Well," laughed Barbara, "spending exhilarates me."

These Cartier orgies invariably made the Woolworth cousins elated, but it was difficult to sustain this euphoria.

They stopped in front of the Savoy Plaza and the chauffeur took the gold horse to Alex. Word had gotten out that Prince Mdivani was staying in the hotel and a curious crowd had gathered to see the famous young man. The appearance of the richly liveried chauffeur and footman caused a lot of attention, too, and suddenly somebody yelled, "That's Barbara Hutton's car! Let's get her!"

"She spends one hundred thousand a week, while we live on two dollars a week!" cried a disgruntled young man who worked at Woolworth's.

Every day the newspapers had been full of Barbara's spending: her parties at the Central Park Casino, the wildly extravagant presents she gave her friends, and the $150,000 a year it cost to maintain her private railway car.

As the mob converged on her Rolls, Barbara panicked and told the chauffeur to drive home to 1020 Fifth. Once again the doormen and elevator men were cold and indifferent, and when the doors were opened into her marble foyer, the familiar New York depression settled over her. Like William Randolph Hearst, Frank Hutton thought medieval and Gothic objects the most refined and esoteric. Barbara found the heavy oak and walnut Louis XIII chests, carvings, bronzes, sofas, and tapestries oppressive. All the brocade curtains were always draped over the tall windows so very little light came in. The whole apartment had the smell of a museum, slightly dank and stale. Ticki was nowhere in sight. She couldn't bear to be alone so she wandered into her stepmother's gaudy sitting room that was Louis XV in style—at least the way Joan Crawford would have imagined Louis XV to look. Everything was gilded and there were mirrors and rock crystals and gilded cupids everywhere. For Barbara it was a horror show. She had never seen anything like this room in any French château.

"You look very distraught and high-strung," observed Irene. Bing Crosby was singing on the radio and she was buffing her red-lacquered nails.

"People are so hostile in New York. I must get away somewhere!"

"You'll never be able to escape from yourself," said Irene, who was a great drugstore philosopher. "You won't have a Chinaman's chance, Barbara Hutton, wherever you go."

"China's just where I'm going," flung back Barbara angrily. "You can't imagine how mean those doormen and elevator men are to me!"

Whenever pressures became too strong for Barbara, she took to her bed. Now she lay between the crêpe de chine sheets with the coverlet pulled up over her head and the pillow clutched to her like a friend. She felt safe and secure. Nothing could hurt her. Barbara continued that habit, which caused husbands and courtiers much dismay, for the rest of her life.

At twilight, Ticki entered the room and sat on the edge of the bed. "Your father's giving a big dinner party tonight, Barbara."

"To which I'm not going," said Barbara defiantly. "All those bankers and stockbrokers and lawyers talking about General Motors and Eastman Kodak and General Electric until I could scream!"

"Tonight your father's seating you next to that handsome athlete Gene Tunney."

"I'm not coming down," cried Barbara.

"But chérie, don't you think it would be prudent to try to please your father? And this Tunney is very handsome and has a body like Greek sculpture."

"Perhaps," said Barbara, remembering Tunney's good-looking face and physique. For a moment a rapturous daydream took shape in her mind.

Jimmy Donahue's phone call interrupted her Tunney fantasy. "Alexis and I are giving a big party at the Central Park Casino tonight," bubbled Jimmy. "Alexis told me he's insane for you, but he respects your feelings so much that he won't ever pounce on you until you're ready. He's really a gentleman, Barbara— classy!"

"Jimmy, what do you think of Gene Tunney as a husband for me?"

"Gee," said Jimmy, "how did you meet that fabulous bruiser?"

"Father's giving a dinner tonight and is going to seat me next to him. Do you think he's a gentleman and sensitive?"

"Jesus, girl, those muscles would strangle you, and he'd probably knock you out cold on your wedding night."

"You mean he's a brute?" asked Barbara.

"Aren't all prizefighters sex fiends?" cried Jimmy. "Now listen, Barbara, get into your ermine and pearls and join us at eight o'clock. Dinner at eight, you know. Ruth Etting said she'd sing for us. Or would you rather have Ethel Merman? Well, I've got to hang up, baby, because I must lasso a hundred people together for the party tonight. . . ."

As Barbara was trying to slip through the hall without her father seeing her, Frank Hutton seized her arm. "Where are you going?" he yelled.

"Jimmy and Libby Holman are giving a big party for me at the Casino," replied Barbara, glaring back.

"You little fool," said Hutton.

"You idiot," said Irene.

Husband and wife watched Barbara disappear into the elevator and sadly shook their heads.

Barbara could just imagine the conversation.

"We should have paid more attention to her, Frank," said Irene.

"Fine time to bring that up," snapped Hutton.

"She's going to fly the coop," cried Irene.

"But I'm going to get a big cut before that Russian guy gets his mitts on her dough. . . ."

CHAPTER 11

Knowing that the prominent Louise Mdivani was her enemy sent Barbara into a state of panic. Her maids packed her suitcases and she rushed to San Francisco to make a round-the-world trip. Jimmy, Aunt Marjorie, and Aunt Jessie all tried to dissuade her but she stubbornly refused to listen. Irene and Frank Hutton made such unpleasant remarks to her over the suitcases and trunks that she was never to forgive them.

A week later there were headlines in all the newspapers saying that Barbara Hutton was sailing to Honolulu and Australia. There were rumors that she was going to marry Count Borromeo, one of the most handsome men in the world. His family even had a castle in a fabulously romantic spot overlooking the waters of Lake Como.

In every port of call Barbara received letters and telegrams from Alex Mdivani. She was even hoping that he would be on the dock in Shanghai to meet her, but he wasn't. He did turn up in Bangkok. In this romantic city that so resembled Venice with its canals and pretty buildings, Alex proposed to her again. He was in jodhpurs and riding boots and a white polo shirt with a coronet over the nipple. She always liked him best in riding clothes. She felt the old attraction for him. Today he looked every bit as good as he did in her fantasies. Alex proposed again and she stared at him speculatively in the springtime sunshine.

"Do you really love me?" she asked with a troubled air.

"I want you," he said, pushing his muscular thigh against her. "God, I want you and need you." His eyes became so heavy lidded that they almost closed.

"What's your answer?" said Alex seductively.

"When?" she said, "and where?"

"Paris," he replied. "Paris, the most beautiful city in the world. Where we'll live! I've arranged to have the whole cast from *Flying Down To Rio* perform the Carioca for us. And Anna Gould's house in Paris is for sale. It's the only way," he added, suddenly brightening.

"But how can we marry?" asked Barbara, "if you're a Roman Catholic?"

"I am a Russian Orthodox," he grinned.

"Oh?" she uttered as she always did when she was stalling for time.

"The Orthodox faith," he said, "is the official church of exiled Russian nobility, since the revolution. We'll marry there."

"Yes?" She hated herself for being so indecisive, but she wasn't quite certain about him.

He felt her bewilderment and kissed her. "When I shall be your husband, darling," he whispered into her ear, "you shall know love and passion such as you have never imagined, and I'm a man who understands your loneliness and the poetry inside you."

She felt better and smiled at him. In the sunshine his young face looked strong and masterful. He would take care of her. What if he was a rotter? Anything was better than her father. Besides, it would be exciting to be married to a scoundrel.

"Do you really think you can make me happy, Alexis?" she asked, gazing up at him tenderly.

"We'll go on the biggest spending spree of the century," he cried in his energetic manner.

"Oh Alexis, you've read my mind."

"You'll find I always will, Barbara darling," he told her. "You see, Barbara, despite my masculine appearance and masculine personality, I understand your feminine needs completely. I was brought up by my two sisters, so I understand the feminine mind."

"When shall we be married, Alexis?" she asked excitedly.

"In summertime, my darling," he exclaimed. "You'll be a June bride and have a fabulous white satin dress from Patou with a train a mile long, and you'll wear a diamond tiara and all the jewels of the Romanovs that I can buy you. All those Farmington girls will be pea-green with envy reading about you, and then we'll buy a palace in Venice and give the biggest party since Anna Gould's and Boni de Castellane's. How does that strike you, my beauty?"

"Dearest Alexis, I can hardly wait for June. And do you really think that Father will turn over all my money to me when I'm twenty-one?"

"He'd better," grinned Alexis.

The young people smiled happily at one another.

What a future they would share!

That evening Alexis cabled Roussie: "Have won the Prize."

CHAPTER 12

In June 1933, 4,000 people were standing in front of the Russian Cathedral in Paris to catch a glimpse of the world's most famous heiress, Miss Barbara Hutton, on her marriage day. Miss Hutton had just stepped out of her father's limousine in a fabulous white satin dress with an eight-foot-long train especially designed for her by Jean Patou. Mobs pressed around her as she and her attendants gathered up her heavy train to move up the steps of the church. She was wearing a single strand of enormous pearls that were rumored to have cost a million dollars, a diamond bracelet, and a diamond tiara. The newspapers reported that her lingerie of real lace made by a dozen nuns in a cloister cost $20,000. Both the bride and her father were smiling for the photographers, but they had exchanged some sharp words in the Rolls and Barbara felt faint with suppressed rage.

"This is supposed to be the happiest day of your life, Barbara," Frank Hutton told her, "but it's going to be your ruination, I can tell you!" Hutton was dressed in the inevitable morning coat, striped pants, and top hat.

"Shut up!" cried Barbara. "I hate you and I've always hated you and you don't frighten me anymore."

Father and daughter were walking over the red carpet that had been laid over the pavement. Two hundred exquisitely liveried gendarmes lined the steps to control the crowd.

The church itself was a heavy Byzantine monument. The altar was banked by 2,000 lilies. Their heady fragrance was overwhelming. Summer sunlight streamed in through the stained-glass windows lighting up the gloomy mosaics. Hundreds of candles blazed in tall bronze candelabra. The ceremony was long and complicated. Two hundred reporters and twenty cameramen were grinding away to immortalize this famous event for the newsreels.

"Are you pregnant?" asked Jimmy Donahue.

"Certainly not," whispered Barbara.

Jimmy and his brother, Woolworth Donahue, were holding crowns over Barbara and Alexis's heads. Jimmy was almost paralyzed by the heavy incense and perfume of the lilies, not to mention six Brandy Alexanders at breakfast. Nearby, Aunt Jessie Donahue, elaborately dressed, watched the ceremony with a sad smile. Like all the Woolworth women, she was plump; indeed her friends described her as a marshmallow with snowman's eyes.

Barbara and Alexis sipped sacred wine, kissed icons, and walked in circles round and round the altar. A huge Russian choir sang soulful renditions. The ceremony seemed endless to Barbara. A terrible headache started to throb behind her eyes; her lips felt dry and taut. Jimmy's remark about being pregnant filled her with dismay. She and Alexis had kissed passionately many times but had not gone any further because of Barbara's sense of propriety and her fears. She endured the service and became Princess Mdivani.

Barbara and her entourage swept into their waiting Rolls-Royces and were carried back to the Hôtel Ritz. Louise Van Alen had already given Alex a string of polo ponies and a pair of Oriental pearl-and-diamond cufflinks, but he had sold the gifts to pursue his courtship of Barbara. Barbara gave him a fresh parure of pearls and some new polo ponies from the Argentine. The groom looked particularly happy in his swallowtail coat, striped pants, and silk ascot flashing a pearl-and-diamond stickpin. Someone remarked that he looked like a gangster. Unfortunately, he wasn't going to be the last one in Barbara's life.

Back in her tall, palatial chambers at the Ritz, Barbara gave a newspaper interview. "He's amusing, smart, interesting. All the American men I know are businessmen, or want to be businessmen. Once they marry a girl, they wrap themselves up in their business again. It's going to be fun being a Princess."

What Barbara really said was that now she was married to an idle aristocrat, she intended to pleasure herself like all the others with inherited money. She might just as well have said that work was a bore and that European men really knew how to have a good time and devoted themselves to their wives. In other words, she wanted no part of the American way of life. Needless to say, her words did not sit well with the U.S. public.

"Talk about all the presents I gave you," said Frank Hutton, standing by his daughter's side. "Tell about all the money that I've made for you."

Barbara winced at his crassness. Gently, she continued to the reporters, "Alexis is so kind and gentle. He listened to all my hurts and problems . . . he didn't seem bored with it all the way most people did. He didn't dismiss my fears with a laugh the way other people did. He just told me that anybody who had as much money as I do shouldn't worry about anything!"

In his daughter's spectacular apartment, Frank Hutton and Irene viewed the wedding presents with rage and fierce envy respectively. There were half-a-dozen diamond bracelets, a diamond brooch in the shape of a polo pony, ruby and diamond earrings, jade bracelets, and jade necklaces—all important gemstones, of course, paid from the coffers of General Foods and other Wall Street victories. Of course there were the inevitable gold toilet sets, heavily coroneted, the usual silver tea services, heavy boxes of George III silver flatware, and sets of Baccarat crystal.

"I'll bet that terrible Russian crook steals all this away from her," hissed Irene.

"Think what he'll do with the stocks and bonds he will get," said Frank.

"And you schemed so hard to increase her fortune," cried Irene, taking her husband's arm.

The butlers were passing around trays of vintage champagne and Frank downed a couple rapidly, then felt violently sick to his stomach. He could literally see those stock certificates from General Motors and RCA and Du Pont being devoured by that terrible Russian wastrel.

"She'll give you something," cooed Irene. "Don't worry."

Hutton was the second person to dance with his daughter at the wedding reception. As he held her plump figure, dressed in shimmering ivory satin and an endless lace veil falling from her diamond tiara, he could barely utter congratulatory words to her.

"Oh, Father, I'm so grateful to you," she said radiantly. "All my good fortune is due to you."

"I'm glad you realize that," he said with a grim smile.

"I've decided to turn over five million dollars to you right away."

Barbara saw the look in her father's face and realized that no matter how much she did to please people, it would never be enough. She felt an incredible sense of despair.

Jimmy Donahue was the next person to whirl her about the parquet floor. "You don't look very happy, Barbara," he remarked.

"No matter what good things I do, people will resent me. I can never do enough."

"It's a rotten world," said Jimmy, nodding.

"I dread my honeymoon," said Barbara.

"A fine way to start your life," said Jimmy bitterly. "Sweet twenty-one with everything in the world."

"Well, I do have everything in the world, don't I?" she said with irony. "Every woman in the world would give her eyeteeth for Alexis."

"And so would I," lisped Jimmy. "Listen, Barbara, can I come along on the honeymoon and help out a little?"

"I don't think Alexis would like that," said Barbara, raising her eyebrows in a humorous gesture. "But perhaps you could join us in Venice, later on."

"And think about all those happy little Mdivanis trotting about in a few years!"

"NO, I don't want any children," said Barbara. Jimmy suddenly smiled. He felt happy. He didn't want Barbara to be a mother. He didn't want her to love anybody else. He knew that she gave him something special, more than she gave anybody else. No money was involved between these two first cousins. Not then anyway.

Later the honeymooners boarded the train for Lake Como. Barbara's twenty suitcases were full of her new wardrobe from Chanel and Molyneux. She held her breath when her personal maid brought in the beautiful flesh-colored chiffon nightdress. Roussie had picked it out for her and said that Alex would greatly admire it, but Alex seemed in a terrible temper. He gave her the dreaded silent treatment and stared moodily out the window at the passing landscape.

"What have I done, Alexis?" she asked, as she was to ask him a thousand times. The butler had brought in the basket of champagne and the bottles rattled in the silent sleeping car. Below them the heavy wheels clattered on the iron tracks and the locomotive let out a mournful wail. Train whistles always made Barbara feel sad, reminding her of being shifted from one boarding school to the next, from one relative to the next. Looking at Alex, she had a terrible feeling that her days with him would be as unhappy as the ones at boarding school. "Oh Alexis, what have I done?" she wailed again, on the verge of tears.

He took off his coat and tie, unbuttoned the top four buttons of his shirt. Then he pulled her to her feet and roughly kissed her on the lips. "Come on," he said coldly, "let's get down to business!"

CHAPTER 13

"God damn it, Barbara Mdivani! You're too damn fat!"

"Oh Alexis, what a thing to say to your bride."

Just a week after her wedding Barbara was lying in bed in their suite at the Palace Hotel in Saint-Moritz. Alexis was walking around naked. He had a splendid body and never wore any clothes in the house. It was rather terrifying for Barbara to reflect that his body was now hers and that he could do anything he wanted to her.

Alexis flung himself on the bed and slapped her bosom. "Look at your breasts—they're too fat!"

"Oh Alexis," she sobbed, "you're horrible."

"Look at your stomach!" he said, slapping her middle, then slamming out of the room.

"Ticki, what can I do?" said Barbara a little later.

"We'll go to one of those good weight doctors in Switzerland."

Barbara didn't pay any attention to the doctor's advice. Painfully sensitive to any criticism, she went on a rigorous diet and lost sixty pounds in six weeks. She drank black coffee three times a day and began to exercise a great deal. Though she never appeared more beautiful, the diet wrecked her good disposition and ruined her health. She became thin, nervous, and more willful than ever; she had trouble sleeping. The biggest irony of all was that her husband fell madly in love with her.

Her new image sent Roussie into a state of ecstasy. "Darling Barbara," she cried, "*Vogue* will be hounding you day and night now. And Captain Molyneux and Schiaparelli are panting to have you wear their lovely clothes. You're far more ravishing than Millicent Rogers and Audrey Emery! Darling, you must start a legend about yourself. You already have splendid jewelry, but now make it a famous collection, like your Aunt Marjorie Hutton and the Russian Grand Duchesses. There's an emerald necklace at Cartier that came from the Romanovs and I can get you a special price. . . ."

Roussie's words all seemed to come true. French *Vogue* and French *Harper's Bazaar* paid court to the Princess. Barbara could hardly recognize the pictures of herself, so fantastic was the transformation. Her freckles were removed. She dyed her light brown hair to a silver-gold color, rather like Jean Harlow's platinum. She allowed her dark brows to grow full again. The thick blackness was a startling contrast to the waved golden hair, vivid blue eyes, and startlingly red lips. Her remarkable emeralds, rubies, and sapphires further helped to enhance her image, along with seventeenth-century lace blouses and sumptuous Renaissance velvet skirts. She passed every mirror with surprise.

The honeymooners stayed at all the grand hotels in Europe, in royal style. Beautiful orchid plants and palms were installed in their luxurious apartments at the Excelsior, Grand, and Palace hotels. Once when Barbara didn't like the décor of a rented villa, she had a decorator change all the rugs and curtains. Another time in a Capri *palazzo* she sent all the furniture to a warehouse and had frail painted Venetian décor installed.

Rome was thrilling, Florence marvelous, but Venice, incomparable Venice, captured Barbara's heart completely. She was greatly impressed by the ancient palaces and churches lining the wide spaces of the Grand Canal and was charmed by teatime in the colonnades of the Piazza San Marco, but she found the motorboat rides in her enormous Chris-Craft most exciting. Every morning this great boat, like a Rolls-Royce on water, stood waiting at the red-and-white striped poles in front of the Grand Hotel. Three liveried boatmen stood at attention. At noontime Barbara and her retinue of liveried servants and titled friends appeared in the vivid sunlight. They rode across the waves, past the great architectural monuments of Palladio and Longhena, covered with a rainbow-covered spray from the sea. Roussie had dressed Barbara in Chinese beach pajamas. With her new slenderness, Barbara was an exotic and desirable figure.

In the plush cabin of the motorboat, Alex, smoking his Turkish cigarettes in his ebony holder, began to be disturbed by his passion for Barbara. The first rule of the successful stud was always to be in control of the situation. He knew that Barbara would have the upper hand if he fell in love with her. Dutifully, Barbara responded to his lust: after lunch, before dinner, and when finally they went to bed at daybreak.

"He's tireless," Barbara would sigh.

"Don't complain," came the inevitable response of one of her courtiers.

Living on black coffee and RyKrisp crackers, Barbara became keyed up and nervous. The enormous lunch parties at the Lido, served right on the hot sands by her liveried footmen, the endless dinner parties and after-dinner entertainments were a tremendous strain for her. Barbara had never been a hostess, though she admired her Aunt Marjorie's talent for getting the right people together and making them have a good time. Now she forced herself to seek out people who would enhance their lives. Under Roussie's tutelage her dinner parties became great successes. She took pride reading about the brilliance of these affairs in the European newspapers and magazines.

The first thing they did when they arrived on the steamy sands of the beach was to order a pile of journals, which Alex and Barbara would read in amusement. With their friends they would carry on the merriment of the night before. In an Italian newspaper Barbara was labeled the most famous playgirl of all times. Barbara was learning that it was enchanting to be a young and lovely Princess. She believed that the Mdivani brothers and sisters really knew how to live, with a capital "L."

Alex had a restless and driven nature. Every day was a new adventure for him. Barbara soon adopted this philosophy, and his spontaneity.

Roussie certainly had not lied when she said the Mdivanis were physical people. Barbara found it gratifying to have such a passionate husband. Years later, looking back on this period, it seemed the brightest spot in her life to her. None of her other husbands were so physically demanding.

Every day was a holiday with Alexis. She began to live as he did—impulsively and compulsively. She'd return home and say to the butler, "I'm having a dinner for eighty tonight. Can the chef cope?" If she got tired of the heat of Venice, she took a fleet of cars and a whole group of friends and went up to the coolness of the mountains a few hours away. She almost bought a chalet in San Cristina de Val Gardena, but bought a palace on the Grand Canal in Venice instead. Once she felt the urge to go to Istanbul, so they boarded the Orient Express with an abundance of champagne and wicker hampers and clattered across to Turkey. In August the Mdivanis tired of Venice and sailed majestically across the Mediterranean in a three-masted schooner and landed at Tangier. Barbara had an instant love affair with the Arab world. The mysterious Casbah with its veiled women and lute music enthralled her. A decade later she would buy a palace in the Casbah.

To top this memorable summer in Venice, Barbara decided to throw a Casanova costume party in early September. During those sultry weeks, Barbara spent every day embellishing her beautiful lace and taffeta costume, which was emerald green and copied from one she had seen in a portrait of Princess Colonna.

Alex was wearing a plum-colored jacket trimmed with gold bowknots, a white lace jabot, and a black tricorn hat. His shapely legs had never looked more fetching than in his tight breeches; his muscled calves stockinged in white silk.

As Barbara, her consort, and friends trailed out into the late summer evening and prepared to step into waiting gondolas strung with colored lights, a fleet of reporters surrounded them.

They all asked her where she was going when she left Venice the day after tomorrow.

"To Paris," replied Barbara.

"Will you give more parties in Paris?" asked a Milan reporter.

"Oh, yes," laughed Barbara, "more parties. My husband adores them."

"And you, *Principe*?" cried a Roman photographer. "Will you play more polo?"

"Yes," nodded the handsome *Principe*. "But when I arrive in New York I shall get a job as a stockbroker, like every other American I know."

As they swept down the dark waters of the Grand Canal, a round pink moon was rising above the Renaissance palace which Cole Porter had rented a few years ago and which Barbara was thinking of buying.

"Alexis, darling," said Barbara, "are you really going to be a stockbroker and devote all your time to making money, like Father?"

"It would please him," said Alex, kissing her hand.

"Well," replied Barbara coolly, "it doesn't please me. I'm most jealous of all the time you spend away from me."

Alexis was delighted and felt that she had fallen as much in love with him as he with her.

On the night train to Paris, Roussie inspected the honeymooners' compartment. "To think," she cried, "in a few short months you will have fifty million dollars, with no strings attached."

Barbara looked up at her and laughed playfully. "Father says its only forty-two million now, because of the market drop."

"A mere pittance," grinned Alexis.

Those were gay, careless days, but as they boarded the ship in early November to take them back to New York, Barbara's lightheartedness changed into a mood of solemnity. In the bar she toasted Alex after dinner, stared over her cocktail glass, and said, "It doesn't seem possible that there is that much money in the whole world!"

"We'll go on a buying orgy!" cried Alex. "Why don't we buy a high Fifth Avenue mansion like Doris Duke's?"

"Oh, Alexis," cried Barbara, "Aunt Marjorie sold her huge Fifth Avenue house because the taxes were so high. And I don't want to live so grandly in New York. Why, everyone will tear me to pieces with their criticisms, and you know I just can't stand criticism, Alexis. I'd rather face lions in the arena than those New York reporters."

"You have nothing to worry about," said Alex, giving her his usual support.

"But everyone in America hates me," she cried.

"No, they don't," said Alex solicitously.

"Yes, they do!" she responded edgily. "They blame me for everything. Why, there are girls richer than I am, and they aren't criticized morning, noon, and night by the press. Why, you would think I was a film star or something."

"Talking of film stars," laughed Alex, "don't pay any attention when reporters ask you about my brothers' affairs with Mae Murray and Pola Negri."

"What have they done now?" said Barbara with a little laugh.

"The usual crookery," said Alex, finishing his drink. "But don't think about that, Barbara. And take that worried frown off your pretty face." He bent down and kissed her bare shoulder. "Forget about everything, darling, but giving me pleasure and love. You do love me, don't you?"

"Yes," she said as they were going down the stairs to the stateroom, but she wondered if this really was love. Alex was more than passionate in those early morning hours and some of his feelings affected her. For a while she forgot the dreaded reporters and their rude questions.

CHAPTER 14

The night before they were to arrive in New York, Barbara barely slept an hour. Ticki entered to inform her that the boat had docked and the reporters were waiting in the lounge. Barbara's dread was so intense that she felt a dull ache in the back of her head and a certain vagueness which prevented her from gathering her thoughts together. When she didn't sleep a full seven hours, she invariably felt unnerved and her self-destructive tendencies grew stronger in these moments.

In the lounge, Barbara was her usual polite self to the probing reporters, but she felt a fierce anger surging through her. She resented their asking such personal questions and their trying to make Alex a figure of ridicule. They focused on the fact that Alex didn't have a job. Finally she snapped, "He certainly does have a job—he looks after me, and that's quite an undertaking."

"A fifty-million-dollar undertaking," said a *Daily Mirror* reporter.

Barbara gritted her teeth and said nothing.

"Well, Babs," said a reporter from the *Journal-American*. "I hope you've got a good lawyer, because you're going to need one now, badly."

"Oh?" said Barbara, her heartbeat sounding in her voice.

"Yeah, Princess, your husband's brothers are probably going to prison because of what they're doing to their wives."

"Oh?" gulped Barbara.

"Yes, Mae Murray is bankrupt and on a park bench, and so is poor Princess Pola. Prince Dave and Prince Serge are piranhas."

"Are they?" said Barbara, feeling queasy. Removing herself from them, she retained her air of dignity. Her head was high but her knees felt as if they would buckle under her; she was grateful for Alex's arms and his reassuring smile.

As they waited to have their trunks opened and examined by Customs officials, a crowd of some hundred people began to heckle them.

"Why don't you get a job like everybody else?" a man yelled at Alex.

"Perhaps I'll be a champagne salesman," said Alex, without thinking.

"Yes," cried a hostile man, "I'll bet you and your wife swill down a lot of that bubbly stuff. How does it feel to have everything paid for by your wife?"

Barbara closed her ears to other, more hurtful remarks. Finally Frank Hutton, Jimmy Donahue, and some police came to the rescue. Barbara was on the verge of tears and clung to Jimmy. In their Rolls-Royce racing across the grim West Fifties streets near where the boat docked, Barbara broke down.

"In Europe, they write glowing things about me. Why are they so vicious here?"

"Your father's press conferences don't help matters," said Jimmy, an unhappy boy who loved to cause friction among others.

"I only told the press the truth," said Frank Hutton. "My brother is married to a woman who has twice what you have, Barbara, and no one throws rocks at her or him. I'm afraid you're just too conspicuous.''

She turned away with her mouth in a set line and drummed her long lacquered red nails on her ribbed gold cigarette case. With her coffee diet she had become a chain smoker. Inhaling seemed the only thing that calmed her these days. She drew her sable coat more tightly about her.

Her dark thoughts were interrupted by Alex putting his arm around her. ''Barbara,'' he said gently, ''anybody who has as much as you shouldn't worry about anything.''

To her great annoyance, she often heard this from Alex. And from everyone. Money, money, money was all anyone ever talked about around her. Such rage swelled through her that she thought the top of her head was going to explode. Aloud, she said, ''I'm sick to death of all this money talk.''

''Come on,'' said Alex playfully. ''Be a good sport and smile at your Russian bear. Listen, darling, you're only twenty-one years old and you have the world on a silver platter.'' He tickled her under the chin. ''Smile? Pretty please, fair Princess.''

''Let's give a party,'' said Jimmy Donahue. ''A party will make her feel better. Why can't we get Fred Astaire and Ginger Rogers?''

Barbara perked up. ''Does he flirt?''

''I'll kill him if he does,'' cried Alexis, winking. ''But I'll let you tap with him.''

''Ethel Merman and I want to give a birthday party for you, Barbara, next week. Gee, we've really got to celebrate that day!'' said Jimmy.

''That's our forty-two-million-dollar day!'' sang out Alexis gaily.

''Yes,'' said Frank Hutton, ''I'm turning your whole fortune over to you next week. I hope you guard it well in these hard times.'' His eyes watched her from behind his pince-nez, and he looked round and bloated. He'd obviously been drinking a lot.

''Pray God I never become like that,'' she thought. Why

couldn't her father have been tall and distinguished like her Uncle Ed, who at least looked like a gentleman?

To cause more trouble, Jimmy added, "Oh Barbara, won't we have fun spending all that money, and we'll really give a party that will set New York on its ear."

"Fiddle while Rome burns," said Frank Hutton. "If you give this party, I'll wash my hands of all of you."

CHAPTER 15

The next morning was a cold wintry day. Barbara was staring out the Fifth Avenue windows of her bedroom. A pile of newspapers was next to her on the Chinese lacquered table. The latest skullduggery of the Mdivani brothers screamed in the headlines. Mae Murray and Mary McCormick, who had followed Pola Negri, the wives of David and Serge, had teamed up in trying to get their husbands put behind bars. Apparently, the unscrupulous Serge and David were involved in some criminal activities where their wives' stock certificates were concerned.

Wailed Mae Murray Mdivani, "I was worth three million when I married that devil David, and now I don't have a stock or a bond. Nightmares? Why, I just haven't had enough sleep for that."

Serge and David had both been in Paris for Barbara's wedding, and David said the reason Mae was so furious was that she had not received an invitation to the famous nuptials. She had told reporters David had socked her and locked her in her room.

Mary called Serge the world's greatest lover, but after some months of disillusionment, she labeled him "the world's worst gigolo." "He said I must remember that I was a Princess, and I could not associate with common people." Her whole testimony was so full of ironies that it was more funny than tragic. Barbara was always amused when she remembered the telegram she received after her own wedding reception: "Hi, sucker. Love Pola and Mae."

However, most of the brothers' activities left an odious taste in her mouth. David had apparently really ruined Mae Murray and Serge apparently had squeezed the lifeblood out of Pola Negri and Mary McCormick. Now the tabloids in Chicago, Los Angeles, Boston, Philadelphia, and New York had a field day speculating about what Alexis would do with Barbara's fortune. WILL WOOLWORTH QUEEN BE CAMPING OUT IN CENTRAL PARK LIKE SISTER-IN-LAW MAE MURRAY?

Presently, Alexis came into her room with a hangdog expression.

"You look awfully down-in-the-mouth," Barbara remarked.

After a half hour of further details of the hard-luck story, Alexis said sorrowfully, "Barbara, I wish you could help my brothers."

"How?" she asked.

"Don't be naïve," he told her.

Without a word, Barbara wrote out a check.

"Thank you, darling, darling Barbara!" said Alexis, kissing her all over. Flinging up his hands, he raced playfully out of the room with high-spirited cries. Barbara's maid had been listening at the door and now she fell on her knees before Barbara and told the Princess that her mother and father had been evicted from their house in Englewood, New Jersey, for lack of mortgage payments.

With admirable composure, Barbara wrote out another check.

When Jimmy called up at twilight to inquire about her twenty-first birthday party, she sounded so glum that he asked her what was the matter. "All I ever do, Jimmy, is write out checks."

"Join the club," said Jimmy bitterly.

"Everyone's after me," said Barbara. "Why, you'd think I was the goose that laid the golden egg."

"But you are, darling, you are the golden goose. Now listen, Barbara, dry your tears and I've got the famous dancer Clifton Webb to be your dance partner. Fred can't come because of some contract at R.K.O., so we'll just have to manage without him. However, I *did* get every Astor, Vanderbilt, Whitney, Goelet, and Harriman that's around. Gee, Barbara, why can't you marry Alfred Gwynne Vanderbilt? He's nifty-looking, and he's got almost as much money as you, and he'd certainly stop the rape of your checkbook."

"Do invite him," said Barbara.

What with the scandal of Serge and David Mdivani, Barbara's twenty-first birthday party at 1020 Fifth Avenue caused another tidal wave of hostility against her. The *Daily News* acidly commented on the princely style of the Mdivanis' existence. They described Barbara's gold brocade dress, her jade necklace, and jade bracelets, which she wore at this scandalous party. The press even commented on Barbara's reaction to her father giving her the $42,000,000 check.

Barbara drank a lot of champagne that evening and woke up at noon the following day. Ticki rushed in and said there was a mob outside the building. "They're out for blood," said Ticki.

"It's a lucky thing I'm in good condition," said Alexis, throwing back the sheet and running naked to the window. The man had absolutely no modesty at all and paraded about like this in front of all the maids.

Irene Hutton came running into the room in a satin negligé trimmed with maribou feathers at the sleeves and hem. She still wore the emerald necklace that she'd worn at the party the night before. "Listen, Babs, you've got to get out of town quick! Your father's hired some policemen and they'll take you out through the servants' entrance and rush you into our private railroad car at Grand Central."

"We'll go to Los Angeles," said Alexis, "and then take a ship to Tokyo."

Aunt Jessie Donahue telephoned and implored Barbara to take

Jimmy along. Barbara felt sorry for her aunt. Her handsome husband had already committed suicide, when his young sailor boyfriend left him. Now Jessie Donahue saw the same terrifying future for her son, who was constantly being blackmailed by greedy chorus boys and sailors, whom he picked up at Broadway bars.

"Of course I'll take him," said Barbara gently. Though she realized Jimmy was a troublemaker, she wanted to please everybody. In any case, she did find Jimmy amusing and she really needed a good laugh.

Even Barbara could not take care of the mounting Mdivani scandal. Alex had told her he had nothing to do with his brothers' business, but of course he had. The press took advantage of his plight and a thundercloud of scandal was unloaded on Barbara. As usual she was blamed for everything.

With their bodyguards, Alex and Barbara raced through Grand Central Station followed by servants with their luggage. Years later, Barbara told me her getaway seemed like a cloak-and-dagger thriller, with Sydney Greenstreet and Peter Lorre in hot pursuit. Fresh humiliations greeted her. Apparently Alex had been involved with his brothers' finances. There were hints that process servers would greet them in Chicago. The way the press tagged along, hounding her, made Barbara furious. They implied that she brought bad luck to her husband. Anyone could have told them it was the other way around.

Finally, the Mdivanis were ensconced in their gilded sleeping car. The reporters began to beat on the windows and a hostile crowd caught the fever and began shaking their fists at Barbara.

"Keep all the doors locked," she told her servants. "Lower all the blinds. And Alexis," she said, gazing at her husband, "for heaven's sake, keep out of sight."

The bad news accelerated. Hearing that the Los Angeles district attorney had issued a subpoena for him, Alex jumped off the train in Reno, Nevada. Barbara was terribly embarrassed by the fresh advances of the newspapermen. As the train pulled out of the Nevada station, the poor, abandoned woman dissolved into a flood of tears. She was further mortified by a wave of hostile reporters who met her at the San Francisco station, and she was furious when she found policemen and investigators waiting outside her hotel.

Jimmy Donahue had kept Barbara's spirits up during this grueling transcontinental trip, but there were times when his loudness irritated her. All through the cross-country ride Barbara could not help resenting the way she spent her twenty-first birthday. Reading about the sordid machinations of the Mdivani brothers made her ill. Alex was responsible for dumping all this unpleasantness on her. They all kept bothering her for money morning, noon, and night.

Jimmy offered a good suggestion. "Why don't you get a rich French or English title the next time? They say the Duke de Valencay is up for grabs. And the Duke of Argyle is a handsome stud, I hear. And at least they speak your language."

In this troubled state of mind Barbara and her entourage set sail for Honolulu and the Far East.

In Washington, President Roosevelt said that the only thing Americans had to fear was fear itself, and that soon prosperity would be here once more. At the same time a Senator blasted the very rich and made Barbara and the Mdivanis his special target. "Why should one woman be permitted to have control of such vast wealth?" he bellowed. "And why should this same woman be allowed to squander money on worthless Russian immigrants who think they fool the world by calling themselves Princes?"

This last sentence bothered Barbara a good deal. "Jimmy," she said on one of their morning shipboard walks, staring out at the endless horizon of water, "Jimmy, do you really think that the Mdivanis are phony?"

"They're the shrewdest operators in town, and Alex is about as much a Prince as I am."

"Then I shouldn't call myself a Princess, should I?"

"No, unless you want to be put behind bars," laughed Jimmy, making fun of the Mdivanis' newspaper notoriety. "All Europe is laughing at you, Barbara, and I think it is a devil's trick to make such a fool of you. The next time, I'm going to steer you into a real title. My fantasy is to see you as the Duchess of West-minster, living in a palace like Blenheim, surrounded by thousands of acres of rolling countryside. Like a Gainsborough!''

"So your dream is to be an English country gentleman?'' said Barbara, looking at her dear friend lovingly.

Said Jimmy, "I'd like to be best friends with the Prince of Wales.''

Twenty years later, Jimmy was to have his dream come true. Barbara was amused to pay for presents that Jimmy sent to the Duchess of Windsor.

Barbara's mood at being deceived faded some when the liner docked in Tokyo. Even in Japan they had heard of the amazing heiress, Miss Hutton. She was given the royal treatment by the passport officials in the smoking lounge when Alex breezed in. He looked robustly handsome and Barbara felt herself falling for his old allure.

"I've missed you, Barbara,'' said Alexis throatily, kissing her hand.

"I, too.''

Jimmy watched the seduction scene with a bitter and envious smile and remarked later that Barbara was always a fool for a pretty face. The Japanese newspaper *Hochi* wrote a long article about the reunited couple and quoted Barbara as saying, "His expertness in wise spending and in gaining access to the choicest circles is one of the reasons I married him.'' She went on to say that she was fascinated by the Orient, that she was thinking of adopting a Chinese baby, and that she was mad to buy a priceless Coromandel screen. Barbara always seemed to say the wrong thing to the press, whether deliberately or not, no one knows. In any case, it wasn't very wise to praise the Chinese, who were mortal enemies of the Japanese.

"Let's go to Shanghai tonight,'' suggested Alexis brightly.

"Why not!'' said Jimmy.

"Okay,'' agreed Barbara. They hired a twin-engine plane and after a terrifying, bumpy ride, circled the airport of cosmopolitan Shanghai.

How thrilling to arrive in a new city at night. The lights of the great city were twinkling below them.

"I need a drink," said Jimmy, who was badly shaken up.

"Me, too," groaned Barbara.

"D.P.," said Alexis, ordering the Dom Perignon champagne.

The three spendthrifts dropped a packet in every antique jewelry shop and rug emporium. They picked up people at the racetrack and gave enormous parties in the evening. In Shanghai, the Paris of the East, Barbara was fascinated by the rickshaws, coolies, and opium dens, and sampans going up the river in the harbor. She adopted Chinese dress and minced along in tiny high-heeled slippers.

One evening at the Grand Hotel they threw a gala Mandarin party. Someone introduced her to a charming Chinese man from Peking who got her so excited about the treasures there that she said to Alexis, "We must go to Peking tomorrow."

"I suppose now you want to buy the palace of the last Empress?" said Jimmy.

"No, just some of her fabulous porcelain and jade."

"I will arrange all the details," said the Chinese in Mandarin robes. "The air service is terrible there and the train service is negligible."

"Get a private train," said Alexis.

And they did. Off they went in a rocking old express train reminiscent of Marlene Dietrich's 1932 movie, *Shanghai Express*. Barbara was dressed and coiffed as if she were to be presented at court, with a mink coat and matching hat, and her beautiful double strand of perfectly matched pearls that had taken Mr. Cartier eight years to assemble. Unlike so many women, Barbara could be bathed and dressed in ten minutes flat. She never dawdled but quickly made up her mind about what she wanted, whether it was a dress, a piece of porcelain, or a Coromandel screen.

In high spirits, the trio arrived in the ancient city of Peking. There is a photo of the two gentlemen dressed in the inevitable fur-collared topcoats and Barbara in her mink. In those days, few women wore mink coats, and then only a few film stars. So the sight of Barbara in these extraordinary pelts caused quite a sensation wherever they went in China. Word had spread quickly about the heiress's generosity so everybody from the highest to the lowest was trying to sell her something, whether it be a Pekingese, a Coromandel screen, or a Ming vase—all of which she bought.

Believe it or not, Barbara and party went to the gala premiere of *42nd Street* in Peking, a fantastic Busby Berkeley film musical with Dick Powell, Ruby Keeler, and a budding Ginger Rogers. The film was dubbed in Chinese, which made the trio boisterous with laughter. Alex really did have a great capacity for fun. Even though Barbara always picked up the tabs, she remained forever grateful to him for teaching her how to live. Before she met Alex, she was always saying, "What am I going to do?" Alex's high spirits always carried things on at such a merry pace, one never had time to be bored or reflect. Still, to have to pay for everything, all the time, really rankled. She had given him $2,000,000 and he still didn't even buy his own cigarettes.

One morning Alexis's valet brought him a letter. The Mdivanis were having their breakfast in bed, and Alexis eagerly opened the heavily perfumed envelope and started to read the letter.

"Smells heavenly," said Barbara. "Anybody I know?"

She spoke lightly to him; they had drifted into a kind of brother-and-sister relationship.

"She's an exotically beautiful woman," said Alexis playfully. "The wife of a big German industrialist."

"Greta Garbo-like?" asked Barbara.

"Exactly. Dear Barbara, you're a mind reader."

"Were you having a love affair before you knew me?" asked Barbara gently.

"Yes, I was."

"And you intend to go back to her now?"

"You've made it quite apparent, Barbara, that you find me boyish and irresponsible. Frankly, I think you need an older man who can give you a more serious life. I am a lightweight, after all.''

Barbara put her arms around his neck affectionately and kissed him on the cheek. ''Remember, dear Alexis, that whatever happens, you'll always belong to me and have a home wherever I am.''

Her words touched him. She spoke with such feeling that he felt a little pain in his heart. ''Barbara, do you think people like ourselves ever have a home? I mean you've always said we're the original wayfarers.''

''Someday we'll settle down,'' said Barbara,'' . . . when we're older.''

''I don't want to be old!''

''Talking about getting old,'' said Barbara, ''what kind of a twenty-second birthday party are you going to give me?''

''An Arabian Nights fantasy,'' cried Alexis excitedly, for his introspective moods never lasted more than two minutes. ''Why don't we have a Night in Casablanca party, and everyone will have to wear exotic Bedouin dress. And we'll have Roussie's husband, Sert, design some wonderful screens for us.''

Later, when he had gone out to do some shopping, Barbara took a pencil and wrote:

Wayfarer
These are the wayward,
The homeless, the unblessed,
Who by the grace of God
Find their refuge and their rest.

Two days later they landed in India. Barbara and Alexis held court in the Taj Mahal Hotel in Bombay, awakened at noon, and went to the colorful racetrack. All the maharajahs fell in love with the dazzling young couple. They spent February with the Jaipurs in their magnificent palace and March and April with the Cooch-Behars. Barbara and Alexis, great spenders that they were, took to the brilliant life-style of the last days of the Raj.

Alexis, of course, went mad with all the tiger hunts on elephant backs. He became intimate friends with Jaipur and Baroda, who were sportsmen, happy-go-lucky daredevils, as he was. They constantly played polo together. And Barbara dressed in saris like the Baroda Cooch-Behars and Jaipur Queens.

Left to her own devices, Barbara took a car and toured all through India. The country became her second home. She returned every year for three months for the rest of her life.

They could hardly be torn away from their brilliant activities in India and lingered in Jaipur long past the cool season of the winter months. May found them in the sweltering heat of the Cooch-Behars' private railroad car headed for Cashmir in the north. Both were laid low with that dreaded virus that attacked nearly all tourists: dysentery. Ticki was the only one in their party who was well and strong. She advised them to return to Paris and London. The season had started there, she told them: Ascot and Epsom and the great horse race at the Grand Prix. Elsa Maxwell was giving a big bash for the Duke of Westminster in July. Though her cable was thrilling, India was more enthralling.

Reluctantly they left their houseboat and their turbaned servants and assembled the ever-growing caravan for the European journey. The honeymoon was over; so was the marriage.

Looking back, it seemed to Barbara that this was the happiest time of her life. It was certainly her most carefree, and she didn't have any trouble with her health then.

CHAPTER 16

Barbara had many stimulating lunches in the Victorian red brick London hotel, Claridge's. In the main dining room, the haughty Claridge's majordomo seated all the most influential people at tables directly to the right and left of the entrance. Many climbers and rough diamonds, directed into the rear of the dining room, which was called Slobovia with supercilious smiles, would gladly have paid a fortune for one of these celebrity tables. This early November morning Barbara and Elsa Maxwell found themselves seated between Hoare Belisha, the diplomat, and the Duke of Westminster; both men flirted with her charmingly. Across the way, Baron Rothschild ogled her through a monocle. Somerset Maugham was lunching with the Duchess of Sutherland, and they smiled graciously in Barbara's direction. Barbara had met them all at different parties. A new star in the social world is always welcome. Barbara was still a new face, and everyone was curious to see how she would handle her future. It's easy to fall and hard to stay on top. Unfortunately, the downward spiral was always more fascinating for Barbara than the positive, upward one.

In any case, all the attention of the rich, grand, and famous was gratifying to young Barbara, who was not yet twenty-two. Elsa was talking about her birthday now, and suggested that this extravaganza should be held at the enormous Regency Room at the Paris Ritz next week.

"Last night Alexis and I invited a divine American orchestra leader to fly over for the party, and we're scouring London for a heavenly rumba band."

Elsa swallowed some smoked salmon. "What about your marriage to that Russian rascal?" Elsa asked, chuckling.

"Here's your answer," said Barbara. Alexis strode in with a striking German girl on his arm. There was an exciting physical aura about them—as if they had just gotten out of bed.

"Good morning, Barbara," said Alexis.

"Good morning to you," replied Barbara.

At neighboring tables, all conversation came to a halt. Then with polite smiles Alexis and the girl were directed into the rear of the dining room. Word was out that the Mdivanis were finished, so Alexis had been demoted by the head waiter, a fact which greatly amused the two women.

"Hurt?" asked Elsa.

"Just a little," sighed Barbara, over her inevitable black coffee. "You see, Elsa, I've grown very fond of him and I'll miss him."

Elsa watched the heiress speculatively. "What you need now, my beauty, is an older, experienced man of the world, an established man, in business if you like, like Rothschild, who can structure your life. After all, the Mdivanis are merely houses of cards built on quicksand. They're here-today-and-gone-tomorrow people. They're an old story, and people are tired of their gold digging. Oh, if only Westminster here were free!"

"Anyone else in mind?" smiled Barbara.

"Hoare Belisha wouldn't be a bad bet," replied Elsa. "Would you like a life in politics?"

"Don't understand politics," said Barbara.

"How about that one?" said Elsa, pointing at a tall, incredibly good-looking man, most stylishly dressed. "He's Count Haugwitz-Reventlow, and he's never been married, Barbara."

"Yes, I met him at a polo match last summer. He *is* incredibly handsome."

"He's called the handsomest man in Europe," boomed Elsa.

As if on cue, Count Haugwitz-Reventlow presented himself before Barbara, clicked his heels, and kissed her hand. "Delighted," said Reventlow, in a deep, manly voice. When he smiled, he was particularly appealing.

"Enchanted," said Barbara, fluttering her long black lashes at him.

"I hope you're going to Paris, Count Reventlow," said Elsa, carrying on the intrigue.

The Count replied that he was, and Barbara put in, with her charming manner, "Do by all means come to my birthday party next week at the Ritz. Where will you be staying? I'll send you an invitation."

"At the Ritz," he replied.

"Well, that makes things awfully cozy, doesn't it?" said Barbara.

"Looking forward very much," said Count Reventlow warmly. He clicked his heels, bowed low, and walked sedately into the dining room. His profile and head had great aristocratic distinction. Barbara felt a little weak flutter in her stomach.

"What a fast worker you are!" observed Elsa.

"Look who's talking," said Barbara.

"I'm an old hand at helping these infatuations along."

"Oh, this isn't an infatuation," said Barbara, her eyes wandering over to Reventlow again. "This is something special."

Barbara's twenty-second birthday party at the Regency Room at the Ritz became notorious. "Luxury stains everything it touches," said Charles Ritz, the owner of the hotel. In Barbara's case it certainly proved to be right. This party brought an avalanche of more distasteful publicity on her. It also brought her her second husband—and the greediest bloodsucker of all.

When Barbara entered the Regency Room at eight o'clock that

evening, six dozen champagne bottles were being opened, and the sound of the popping bottles exhilarated her. The orchestra was playing lively strains of Cole Porter's "Let's Do It."

Hoagy Carmichael was singing at the piano. Barbara crossed over to him and embraced him warmly. She put her arms around his neck and began to sing along with him. The champagne corks continued popping, and Barbara laughed. "Hoagy, dear, I'm drunk before the evening's started, and I don't even drink."

"You will soon, baby," he said, giving her a knowing look.

"How do you know that?" she asked.

"It's a look drinkers have," Hoagy replied in his intelligent way. "You're a dreamer, Barbara, and you'll always be disappointed."

"She's never disappointed in me," said Jimmy Donahue, breezing over. He wore a mustache like Hitler's little black one. "Feel like playing a new role tonight," said Jimmy.

"Me, too," said Barbara. "Tired of the old Barbara."

Two thousand guests had been invited, and the room began to fill up. Elsa Maxwell watched Barbara's slender figure enviously. "It's time I get a chunk of some of that money," Elsa thought.

At that moment, the handsome figure of Kurt Reventlow strode into the glittering cream and gold room. Knowingly, Elsa's eyes traveled up and down his athletic figure and well-tailored dinner jacket. Reventlow was unknown among the international set, and Elsa suddenly had a brainstorm. She'd form an alliance with Reventlow and then they'd split what they squeezed out of Barbara.

As if reading her thought, Kurt Reventlow joined Elsa with a polite "Good evening."

"What a welcome surprise you are in Paris," boomed Elsa. "Everyone says you're the handsomest man in Paris this season."

Alexis Mdivani strode cockily into the room and greeted Countess di Frasso and Lady Mendl.

"Do you think I'm as handsome as that Prince?" said Reventlow.

Elsa's shrewd eyes studied his features. "You're better-looking and you're much more clever, my friend . . . at least if you play your cards right."

"Can you help me play my cards right, Miss Maxwell?"

"Elsa," she corrected with a chuckle, putting her hand on his shoulder. "Yes, I'll show you how to play your cards right."

A waiter was passing an enormous silver tray of champagne cocktails, and Elsa and the Count took glasses and clinked them.

"Let's drink to our friendship," said Elsa. "It should prove profitable."

"I like that word 'profitable,' " said Kurt.

"I knew you would, Kurt," chuckled Elsa, her jowls shaking in mirth.

On the dance floor Barbara's exquisite white chiffon dress whirled gracefully about her lean, slender figure. The diamond bracelets glittered on her frail wrists. Her pendant diamond earrings flashed alluringly as she tossed her golden head.

"I'd make a beeline for her if I were a man," announced Elsa. "But I'll have to live vicariously through you, my noble Count."

"I can't believe that any woman today has as much money as Barbara," said Kurt.

"Well, she does," boomed Elsa, "and it's not a myth."

Barbara stared wistfully up at Jimmy Donahue's pretty but somewhat dissipated features. "You're drinking too much, Jimmy," she observed.

"On a pink cloud," sang Jimmy.

Barbara caught the eye of Kurt Reventlow watching her. "Do you think Mr. Right is going to come along and save me?"

Jimmy tittered. "Not here at the Ritz, baby. You'll only find the bad guys here at the Ritz."

"What have you heard about the extraordinary-looking Kurt Reventlow?"

"He has a lean and hungry look, Barbara."

"Ticki told me he is really a very serious man. And clever, too."

"Yeah, he looks clever," said Jimmy, gazing at Reventlow's hard Germanic features.

"Do you think he'll hurt me?" asked Barbara tensely.

"Destruction is so delicious, Barbara," replied Jimmy. "And that's the quickest way to get back at your father."

The music and the Count's admiring glances shot Barbara into a vicious mood. She'd love to see her father's expression when he heard the news that Kurt Reventlow was after her. And wait till he heard how costly this party was.

With her new cohort in tow, Elsa broke up the Woolworth heirs' merriment. "Well, Barbara, here's a delicious fairy-tale Prince who's dying of love for you, and he's poetic, darling, like Hamlet."

"You're a Dane?" said Barbara, flashing a flirtatious look at Reventlow from her beautiful eyes.

"Yes, a melancholy Dane."

"He won't be melancholy for long," said Jimmy and pranced over to Dorothy di Frasso.

"Are you a poet?" asked Barbara, gazing up at the splendid profile of the athletic man.

"I'd like to write," he said, smiling, and the smile was deceptively sweet. "I've got so many feelings that are dying to come out. And looking at you tonight, I thought you could help me with this."

"Oh?" said Barbara, really stuck on the man now.

"Yes, I heard that you were a poet yourself and were interested in knowing about people's feelings—deep feelings. That is . . . that's what love is all about . . . don't you think?"

Barbara was hooked.

CHAPTER 17

In Reno, Nevada, on May 13, 1935, Barbara shed her Prince and the Mdivani name. After a few breathless hours she became Countess Haugwitz-Reventlow. Kurt was hers!

Newspaper headlines flashed around the world: newsboys in Paris, London, Los Angeles, and New York yelled the latest marital—and financial—developments.

PRINCESS BABS BECOMES COUNTESS BABS
WOOLWORTH HEIRESS TAKES ON NEW TITLE
COUNT REVENTLOW BECOMES BARBARA'S
NEW MILLION-DOLLAR BABY
MUCH WOOLWORTH STOCK CHANGES
HANDS IN RENO, NEVADA

Barbara was quoted in the tabloids: "Alexis cared more for his polo ponies than for me. . . . I didn't know Alexis had planned to marry me when I came of age, ever since we had met when I was very young. . . ."

So now the lucky, or unlucky as you might say, Prince Alex Mdivani had three million dollars in securities from Miss Hutton, furniture, jewelry, polo ponies, automobiles, and a fifteenth-century palace in Venice that had formerly been an abbey. Barbara had told him to buy the house, but he had the deed put in his name.

To the newspapers Barbara bubbled, "Now, at last I have found happiness. My search is ended. I know this is safe and sure." She went on to say that Kurt was the handsomest person she'd ever happened to see. She, couldn't take her eyes off him. "Then when we met and he looked at me, that was that!"

The New York *Mirror* bannerlined about the honeymooners:

COUNT AND COUNTESS REVENTLOW WILL LIVE IN
EUROPE FROM FEAR OF GANGSTERS IN AMERICA

If you happened to wonder where Barbara Hutton was at this time, you had only to pick up the newspaper and read the headlines.

REVENTLOWS LEAVE CAIRO AFTER
COLOSSAL SPENDING IN THE BAZAAR
COUNTESS BARBARA WANTS TO BUY
SPHINX BUT IT'S NOT FOR SALE
REVENTLOWS ARRIVE IN DENMARK:
Family Home Renovated
REVENTLOWS ARRIVE IN CZECHOSLOVAKIA:
Countess Is Said to Be on Hitler's Most Wanted List
COUNT AND COUNTESS PROVOKE BLACK SHIRT
FASCIST ATTACK IN ROME BY CHEERING
FOR ETHIOPIA
COUNT AND COUNTESS ASKED TO LEAVE
ROYAL SUITE IN GRAND HOTEL, ROME,
TO MAKE WAY FOR FORMER KING OF SPAIN,
ALFONSO. COUNTESS REFUSES
COUNT AND COUNTESS COMB ENGLAND FOR
SUITABLE RESIDENCE

COUNTESS REVENTLOW HEARS OF DEATH OF
FORMER HUSBAND AND GOES INTO
SECLUSION IN LONDON

On August 1, 1935 the handsome daredevil, Alex Mdivani, slammed into a stone fence somewhere between Palamos and Figueras. He was racing his Hutton Rolls-Royce 100 miles an hour. He was killed instantly. The car turned over five times, the Prince was decapitated, and his companion—Baroness Maude Thyssen—estranged wife of a great German industrialist—escaped injury when she was thrown clear.

Roussie, who loved Alex more than anyone in the world, hurried to the accident site. She could never forget seeing her brother's splendid body sprawled on the hay of a peasant's cart. She refused to believe that this young, vigorous man was gone. She would never fully recover. A little later, Roussie developed tuberculosis, got hooked on drugs, and her friends said she looked like a ghost.

As for the beautiful and notorious Baroness Thyssen, she not only lost her lover in the accident, but also an alligator bag containing $400,000 worth of jewelry. In her hospital room, when she learned of Alex's death, she had a relapse. The police were never able to find any trace of the jewels. The press claimed Barbara was bad luck to her mates.

A story went around that a woman, dressed all in black and veiled, visited Alex's tomb every morning at dawn. No one knew who this woman was. There was much speculation that it was Baroness Thyssen. Some said that it was Barbara herself. Another rumor pointed to Louise Van Alen. The Mdivanis became sort of an obsession to her. Serge Mdivani comforted her so well after her divorce that soon she became his third wife. A few weeks later, Louise was watching a polo match when Serge was knocked off his horse. As he got to his feet the horse kicked him in the head and he died. Louise ran over to the body and flung herself on him. She wore widow's weeds for years afterward.

Barbara was happy with Kurt Reventlow for a time. He was attentive and Barbara always demanded that her husbands be solicitous. He had beautiful manners. If he was a little stiff and formal, she forgave him. No love could be quite perfect, although she had hoped that this one would be.

Barbara's courtships and honeymoons were always joyful. The trouble came when the romantic period was over and husband and wife were left staring at each other, face to face, every illusion gone. In any case, her poetry flourished and people remarked that her verses had never been better. Elsa Maxwell even put them to music and Lawrence Tibbett sang the verses. The public didn't buy them.

A vague uneasiness began to grip Barbara when they arrived in London. Suddenly, with the days no longer busy with packing, no longer new people to see and fresh places to explore every day, they had the reality of daily monotony to cope with. Over lunch and breakfast Barbara would look at Kurt and wonder if she could remain with this man until death did them part.

As the days dragged by she began to wonder if they had anything in common. He was a man's man and liked to spend his time with male companions in his pompous clubs. Before the marriage he seemed quite fascinated by her poetry, but she soon discovered that he never opened a book. Even more important, he didn't like her friends any better than she liked his.

By 1936 Barbara realized that she had made a terrible mistake, but her pride prevented her from admitting it. Besides, she was six months pregnant and the idea of motherhood gave her moments of exultation. She believed a child might be the miracle that would stabilize her life. A child would make her a mature woman.

One morning in their hotel suite at Claridge's, Barbara could think of nothing to say to her husband. Finally, feeling the uncomfortable silence between them, she blurted out, "Where would you like to live, Kurt?"

"I think London would suit us best," he replied in his thoughtful manner.

"You wouldn't prefer Copenhagen?" she said sweetly, hoping to please him.

He shook his handsome head. "There exist a more important King and Queen in London," said Kurt, who cared greatly for royalty and protocol and all the trappings that went with the English monarchy.

"And that is so important to you?" she asked.

"Yes," he nodded. "London is the ideal place for us."

"As you like, beloved," she replied.

"We can make a big position here for our children, Barbara. Position is important."

"Yes," she said, "position is important."

"In America," he said sourly, "I'm considered merely the husband of a rich woman."

For months she felt there was something unsaid between them. It was her money, of course, that was splitting them apart. Now she said with becoming gravity, "You don't resent me because I'm a rich woman, do you, Kurt?"

"No," he lied.

"My money is yours, darling," she continued timidly.

"You're very generous, Barbara," he managed in a gentle tone, expressing a mood he was far from feeling.

"Father disapproved of my sharing my bank account with you."

"Why should he? Doesn't he trust me?"

"Of course, darling," she said, blushing under his hard eyes. The butler entered, providing a rescue from her acute discomfort.

"The Duchess of Rutland is on the line, m'lady."

Gratefully, Barbara sprang to her feet. "Oh, Kurt," she cried, running to the phone. "Why don't we buy a lovely historical place in the country like hers. Wouldn't you like to live where you could have your hunts and your shoots?"

"Why not?" he ventured. "Why don't we go and investigate today? . . ."

It was a thrilling adventure for them to scour the countryside of Cornwall, Surrey, and even faraway Northumberland at the Scottish border. A fantastic Elizabethan mansion in the style of Long-leat caught their eyes. It had an enormous park with formal gardens, a stable, and a zoo. Kurt was captivated and wanted to buy it immediately. Barbara suddenly thought, "Good grief. What would I do with Kurt all day, trapped here in the middle of nowhere?"

Finally, the Duke of St. Albans told them of a famous Regency house in Regent's Park, London. He reported that it was right in the heart of London but seemed as if it were in the moors of Devon. In a state of heightened anticipation, Barbara and Kurt set out to see this landmark. They drove up an endless driveway that wound through landscaped gardens and stately trees. Barbara's poetic nature was moved by the vivid greenery. Kurt's materialistic bent was moved by the splendor of the mansion. This was the place where his son must be born.

Barbara always made up her mind with amazing alacrity. When she saw this noble, cream-colored mansion she cried, "Oh, darling, it's pure enchantment. We must have it!"

"Agreed," he said, his stern face breaking into one of his rare smiles.

The Duke of St. Albans escorted the couple through the grand columned rooms with their Adam chimney pieces and scrolled ceilings. A few full-length portraits from Van Dyke looked down from the walls.

After viewing the endless magnificence of the lower floor reception rooms, the Count and Countess were led upstairs. The bedroom windows opened to a sweeping panorama of trees, sculptured fountains, and balustraded gardens. Amid all this splendor, there were no closets and no bathrooms.

"Of course I'll have to make a few changes," Barbara said.

The Duke said, "Our English houses never seem to meet American expectations."

"Oh Kurt, sweetheart," Barbara murmured, taking her husband's arm, "do you think it would be nice to have all gold fixtures in our bathrooms?"

"It's your money," he muttered.

"Ours, Angel, ours," replied the world's prize people-pleaser. "Besides," she added, "we should thank Grandpa Woolworth. In fact, I'm going to call this place Winfield House, for that was Grandpa's middle name."

"Uh-huh," Count Reventlow replied.

"I'm going to get Grandpa's very own decorator, whom I call Uncle Hans. Darling, he'll whip it into shape for practically nothing. He's such a sweet old man."

Kurt was ready with another "Uh-huh," knowing Uncle Hans for the vulture he was.

Uncle Hans clipped the Countess for three million. Gutting the house, he called for major alterations—new floors, stairs, and chimney pieces, not to mention 14-k shower handles, bidet trimmings, and towel racks. Hans conscientiously tried to give full value by being a stimulating companion. He thoughtfully took the titled couple to grand and smart dinner parties. All the great estates had storied treasures to unload, which they greedily sold to the Woolworth Queen for top dollar.

"I've found Marie Antoinette's Savonnerie rug for you, Barbara," cried the crafty Hans. "And I've persuaded a Romanov Grand Duchess to part with a matchless pair of black-lacquered commodes made for Versailles."

Barbara was thrilled that the project gave her life a new meaning. It also provided something to discuss with Kurt. The haggling over treasures proved diverting. Like the Bourbon Kings, the Vanderbilts, and Goulds, Barbara was also bitten by the building bug. The house formerly had been a cream-colored Regency mansion called St. Dunstan's, a home for blind soldiers. Now the walls had been ripped down and the facade was red brick Georgian.

Newspaper reporters converged on the site daily. Photographs of Countess Reventlow abounded in the London press. A frail, wan Barbara was pictured alighting from her gray-and-silver Rolls-Royce, her face shaded by a black cartwheel hat quivering with egret feathers. Her silk dress was gray, too. A silky silver fox complete with head and tail trailed from her shoulder. Size

2A lizard pumps encased her tiny feet. A collar of pearls completed the elegant picture.

"Oh, Kurt," she said, searchingly gazing at her husband, "this is the first time I've had a house of my own."

"And your first child, too," replied her husband, as he put his athletic arm around her swollen waist. Their baby was due any day.

"I hope we'll have many," she said.

"I'm a potent man. I intend that we shall."

"Heavenly," she murmured—a trifle uneasily. After a moment she whispered, "Happy?"

"Yes. But I wish you'd eat more."

Barbara's starvation diet had given Kurt many troubled hours. She still adhered to her coffee and RyKrisp routine from her Mdivani days. Kurt found it supremely annoying to lunch and dine with his wife in the best restaurants. He had a fierce appetite and it was boring for him to sit at the table and gorge on succulent dishes, while Barbara sipped cup after cup of cappuccino. His irritation peaked when he would watch his wife standing on the scales every morning having a fit if she'd gained a pound. The stubborn girl disregarded her doctor's advice to feed the infant she carried. Kurt, as well as her friends, were frankly worried about her. Her chief lady-in-waiting, and best friend, Sylvia de Castellane, constantly urged Barbara to change her eating habits. Sylvia, formerly married to the old and rich Duke de Valencay, preferred the company of a younger, richer person—which she found in Barbara.

"Dear Sylvia," moaned Barbara, "you don't want me to be fat as a piglet, do you?"

"But darling," warned Sylvia, "you're pregnant."

"Forget your vanity, Barbara," said Lady Diana Cooper, one of the great beauties of Europe.

"It's a matter of life and death that I stay thin," cried Barbara illogically.

"Barbara," said Lady Joan Moore—married to the heir of Viscount Drogheda—"forget what Alex Mdivani insisted on!

Why, my husband said you looked like a skeleton. What man would want that?''

Finally the stubborn Barbara took their advice. She tried to eat more, but her surprised stomach sent it right back up. In those days diagnosticians were unfamiliar with anorexia nervosa, which is clearly what the poor woman had. The doctors grew increasingly alarmed. Kurt asked if there were something disturbing her. Barbara, who was anything but a hypochondriac at the time, was puzzled by his concern. When Kurt suggested that he summon her father, she begged him not to.

Only Ticki understood that Barbara's problems stemmed from early childhood traumas. When a stabbing pain bent her double one day, Barbara clutched her stomach and fell onto the bed. Her face was so contorted and white that Ticki summoned the doctors immediately.

"My poor little baby," cried Ticki, sitting on the edge of the bed and mopping Barbara's brow, wet with perspiration.

Doctors circled the canopied bed. Their expressions were grave because they didn't know what to do. An anxious Kurt joined them at the bedside. Overlong heavy brocade curtains—thickly fringed and tassled—bunched in a heap on the Aubusson carpet. Lights burned feebly from the carved jade lamps through their pagoda shades. Her collection of jeweled eighteenth-century snuffboxes glowed in their gilded vitrines. The immense windows facing onto Hyde Park were shuttered; no outside noises penetrated them. The whole house was shrouded in a deathlike air.

CHAPTER 18

No secret is safe from a Fleet Street reporter. In no time at all, Barbara Hutton's illness was front-paged around the globe. The beautiful Woolworth Princess was not yet twenty-four years old and the staid old *London Times* printed that the Countess hovered between life and death. The *New York Times* chronicled: "BARBARA HUTTON, COUNTESS HAUGWITZ, SERIOUSLY ILL" and then went on to say "Lord H., physician inordinary to King Edward, made an unexpected visit to Countess Haugwitz-Reventlow's mansion in Regent's Park where the frail and lovely Countess hoped to enjoy a lifetime of happiness."

Jimmy Donahue, in an emotional state, rushed over to be at his beloved cousin's bedside. As he stepped out of his Rolls-Royce, he told the waiting reporters at Winfield House, "I'm afraid this is very serious." He began to cry. "This is all I can say now."

For weeks Barbara lay in bed, unconscious most of the time. She barely recognized the faces around her. In later years, she recalled that everything was enveloped in a gray mist. Sometimes, she told me, she felt she was in a dark tunnel with no light at either end. There were moments when she floated in the clouds—detached from her body. Once she saw herself lying in a coffin, with Kurt and Jimmy and all her friends crying. She claimed it wasn't unpleasant.

On February 18 Barbara's son Lance was delivered by cesarian operation. Headlines reported on the condition of mother and the infant heir.

Bannerlines trumpeted:

COUNTESS GOES FOR A DRIVE
FOR THE FIRST TIME IN MONTHS
CHILD WILL BE REGARDED AS CITIZEN OF DENMARK
SON HAS FIRST TRIP OUT OF DOORS,
FOLLOWED BY ARMED GUARDS:
FEAR OF KIDNAPPING

In the following weeks, numerous photos appeared in the press of Barbara being assisted by a platoon of nurses out of Winfield House and into her Rolls-Royce. She weighed less than 100 pounds and looked defeated. She had the appearance of an old woman.

The American public felt some sympathy about the birth of her son, but then fresh revelations made Barbara even more hated.

COUNTESS BUYS EMERALD COLLECTION OF
GANNA WALSKA FOR OVER A MILLION DOLLARS
BARBARA HUTTON, COUNTESS HAUGWITZ,
SAID TO HAVE SPENT
OVER FIVE MILLION TO COMPLETE LONDON MANSION

Her illness had made her unbalanced. As the summer season opened, she plunged headlong into social activities. Having made a conspicuous entrance to the Ascot races, Barbara sat in the Royal Enclosure. She also loved the tennis matches at Wimbledon. One of the men she admired on center court was Baron Gottfried von Cramm. She had seen this German tennis ace play in

Cairo the winter before and she marveled at his grace and agility. The Baron was one of the best-looking men she'd ever seen—with his shining blond hair, glorious tan, and lithe figure. His smile was blindingly vivid.

One day, watching him from her box, Barbara—in a black-and-pink chiffon frock, collar of pearls, white gloves, tiny straw hat tilted forward—turned and said to her husband, "Kurt, dear. I wish you would introduce me to von Cramm." It was a request disregarded by Count Haugwitz. He had recently taken to giving his wife the cold shoulder with less reason. There were so many younger and more handsome men about London at the time. Word of the Woolworth heiress's stupefying generosity had spread like brushfire. Reventlow was especially piqued at the attentions of a budding English actor named David Niven. In his book, *The Moon's a Balloon*, Niven has written that Barbara was the prettiest, gayest woman in London, and they laughed and joked at the formality of balls they attended. Niven acknowledges that Barbara had given him the fare to come to America—to pursue his movie career in Hollywood. No one liked to have a good time more than Barbara, he wrote.

Many times when Barbara and Kurt sped up the long driveway leading to the grand rooms of Winfield House, Barbara felt that some of her daydreams had been fulfilled. A regiment of footmen outfitted in yellow and blue livery greeted them at the door. Her panoramic Canalettos of Venice blazed from the damask walls. Her fragile, Paris-shod feet tripped lightly over the blue and gold threads of the famed Savonnerie carpet. Up the curving marble staircase waited her baby son, Lance, a little blond angel in a crib centered in his turquoise-and-white nursery.

Kurt claimed Lance resembled his side of the family, but the appealing child definitely had Barbara's eyes. Barbara seemingly had everything she wanted—a real title, a handsome husband who was intelligent, impeccably dressed, and impeccably mannered, a galaxy of friends from Europe's most distinguished lineage, invitations to the most elegant parties in London, and a child whom she could smother with all the love she never received when young. Noel Coward and the Duke and Duchess of Kent, whom she met through decorator Uncle Hans, were all part of her new circle. Noel was even said to have written a song especially for Barbara, "Poor Little Rich Girl."

There was a very definite change in Barbara after the birth of little Lance Reventlow. On the surface, everything was very much the same. The Count and Countess went out a great deal in society, but their relations at home were strained. Barbara flung herself into the social arena with a vengeance. There wasn't a luncheon, cocktail party, dinner, or ball that she didn't attend. To escape gnawing miseries and insecurities, she commenced an astonishing spending spree. At the end of each day, she returned home with some new treasure. And invariably, when she viewed this new piece of silver or porcelain, or new tapestry or new bronze, the object would no longer seem so intriguing to her and she would wonder why on earth she had bought it. A terrible sense of anticlimax would settle over her in late afternoon. Kurt was playing squash in the club. Lance was being looked after by his nanny. There seemed no place or need for her in the household at all.

Of course, everyone needed her to write out the checks. Make no mistake about that. She began to develop her body and took narcissistic delight in her flat stomach and lean hips. A gymnast worked on her every afternoon for two hours, followed with an hour's massage by a fiendish Swedish masseur. He forced her into the most terrible positions to improve her posture and to make her neck long and swanlike.

"Beauty," Roussie said, "beauty is all that matters."

Yes, Roussie was back in her life again. One afternoon at the tea hour the butler ushered Madame Sert into the splendidly carved oak-paneled library. Roussie was the only person who understood that Barbara was two separate individuals: one a lovely woman who moved about in fashionable society, and the other a troubled and confused girl who liked to be alone and write poetry. Both women had no need for small talk, which was a welcome relief. They could talk about their true feelings.

"You don't look very happy, Barbara," Roussie remarked with concern.

"What's happiness?" Barbara retorted, pacing over the Queen Anne needlepoint carpet.

"Are you content with Kurt?" she probed further.

"We scarcely have a moment to ourselves," Barbara replied, her thin lips set in a taut line.

"Why are you so distraught?"

"I feel something ominous is about to happen," a tense Barbara continued. "I have bad dreams about the future."

"You, too?"

"I try not to think about it. Now I must get dressed. Come upstairs with me. We're all dining at Diana Cooper's ball. . . ."

The two women moved upstairs through the gilded opulence and stepped into the ornate bedchamber. "Prince George will be there," Barbara announced shrilly. "He's as good-looking as a film star. And I wish he would flirt with me. We're all flying down to Venice tomorrow. Won't you join my party?"

"You've become as restless as poor Alex," Roussie observed.

"Yes, perhaps I am."

"I thought this beautiful house, your child, and husband would settle you down and end your traveling days."

"*Au contraire,*" Barbara said as her personal maid proceeded to help her dress. "Traveling is the greatest escape I've discovered."

"Why should you want to escape?"

"I've always wanted to escape," Barbara said.

"Have you tried drugs?" purred Roussie, already deep into the habit herself.

"Drugs are terribly sordid," Barbara said with a shiver.

"Drugs would help you, my darling," suggested Roussie.

Barbara shuddered. "I have a Victorian horror of drugs. Probably inherited from my Aunt Jessie and Aunt Marjorie."

"Well, Seconal pills have been a great assistance to me in this terrible time," said Roussie.

"Is that sleeping medicine?" Barbara innocently asked.

"Yes, they help the spirit to rest," said Roussie.

"And you don't have any hangover from them?" Barbara asked. "Recently, when I was ill the doctor prescribed so much sleeping medicine, I felt I was sleepwalking like Lady Macbeth."

"With murder in your heart, my dear?" asked Roussie.

"Yes, toward Kurt! And toward Father! Men! If only we could do without them."

"Well, we can't," replied Roussie, thinking of her beloved Alexis and Serge, both in their graves now.

A footman entered with a tray of drinks, and the two ladies sipped their cocktails delicately.

"Fortunately, I've never liked the taste of alcohol," drawled Roussie, her eyes wandering about the beautiful room with all its priceless objects.

"I rather like drinking on an empty stomach," said Barbara with a tight smile.

"I have to drink a lot before the phantoms fade," Roussie continued gravely.

"Are there so many phantoms?" asked Barbara, watching her friend apprehensively.

"Alexis—just dearest Alexis; I can't accept he's gone." Roussie opened a yellow enamel-and-gold box studded with diamonds—a gift from Barbara—and extracted two pills. She put them into her mouth, then tossed back her head and swallowed them down. Presently, a sort of peaceful expression came over her distraught face.

"They're marvelous," she sighed.

"Dare I try one?" Barbara ventured, with a sinking sensation.

"I don't want to initiate you into any bad habits," Roussie said gravely.

"Oh, I'm strong as a horse," tossed Barbara. "Nothing affects me. I've inherited my grandfather's constitution, the Lord be praised."

Roussie handed her the box, and Barbara swallowed two pills. It was a turning point in her life. We rarely are aware of these milestones, but what grew into a new dependence heightened the downward spiral.

Presently, Roussie was gone and Barbara wandered up the great staircase alone. Now she knew what Jimmy meant by floating on a pink cloud. It was nice to float like this and nice not to feel anything anymore. Even when Kurt came in and made some ugly remarks about Roussie it didn't matter much. Indeed, nothing seemed to matter at all.

CHAPTER 19

"What was that Russian operator doing in my house?" Kurt was saying.

"She was my sister-in-law, in case you've forgotten," replied Barbara vaguely.

"I'd like to forget it," said Kurt. "And I wish you would, too. I don't want any of the Mdivani notoriety to taint my son's future."

Two maids were putting the finishing touches to his wife's coiffure. She was dressed in rustling mauve taffeta caught up with a bustle. Her thick gold hair was upswept and held by half-a-dozen diamond stars that Kurt had given her. She felt wonderfully remote.

Dismissing the servants in his grand manner, Kurt told Barbara he was tired of this party life and wanted more time with her alone. On her fragile Louis Quinze beechwood chair, she turned her darkly outlined, tragic eyes to her husband.

141

"Why do you want to be alone with me?" she asked in a faintly mocking tone.

"Because I love you," he replied, moving closer to her.

"Do you?" she inquired with a mysterious smile.

"Have you any reason to doubt it?" He put his arms around her and tried to kiss her but she turned away. "Don't you love me, Barbara?" he asked.

She watched him in the many beveled mirrors that reflected him a dozen times. It seemed that whenever anyone loved her and grew close to her she became suspicious of their feelings. Lightly she said, "Of course I love you, darling."

"Can't we cancel the trip to Venice?" he said.

"No, no!" she objected, her voice rising almost hysterically. "No, no, I must go to Venice. Everyone will be in Venice, and there are the most beautiful parties in early September."

"Why are you so frivolous, Barbara?"

"The newspapers call me a playgirl," she snapped. "Don't you read the newspapers, Kurt?" Suddenly and perversely, she wanted to put herself in the worst possible light—to make herself unattractive to her husband. "Don't you know," she added, "that we American women marry foreigners only for their titles?"

Kurt was stunned. "You have no feelings for me at all?"

A madly capricious mood took hold of her. "No. No feelings at all." She felt compelled to make him hate her.

When they returned home at four in the morning, Kurt removed all his clothes, stood naked before his wife, then tried to make love to her. She pushed him away.

"I have my rights," he said roughly, his voice husky with desire. "The rights of a husband!" he added. He began to fondle her breasts, hoping to arouse her. When she refused his desperate advances, he turned away and went to sleep on his side of the bed.

The next morning Kurt was seized by a brainstorm. He decided to take her to some orgies in Paris and force her to watch the exhibition. He believed that Barbara was innocent about sexual matters and needed to have her eyes opened. Kurt, a clever manipulator, was extremely frustrated because he could not control his wife. He set his mind to break through Barbara's detachment. He intended to have the upper hand. Her will must bend to his.

"I want to go to Paris this afternoon," he announced over breakfast.

"As you like," she said, feeling guilty about the way she had treated him the night before. Her self-esteem was at a new low. She justified her behavior by telling herself that Roussie had upset her.

Kurt felt a warm surge of power when she acquiesced. His next plan was to make her sign some papers renouncing her American citizenship so that she would become a Dane. Then he'd truly have the upper hand—he would control the vast Woolworth fortune.

That afternoon they took the plane to Paris. In the City of Light, unspeakable humiliations awaited Barbara.

CHAPTER 20

The first person she saw in the Ritz lobby was her dear childhood friend and soulmate, Jimmy Donahue. The two cousins fell on each other with affectionate greetings. Kurt jealously watched them carry on. He loathed Jimmy, whom he considered a bad influence on his wife, with his lack of discipline. Kurt also was offended by Jimmy's behavior, by his flaunting of the conventions.

"Why are you here, Jimmy dear?" Barbara was saying in her gentle voice. Despite his youth, Jimmy looked dissipated, and she watched him compassionately.

"I'm here, Barbara," Jimmy said, "to be near you."

He spoke with such unusual solemnity that she stared at him. Gazing into his eyes she realized suddenly that her cousin loved her in a physical way—as a man loves a woman. It made her uneasy that a childhood friend, her cousin, desired her. It would create an awkward dimension to their relationship. Barbara had always understood that Jimmy preferred the company of his own sex.

Even Kurt caught the incestuous situation and said in his usual patronizing manner that he adopted with the boy, "Are you here with your mother, Jimmy?"

"Yes. She pays my bills. And I'm sure you understand that." Without a word, Kurt strode off, furious.

Declining Jimmy's invitation for the evening, Barbara explained that Kurt had arranged to take her to a "strange, sinister party" on the Left Bank.

At this point, the plump, fashionable, but overdressed Mrs. Jessie Woolworth Donahue approached to kiss her niece affectionately and said:

"I've seen your Dane."

"Oh," said Barbara with false brightness. "What did you think of him, Aunt Jessie?"

"He's as cold as a barracuda and as dangerous," Jimmy interjected. "He acted rude to me."

"It was Jimmy's fault. He started it," Barbara explained.

"I don't like the looks of him," Mrs. Donahue said in an imperious manner. Then she gave Barbara a level stare, adding, "Your pearls are bigger than mine, Barbara." She returned the wave of the slim, petite, exquisitely dressed Duchess of Windsor. "I wish you'd pay more attention to Wallis," she admonished her niece. "But of course you never listen to advice from anyone, you willful girl." Aunt Jessie was someone to reckon with. Now she moved away toward the woman who had almost become Queen of England, and who was queen of the ultra-fashionables.

At eight o'clock Barbara was sitting at her Adam satinwood dressing table, staring critically into the oval looking glass. A maid was smoothing the waves of her thick white-blond hair— swept up into a regal pompadour. Kurt had told her to dress down for the evening, so she had on a simple Mainbocher suit and her usual assortment of diamonds and pearls. Beside her lay the trays of jewelry that had been brought up from the safe below. The fabled gemstones flashed against the black velvet.

"I wouldn't wear those large diamond earrings to the Left Bank," suggested Kurt.

"Why should I step out of character?"

"Barbara, you have no sense of reality," Kurt replied. "And that's your tragedy." After a pause he added, "But maybe tonight will open your eyes."

She felt a vague tremor of premonition. When they got downstairs and passed into the Place Vendôme her anxiety was compounded when her husband canceled the Rolls and ordered a taxi. "Oh, Kurt, aren't you carrying this thing a bit far?" she said, drawing her silver-fox cape closer.

They rode in silence through the stately streets of Paris. Kurt smoked his cigarette through a long ebony holder and observed her ensemble contemptuously. Suddenly, the streets narrowed and the neighborhood became squalid. Barbara had never seen this side of Paris. "How dreary," she said, looking out the window.

"You won't find the performance dreary," Kurt said with a nasty smile.

Finally they drew up before a shabby brick bar on a dark street. The stucco facade was peeling and one of the shutters on the window hung down forlornly. Bright jazz music echoed from inside. Presently they stepped into a bar that smelled of stale beer and sweat. Drunken women turned to look at Barbara. One made such a vulgar remark that Barbara cringed. The language of the gutter is always comprehensible.

"I'm not amused, Kurt," Barbara informed her husband coldly. Turning to him she said, "Why are we here?"

"We're here," he said touching her arm tightly with strong fingers, "because I want my dear innocent wife to see what life is all about."

"If this is what life is all about," she replied, "I don't want any part of it."

"Come," said Kurt, leading her up the grimy stairs. "I want to show you how men and women handle sex with one another. You've been far too sheltered."

"What's the point of showing me all this?" his wife continued.

"I want to make you a more passionate bed partner."

"Perhaps it's your fault and not mine," she intoned, regarding him coldly.

"You're far too reserved," he complained. "Too shy—too detached."

"That's my nature," she sighed, pausing outside the door. Barbara took her husband's hand. "Kurt, *must* we go through with this?" she pleaded.

"Yes," he said with a cruel expression. "Now you'll lose your detachment, after this!"

The exhibition was performed by two teenage girls attempting an innocent air, and a stocky young Hercules of amazing extremities. All three were nude and acted out their parts with a relish that was embarrassing—at least to Barbara. The audience of fifty people watching the stage with hungry and desperate eyes increased her discomfort. She thought the incidents onstage were bloodcurdling. The youngest girl couldn't have been more than thirteen.

Kurt was becoming more and more aroused by their gyrations and the shrieks and moans coming from onstage.

Barbara had covered her face with her hands, then heard Kurt say, "That's the way you should be."

"Oh, Kurt!" she sobbed.

"This is love," he said.

"This is dirt!"

"But darling," he added smoothly, "when two people love each other and are married as we are, nothing between them can be dirty."

Barbara looked at him in bewilderment, and then seeing his cold gray taunting eyes she shuddered, convinced she had married a sadist! She had heard about Germans and their terrible depravity, and Kurt's mother was German.

What would he do to her back at the Ritz?

CHAPTER 21

The following day, facing Kurt across the breakfast table, she
could not look him in the eye.

"How do you feel, dear?" he asked, grinning.

She blushed to the roots of her hair and dropped her coffee cup.

"Have you ever felt more relaxed? More satisfied?" he went
on. He was pleased with himself and strutted about in his black
brocade Charvet dressing gown with its red moiré lapels. After
breakfast, he removed his robe and inflicted his lust on her again.
Later, at five o'clock, they boarded the night train for Venice,
and in the wagon-lits he made love to her repeatedly. When
friends met her in Venice in Barbara's sumptuous motorboat,
they all remarked on her pallor and frailty. As the launch drew up
before the candy-striped wooden poles in front of the Grand Hotel, the orange-colored Gothic facade made a shimmering reflection in the water. Numerous invitations awaited them; much mail
was held for them at the concierge's desk. Presently, when they

were settled in their red damask and white stucco drawing room, he said, "Here, Barbara, sign some papers."

"What are they?"

"Don't ask, just sign!"

"Later," she replied coolly. "Really, Kurt, why are you always pushing papers in front of me to sign?"

"Because I'm looking after you now."

"But Father looks after my interests," said Barbara nervously. She felt unbalanced and sank onto a gilt wood sofa covered with gold lampas. Church bells were ringing loudly—too loudly.

"Who do you love more, your father or me?" he shouted.

She regarded him angrily.

"Kurt, why don't you go to the beach and take a swim in some cold water? I'm tired of all your domineering ways."

"What a wife I'm saddled with!"

"Likewise."

He stormed out of the room, and the banging double doors set her nerves even more on edge.

A moment later, she heard some powerful engines gurgling from the canal below. She ran to the marble balcony outside the french doors and breathed in the scintillating salt air of Venice. The activity of the harbor, with all its yachts and tourist boats, raised her spirits somewhat. She watched her heavy black launch carrying Kurt in splendid isolation vanish over the deep greenish waters of the lagoon and observed bitterly that the Reventlow arms had replaced the Mdivani shield on the side of the boat. "Not for long," she thought, disgust welling up inside her. She picked up the telephone and called her father in New York. Half an hour later she got through to Frank Hutton at his Wall Street firm.

The first thing he said was, "Has Hitler started the war yet?"

"Good heavens, no," she replied. "But my marriage seems to have turned into a war. And Kurt the Terrible is determined to win. Oh, Father, he's so brutal and revolting."

"How so?"

"He does vile things to me!"

"Don't sign any papers," advised the cunning old man.

"He's always pushing papers in front of me to sign," wailed Barbara.

"Don't sign, you birdbrain!"

"Father, it's imperative that you join me here in Venice."

"Is your boy with you?"

"No. He's joining us later. Oh, Father, please say you'll come."

"The market's in bad shape," Frank Hutton grunted.

"I'm in worse shape," she told him. "Can't you come, Father? I need you."

"You need Dr. Freud."

"Father! Father! Don't hang up—I forbid you to . . ."

But the wire went dead. The old man had hung up.

"Poor Barbara," cried Ticki. "Anything I can do for my poor baby?"

"Your poor baby has a headache and is going to swallow an aspirin." She swallowed a Seconal with some wine.

"You've been acting awfully strange lately," observed Ticki.

"That's because my husband's so strange," replied Barbara.

"I'll draw your bath, Madame," said Madeleine, her French maid. "Do you want the verbena bath salts or would you prefer the geranium?"

"Countess Cicogna is on the phone," said her secretary.

After a time, Barbara was dressed in her exquisite Chinese silk beach pajamas. On her head was a picture hat secured with chiffon scarves under her neck. In such a poetic garb, she joined her husband on the hot yellow sands in front of the 1920s Gothic structure of the Hotel Excelsior. Her whole world seemed to be on that fashionable beach called the Lido. She had Cabana No. 2, directly to the right as one stepped out of the hotel. An orchestra played "You're the Top." A fleet of reporters and photographers surrounded the Countess's frail figure as she moved gracefully down the flight of balustraded steps that led onto the beach.

"How's the Count?" asked one insolent newsman.

"The top," cried Barbara gaily.

In her blue-and-white striped cabana she changed into her bathing suit. Kurt flung back the canvas partition and strode in. "Where have you been?" he snarled.

"At the coiffeur."

"I called the hairdresser and you weren't there." He slapped her across the face. "You're a liar," he shouted. "Whom did you meet and what did you do? Was it von Cramm?"

"What of it?" she cried, suddenly glad to have a scene with him.

"You must respect the name and position to which I've elevated you."

"Elevated me?"

"Yes—from your common five-and-ten-cent-store origins!"

This was the beginning of Kurt's violent scenes. He became fiercely suspicious of any man who even conversed with his wife. To make matters worse, the handsome Baron von Cramm himself was staying at the Excelsior and playing in a tennis match which the Reventlows attended that very afternoon. Barbara, in truth, didn't provoke the German champion, but von Cramm bowed low before her box and gave her a dazzling smile that showed his even white teeth. Kurt's worse suspicions were confirmed.

That evening they attended a film festival and Barbara saw *Holiday,* with Katharine Hepburn and Cary Grant. The film concerned a beautiful Fifth Avenue heiress and a good-looking working man who'd formerly been engaged to her sister. She adored the movie because it brought home so many truths to her. Lew Ayres, who played Hepburn's drunken young brother, was pure Jimmy Donahue. And the father was pure Frank Hutton. And of course she couldn't take her eyes off the fascinating Mr. Grant. Later, the Reventlows and their party were having raspberry ice and champagne in the Piazza San Marco at midnight. A half moon was coming up over the bell tower and waltz music drifted out from the damp colonnades across the square. It seemed for all the world like a scene from her lovely Canaletto paintings.

"Does anyone know that heavenly Grant man?" Barbara was saying.

"I do," said Dorothy di Frasso, a middle-aged and sensual American heiress who lived in a palace in Rome.

"And is Mr. Grant so delicious?" pursued Barbara.

"As delicious as Gary Cooper," replied Countess di Frasso with a naughty wink. She'd often boasted, "Going to Europe under Gary Cooper was the only way to go."

A strapping blond youth called Henry, with a fierce sandy-colored mustache, was sitting across the table from Barbara. His looks were really quite remarkable and Madame di Frasso told Barbara he was a hell-bent racing-car driver. Barbara felt a thrill. It was nice for any woman to be admired, but this boy really stared at her too hard. Kurt the Terrible was sitting beside her and she couldn't cope with another of his jealous scenes. In any case, the stranger's advances worked Kurt up into such a passion that he made even more violent love to her that night. The more he tried, the stronger her resistance became. It was going to be a battle to the finish. Neither planned to give an inch. Yet slowly poor Barbara was weakening.

Kurt's jealousy and possessiveness were becoming extreme. Greed, too, gave him sleepless nights. Unwittingly, Barbara's whole life-style encouraged her mates' avarice. In the end, her very generosity of spirit, her eagerness to please, and her desire to share everything with her beloved-of-the-moment filled both her husbands with ambivalent feelings toward her. If there was a choice between love and money, money always won with these men. And the pattern was to be repeated. Barbara herself was the root of the harm done to her.

"I was always my own worst enemy," Barbara told me, "but my husbands for the most part were pretty rotten, except for Cary Grant. But then he was only a dream at that point. . . ."

It would take three years for Barbara's dream to become a reality.

CHAPTER 22

The September parties, for which Venice is famous, began the new season. The aristocratic English families were still rich then, and they entertained in high style. Across from Barbara's high Gothic windows at the Grand Hotel was the Longhena masterpiece, Santa Maria della Salute. In the shadow of this great cream marble church lay the palace that Alexis Mdivani had bought in his name, and where his sister, Roussie, now resided. W. K. Vanderbilt's white steam yacht and the Duke of Westminster's even larger yacht were anchored in the harbor, almost centered in Barbara's view. In the evening, these boats were strung with lights that made a haunting picture. Every evening there were gala parties on these yachts for all the fresh arrivals. A season wasn't a season without heiresses and international beauties: Millicent Rogers, Audrey Emery, and the two Volpi sisters, Anna Maria and Marina, were all friends of Barbara's. Barbara was always fascinated to hear of their latest marital joys and miseries.

Roussie Sert arrived the first of September and promptly telephoned Barbara. Barbara was heartsick; Roussie was dying and this would probably be their last reunion. Unhappiness, disappointment, and drugs had helped push her into the abyss.

"Why don't you come and pay a call on me here?" said Roussie faintly, and then added with trenchant irony, "unless it would make you feel awkward to come to your former home—which in fact is really yours still, if you want it."

"No, I don't want it," Barbara said quietly. When Alexis died, Roussie had inherited the palace, and Barbara, in her usual generous manner, had let the Mdivanis keep it.

Barbara was shocked by Roussie's appearance. She had the look of death. Barbara knew that her former sister-in-law wasn't long for this world. She bravely tried to keep up a front, but it was silly for her to do so, for Roussie always saw through her.

"It would make me feel better," said Roussie, "if you would make up with your father and then I wouldn't worry about your future."

"You mustn't worry about me, Roussie," Barbara replied softly.

"But you seem like a volcano about to erupt," Roussie remarked with her probing stare.

"I don't want to talk about myself," said Barbara. "Let's talk about you, Roussie."

Roussie gave a hoarse laugh. "But my pretty darling, I certainly don't want to talk about myself in the state that I'm in. Barbara, you have an angry look in your eye that disturbs me. Why not let your hair down and tell everything to old Roussie?"

All emotionally upset people have good and bad days, and this was a bad day for Barbara. It was one of those days when she couldn't get out of herself. Depression weighed on her. Try as she might, her mind kept wandering back to her mother's suicide at the Plaza, to her father's screaming that she was so stupid, and all the Farmington girls calling her common and vulgar, to Alexis's horrible death. Perhaps what triggered all these memories was Kurt constantly reminding her of her "lowly origins." Kurt was forty-two years old, and he represented an authority figure to

her. In any case, under Roussie's probing eyes, Barbara was able
to talk about her feelings. Subsequently, she felt better.

The two women had been talking about Kurt Reventlow for a
time, and suddenly Roussie remarked: "Barbara, has it ever occurred to you why you married Kurt?"

"Freud says all women are masochistic," replied Barbara.

"And suffering is what you want?" asked Roussie.

"I expect bad treatment from men," said Barbara sadly.

"Do you think you'd be bored if a man was nice to you?"

"Probably."

Roussie was puffing a cigarette from her cigarette holder.
"Have you ever thought of going into analysis, Barbara?"

"No," said Barbara, shaking her head, with a little smile.
"No, I'd rather stay as I am. The old me is at least familiar.
Change frightens me."

"You're so American, Barbara. I think you'd be happier if you
returned to America now. Terrible things are going to happen
here, with Hitler on the march."

"Then I want to stay here," said Barbara, attempting humor.

"You and your father should try again," said Roussie. "He'll
help you bring up your boy."

"I don't want any of his interference," cried Barbara defiantly.

"I think he has your best interests at heart, Barbara. Probably
Kurt does, too, in his way."

"You must be mad!"

"Did I tell you that I saw the two of them lunching in London a
few months ago?"

Barbara was startled. "My father and Kurt together? Are you
certain, Roussie?"

"I absolutely swear it. Didn't your father telephone you?"

"No, he didn't," replied Barbara, with a quiver of fear. With
the initial shock over, a terrible anxiety crept over her. What an
unholy pair her father and Kurt would make. What were the two
monsters hatching up for her? In her disturbed state, paranoia un-
comfortably settled in.

A nurse came out and said it was time for an injection. Barbara and Roussie embraced in a tearful farewell, then the nurse led her away . . .

It was twilight in the garden. The light changed from gray to silver to mauve, and finally to midnight blue. Birds trilled on the ancient pockmarked statues of the four seasons, and a rather melancholy fragrance came from the autumn flowerbeds of zinnias and marigolds. The heavy wisteria vine climbing up the ancient walls of the palace seemed to have it in a death hold.

A round pink moon was rising over the dome of the Salute church, and Barbara stared at it sorrowfully. She drifted into the Gothic doorway and into the dim vaulted stone hall. Lamenting madonnas by Raphael stared down at her. It almost seemed preordained that Barbara should suffer. Anna Maria Volpi certainly suffered with her husband, Cicogna. And Daisy Fellowes, whose mother had been a Singer and her father a French Duke, escaped her husband by setting sail on her yacht. Millicent Rogers and Audrey Emery had both had difficult times with their European husbands. Millicent was an exotic creature with a Standard Oil fortune, and had been married to an Austrian Count, Ludi Salm. Audrey was a radiant girl from Cincinnati, a major heiress who had been shot down by the Grand Duke Dmitri in 1926 and now was being pursued by another Russian Prince, also a great ladies' man.

If there were sad moments, there were light ones, too. Very rich girls' problems always had a certain humor for Barbara. One afternoon Barbara, Millicent, and Audrey were sitting in Harry's Bar at five in the afternoon. Each woman had been named the most beautiful woman in the world in the pages of *Vogue*. The trio made quite an eyeful. The bar, as usual, was packed to capacity with standing room only at the bar and a long line of people outside the swinging wooden doors waiting to get in. Word had spread that the celebrated Countess Reventlow was inside. Two overly friendly men from Kansas City asked Barbara for an autograph. A handsome Chicago youth flexed his biceps and made an obscene gesture at her. All the attention was entertaining.

The three famous heiresses had been drinking Bellini cocktails, a lethal mixture of champagne and peach juice that tasted like ice cream sodas, but was surprisingly potent. By six o'clock, the trio was stoned. All three were literally almost starving to death. Society decreed that they be bone thin so that they could be the famous fashion plates they were. And did they have problems! About men, of course.

"To Mister Right," cried Barbara, raising her Bellini glass.

"You can be sure that we'll only meet Mr. Wrongs here," laughed Audrey.

"*In vino veritas,*" said Millicent.

When Barbara returned home in her motorboat, the porter gave her a coroneted envelope and stared at her meaningfully. Walking up the red carpeted staircase she excitedly read the letter. It was from the wild racing-car driver, the blond boy with the fierce mustache. Henry couldn't have been more than twenty-one, but she read his boyish words with rapture. He said he yearned to be with her and tell her all the things that were close to his heart. She had such wounded, sympathetic eyes that he knew she would understand and help him with his problems. He hoped to see her at Charlie Beistigui's party later, and he looked forward to a dance with her.

Barbara was in a reflective mood that evening as she floated through the Renaissance palace of the South American millionaire. Her eyes darted expectantly about the huge ballroom, all painted by Tintoretto in blues and pinks. She was talking to Audrey about her admirer, when the youth appeared before them and kissed Barbara's hand. He looked brilliant in his white tie and tails. They danced awhile in the cream and blue and gold ballroom and talked of a rendezvous in the Alps. Henry was a striking contrast to Kurt. The boy was sensitive and understanding and had a sweet disposition.

The next morning, slamming over the waves in her speeding

launch, Barbara sat in the cabin that was like a little Venetian sa-
lon, with tufted velvet armchairs and spindly-legged tables, and
pondered the budding flirtation. Behind the slanting glass wind-
shield stood two athletic boatmen dressed in her yellow and blue
livery. In the cabin with her was one of her house guests, an English Duchess, her three children, two governesses, a butler, a
secretary, and thirty pieces of luggage. Such was the grandeur of
the English in these prewar days. While Kurt read a German pa-
per beside her, the Duchess described the new Chanel collection.
Barbara, who'd learned the social game, gave all the appropriate
answers while she pursued her own train of thought.

Watching her daydream, the arrogant Kurt asked: "A penny
for your thoughts, Barbara?" He envisioned her thinking of his
masterful lovemaking.

In her reverie, she re-created what the blond man had told her
about Salzburg and how he yearned to take her there. They would
stroll through the flower-filled streets, dance in historic squares
with fountains bubbling and jolly old men squeezing tunes from
their concertinas. They would climb mountains, pick wildflowers
in the forest, and in late afternoon return to their *schloss* and sip
thick hot chocolate heavy with whipped cream.

With an innocent expression she answered Kurt: "I was just
thinking about the Mercedes I'm going to buy you," then lowered her beautiful blue orbs and thought, "That'll get him."

"Barbara, beloved," he muttered. The mention of money and
costly presents always warmed him. "Darling, you're so
thoughtful," he added, resting his hand on her thigh.

"Yes, I am thoughtful," replied Barbara, giggling to herself
and promptly returned to her Austrian fantasy.

Feeling powerful, Kurt was certain Barbara would now sign
away her American citizenship.

June, 1933: Barbara in satin and Marie Antoinette's pearls at the Russian Church in Paris for her wedding to Prince Alexis Mdivani. Beside her is her father, Franklyn Hutton. (*Associated Press*)

June, 1933: Barbara and Prince Alexis Mdivani at their civil marriage ceremony in Paris. (*Bettmann Archive*)

Barbara mobbed by Depression crowds as she arrives in New York on the *S.S. Europa*. Barbara's father is on her right and her mischievous cousin Jimmy Donahue is on her left. (*Wide World Photos*)

Count and Countess Haugwitz-Reventlow. Kurt was to be the cruelest and most greedy of all her husbands. (*Bettmann Archive*)

Miss Elsa Maxwell, the most famous party-giver of the '30s, '40s and '50s, played a prominent part in Barbara's many marriages. The portrait is by Simon Elmes. (*Wide World Photos*)

Barbara's son, Lance Reventlow, is surrounded by mother, father, and grandfather. This child cost Barbara her American citizenship and $4 million. (*Bettmann Archive*)

June, 1936: The forty-room Regency landmark in London with fourteen acres before Barbara transformed it into a red brick Georgian palace, complete with solid gold bathroom fixtures, 31 servants and 6 bodyguards. (*Associated Press*)

June, 1938: A glimpse of the renovated Winfield House, named after her grandfather, Frank Winfield Woolworth. (*Wide World Photos*)

April, 1948: Frail Barbara, weighing 85 pounds, leaves Winfield House. She is about to step into the inevitable Rolls-Royce. (*Associated Press*)

October, 1939: Three-year-old Lance Reventlow being held by Bobby Sweeney as they were about to board *Conte di Savoia*. (Photo by *New York Daily News*)

During the Great Depression years of the 1930s, these signs, hostile mobs and picketing Woolworth workers were a common sight for Barbara. (*Bettmann Archive*)

April, 1939: A beautiful Countess Barbara surrounded by the usual dozen reporters as she docks on the luxurious Cunard liner *Aquitania*. (*Wide World Photos*)

Countess Barbara looks at the cameras as she arrives in New York in 1939. A Danish subject and more than $20 million of her fortune spent, America seemed the place to recoup one's losses. (*Bettmann Archive*)

December, 1939; Countess Barbara dining at the fashionable Colony restaurant. With her is handsome American golfer Bobby Sweeney. Countess Barbara is legally separated from husband number two. (*Wide World*)

January, 1940;
Wearing a blue fox
jacket, Barbara strolls
on Worth Avenue, the
exclusive shopping
district of Palm Beach,
with the Countess di
Frasso. (*Acme Photo*)

January, 1940: Barbara and Bobby Sweeney watch the tennis matches at the
Everglades Club in Palm Beach. (*Acme Photo*)

January, 1940: Countess Barbara
arrives at the Colony Club, a Palm
Beach night spot, for the opening
night of the season. (*Acme Photo*)

May, 1940: Off to Hawaii, Barbara
sails from San Francisco on the
Matsonia. (*Acme Photo*)

"Cash and Cary," the most famous couple in 1942, aside from Hitler and Mussolini. In July at Lake Arrowhead, California, Countess Barbara became Mrs. Cary Grant. Cary was the great love of her life. (*Bettmann Archive*)

Barbara, no longer a happy bride, at Elsa Maxwell's liberation party in Hollywood, 1944. Frank Sinatra is standing with his back to the camera. (*Photo by Bob Beekman, courtesy of the Silver Screen Archives*)

August, 1945: Barbara in a Los Angeles court after securing a divorce from Cary Grant. She testified that they had nothing in common and never would. (*Acme Photo*)

Barbara and her fourth husband, virile Prince Igor Troubetzkoy, descended from Lithuanian royalty. (*Bettmann Archive*)

September, 1951: A frail and freshly divorced Barbara dances with Cecil Beaton. It's the most famous party of the decade, given in Venice by Charlie Beistegui. Barbara spent $25,000 on her costume. (*Wide World*)

September, 1953: Barbara is watching a tennis match in Monte Carlo with handsome ex-tennis champ Baron Gottfried von Cramm. Barbara is unmarried. (*Wide World*)

Barbara becomes Madame Rubirosa in New York on December 30, 1953. This fifth marriage lasted only seventy-three days. Barbara and Rubi were then separated, and she was some $2 million poorer. (*New York Daily News*)

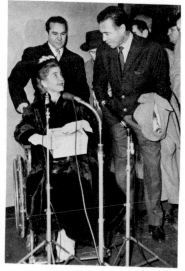

Barbara smiles radiantly at the bridegegroom Rubirosa. She was often confined to a wheelchair now and Rubi was having a flamboyant affair with Zsa Zsa Gabor. (*Bettmann Archive*)

November, 1964: Princess Doan of Champassak, Barbara, and her husband pose in their Paris apartment. Prince Doan was to be Barbara's last husband. (*Wide World Photos*)

Princess Barbara in her famous Casbah palace in Tangier, Morocco. She is approaching sixty but still has a wistful, tragic and lovely look. Barbara loved to wear Indian saris, and emeralds and diamonds were her favorite stones. Her old friend Cecil Beaton did these photos. (*Cecil Beaton, Courtesy of Sotheby's Belgravia*)

November, 1957: Barbara and the author, Philip Van Rensselaer, arriving in New York on the steamship *United States.* Barbara was sick on the boat with Asian flu, Philip was busy writing in his diary. (*The New York Daily News*)

1973: Barbara and her first cousin Woolworth Donahue. Her face is a mask of tragedy. Her son, Lance, had just died, Aunt Marjorie and Aunt Jessie were dead, and Woolworth died a month later. (*Charles Van Rensselaer*)

CHAPTER 23

Barbara swam like an otter through the Adriatic, headed in the direction of the blond man sunning on a raft. She loved to swim, did an excellent crawl, and liked the feeling of warm water surging around her slender body like a caress. She was thrilled by the idea of meeting Henry.

As she called good morning, her blond friend stood up on the raft. His lean hips were covered with the smallest blue-and-white bathing costume she had ever seen. He made a graceful dive and suddenly she felt his arms around her waist. His strong arms were pulling her down beside him. Before she knew what was happening, they were kissing underwater.

They came up for air. Again they kissed and again he pulled her down below the water.

They came up for air. Again they kissed and again he pulled her down below the water.

Barbara and Henry trotted happily out of the sea and ran joyously over the hot sand toward her cabana.

"I'm mad for you, Barbara," the youth was saying. "When can we be alone?"

"Soon."

"Tonight?"

"Hopefully."

She was ecstatic.

"Now, Henry, you mustn't look at me during lunch," she began in a frightened voice—feeling Kurt's eyes on her.

"Silly girl." He looked so fresh and clean and good—untainted, not corrupted.

"No, no," protested Barbara. "You mustn't look at me like that, Henry dear. You'll give the whole show away."

"Promise me that you'll come to Salzburg with me tomorrow?"

"Yes, yes!"

She took special pains to make herself lovely at luncheon. The mirror in her cabana told her that her eyes had never been so blue, her cheeks never so pink.

A naked Kurt came up behind her and cupped her breasts in his hands. "You're awfully flushed, Barbara," he said suspiciously.

"Venezia agrees with me," she said.

"All morning long," Kurt said amorously, "I've been thinking what I'm going to do to you this afternoon."

"Kurt," she said faintly, "I'm limp from exhaustion already. And I have a black-and-blue mark on my thigh."

"You'll have more by tonight," he promised.

"I've fallen madly in love with you," he said. "You've become an obsession to me. Look at my hard brown body and your soft white body. Doesn't it excite you?"

"Yes," she said, thinking of another tan body.

"Why can't we run away and be alone somewhere in the country?" her husband asked as he kissed her bare shoulder.

Barbara almost laughed out loud. "Well, darling," she said—her thoughts racing—"why don't we take the night train to Salzburg tomorrow?"

"Promise?" he asked.

"Promise."

Husband and wife stepped out into the sunshine a moment later smiling radiantly. Each thought they had outwitted the other.

In the blazing sunshine Barbara and her guests sat at the luncheon table set up in front of her cabana. Her footmen served course after course to the dozen guests. Juicy prosciutto ham entwined with the most succulent Persian melon; followed by creamy fettucini Alfredo; then thin slices of veal with tuna sauce . . . all washed down by chilled Orvietto wine, which was like flowers to the palate. Barbara didn't normally drink at all and ate little, but with Henry pressing his firm tanned leg against hers under the table, she devoured the fettucini like a starving person and gulped glass after glass of wine.

Naturally, the conversation during lunch concerned Hitler and his ominous new threats, which might end their good times in the sun. This season the galas were even more splendid. Daisy Fellowes gave her usual sumptuous party at her Renaissance palace. Countess Volpi entertained at a ball in her Grand Canal palace. Tonight hundreds were attending Cole Porter's costume party where the guests would come dressed as their favorite movie stars. The luncheon suddenly became quite festive—amorous intrigues and wine were flowing. The guests enjoyed revealing what identity they would assume in the evening. Barbara loved dress-up parties, loved pretending she was somebody different, and often reflected it was a pity she hadn't become an actress. The Maharanee of Jaipur, a ravishing dark-haired beauty, was coming as platinum-tressed Jean Harlow which caused much speculation. Kurt was going as Erich von Stroheim. For herself, Barbara chose to be Constance Bennett, the sophisticated blonde actress who was similar in appearance to the Woolworth heiress.

"Why did you choose to come as Constance Bennett?" asked Henry, putting his naked foot on Barbara's under the table.

"In her early movies," replied Barbara, "she was always in love with polo players."

"And so you married one?" pursued the young blond.

"Yes," said Barbara thoughtfully, her happiness suddenly marred by the reminder of Alexis and his superb physique.

"And I suppose you identify with Constance Bennett because she married the Marquis de la Falaise?"

"I don't know what you're driving at," said Barbara tenderly.

"I'm merely trying to figure out why you married your present husband."

Kurt heard this. He had a violent temper, but decided to let the matter slide. He decided to let Barbara entertain herself for a little while longer. He believed he would have her under his thumb eventually.

In the midst of all this party anticipation and excitement, Guido, one of Barbara's footmen, bent down to whisper in her ear that her son and nursemaid had just arrived at the hotel. Barbara shot her husband a questioning look.

"I didn't know little Lance was arriving today, Kurt?"

"I thought it would balance you somewhat, Barbara," said Kurt with a chilling expression.

"I'm delighted, of course," said Barbara, drawing her golden hair back from her forehead and running her hands through her curls. "But why did you have to keep it a secret from me, Kurt?"

"One's secrets are always fascinating, don't you think so, Barbara?"

"Yes," said his wife, meeting her husband's eyes. "Secrets *are* fascinating." Suddenly both the Reventlows wondered what devious things the other was up to.

The little boy was brought onto the beach with his nanny. He looked so adorable that Barbara forgot everything.

"My darling angel," she said, drawing the little son to her side. He circled his plump arms around her neck and began playing with her pearl necklace.

"He knows they're real," chortled Elsa Maxwell. "He's clever like his father."

"I take that for a compliment, Miss Maxwell," said Kurt in an icy tone.

All at once a chill mist blew in from the sea. Storm clouds appeared, completely obliterating the sun. The two men who'd been playing the accordions abruptly packed up and fled. A high wind struck the long line of cabanas and newspapers blew wildly about the sand. At the end of the wooden pier, canvas flags began to shake and snap alarmingly.

"Hurry," gasped Kurt. "We must return to Venice before the rain comes."

The boatmen quickly gathered up the wicker hampers and scurried through the tunnels under the hotel that led to the other side where the boats were docked. Barbara and her new friend scampered through these dark corridors hand in hand.

"You look odd, Barbara," Henry told her.

"I feel odd," she replied.

"Is something bothering you?" He spoke with such concern that she wanted to cry.

"Kurt's planning something. Planning something dreadful," she said.

She spoke with such distress that he turned to look at her in surprise.

"You're really frightened of him, aren't you?"

"Yes, I'm frightened of him. He's capable of anything. . . ."

Church bells were chiming wildly in Venice. There were three hundred and sixty-five churches in Venice—the noise was deafening. Church bells had always alarmed Barbara. In her confused and anguished state, the clanging bells represented something fearful to her. In her motorboat, she glanced from Kurt to Henry. She realized she must not let her nerves get the better of her. She stared at Kurt. Her husband was up to something.

Barbara had a very sharp sixth sense. These flashes of intuition frightened her. Always in the back of her mind was the fear that she might wind up insane like Grandmother Woolworth or suicidal like her mother. She knew she was overtired, and when she was overtired she couldn't trust her judgment. She had to keep her wits about her with Kurt. She knew she could not risk doing anything silly with Henry. Little Lance had sobered her up.

When they got back to the hotel Barbara went swiftly to her own room and closed the door. She flung off her clothes, tossing them about, not caring where they fell. She collapsed into bed and pulled the covers over her head. She lay there on the monogrammed crêpe de chine pink sheets, her face buried in the soft satin and lace baby pillows. Her heart was beating queerly and she listened to the uneven jolts in panic.

An eighteenth-century apple-green-and-gold snuffbox on the bedside table caught her eyes. The oval of diamonds flashed. Inside were the Seconal tablets. They gave her a feeling of oblivion, and oblivion was what she craved. Opening the box, she grabbed two red pills and swallowed them down with some Vichy Celestines water. In a matter of moments her fears and anxieties faded and she drifted off into a deep and untroubled sleep . . .

Barbara remembered little about the ball that night. She had discovered that if she took the pills in the daytime they had an odd way of affecting her mind. The drug dulled her senses and made her perceive every incident as if she were in a mist. All she remembered was returning to the hotel at dawn in her wonderful silver lamé evening dress, turban, and emeralds. Nearby the church chimed six times and Barbara put her hands over her ears to blot out the sound.

"Are you ready?"

Kurt stood in the doorway. When she turned to look at him, he opened his dressing gown. She resigned herself to what was in store for her.

As he made love to her, pounding, pounding over her, he said, "Barbara, how lucky we are. How lucky we are."

"Why are we lucky?" she mumbled hazily.

"We're lucky," said Kurt panting over her, "we're lucky because we have our child . . . the love that we share . . . and aren't we the most beautiful couple in the world!"

"Yes, we're the envy of the world," echoed Barbara dully.

"Let me hear it from your own mouth, from your own lips," said Kurt, thrusting. "Tell me how you feel about me . . . tell me that you care about me. . . ."

The pills had taken their toll. Barbara was fast asleep. Kurt was enraged that his woman would go to sleep in the middle of his masterful performance.

CHAPTER 24

Jimmy Donahue appeared next morning in a double-breasted cream-colored linen suit, and awakened Barbara in her bedroom. He sipped on a glass of champagne and offered some to her.

"Why not?" cried Barbara, raising herself up among the silky pillows. It was one of her bad days, when she had trouble organizing her thoughts.

"It tastes better than coffee," Jimmy laughed. "And aren't you getting awfully tired of that beverage?"

"Yes, I'm getting tired of everything—including myself."

The maid entered and began pulling up the cream-colored shirred silk blinds. Brilliant sunshine flooded the red velvet and gilt room. With a moan, Barbara covered her eyes.

"Jesus, Barbara, you look like the wrath of God, with those blue circles under your eyes."

Barbara held up a gold hand mirror. "You'd have them, too, if you had a sadistic husband like Kurt."

"I wish I did," Jimmy said, flinging himself onto the bed.

"Come on now, Barbara, give me details about what that German swine does to you."

"Jimmy," Barbara said coldly. "You know I don't approve of talk like that."

"Well, baby, somebody better talk rough to you or else you're going to end up in the bread line. Uncle Frank and Aunt Marjorie are worried sick about you. They fear Kurt's really going to take you to the cleaners."

"How could he do that?"

"Don't look at me with those innocent blue eyes, Barbara Hutton," said Jimmy. "You're the biggest victim in the world. All of Venice is talking about you and that blond hustler chasing you around every nook and cranny. How much have you given this one?"

"Jimmy!" Her eyes wandered up to the painted ceiling where a lustful naked god was trying to penetrate a Rubenesque goddess.

"Barbara, you're the laughingstock of the continent, and I'm here to open your eyes. Number one, you can't get married again. And number two, you can't leave Kurt Reventlow."

" 'Can't' is not in my vocabulary," flung back Barbara grandly.

"We all warned you about that stallion Mdivani and you stubbornly went through with the marriage. You never think about anyone else. You must think about the future of your son. You've got to give him some sense of continuity and stability. God knows, Barbara, we've never had either."

Lying there in the vast bed with the towering Venetian headboard rising up behind her, Barbara nodded her head. She sighed. "Yes, you're right." Jimmy spoke the truth. She wasn't deluded enough not to be able to see the truth. Not yet.

"All right," she said quietly. "What do you want me to do?"

"Stick it out with Kurt," said Jimmy, "and make yourself a good mother to Lance. Forget all these parties and frivolity."

"Look who's talking!"

"But I'm alone, Barbara. I'm not responsible for anybody else. You *must* be responsible, you know."

Barbara was not unaffected by her cousin's good sense. The phone on the rococo gilded table by her side rang and Jimmy, acting the butler, picked it up. "Countess Haugwitz-Reventlow's residence," he announced, affecting a British accent. "May I ask who's calling, please? . . . No, the Countess is asleep right now, sir, and she's leaving for Happy Hill, the clinic, tonight."

Barbara sat up erect in bed. "Jimmy, how dare you?"

"You're not seeing that blond operator anymore," said Jimmy. "Why, the whole world knows that he's a faggot."

"How do you know?" cried Barbara, stunned.

"It takes one to know one," sang Jimmy.

"I don't believe it," cried Barbara, tears forming in her eyes.

"Barbara," said Jimmy. "When will you see people as they really are and not the way you want them to be? . . . "

That evening the press reported that "the happy reunited Reventlows" returned to London. A week later, Barbara was dressing to go to lunch with the Duchess of Kent. She wore a trim, beautifully tailored black suit with dashing high lapels and a jabot of creamy *point de Venise* lace at the throat. A dashing feathered hat sat on her forehead and was held by a band at the back of her head. Trays of jewels had been brought up from the safe downstairs and she pondered which brooch or which clip she should wear on her blouse. Thoughts raced in and out of her mind with alarming jolts. She reached into a drawer and swallowed a couple of pills.

Kurt strode in.

"Anything the matter, Barbara darling?" inquired the crafty bridegroom.

Her gray days rendered her weak, frightened, and confused.

"Kurt, I can't make up my mind," she whispered helplessly.

"I'll help you make up your mind, Barbara," he said, crossing to her side and kissing her on the cheek.

She tried to act normal. It was an effort.

"Do you think the diamond rose is more becoming? Or is the temple of love more appropriate?"

"The temple of love," he said meaningfully.

"As you like," she said. She pinned on Mr. Cartier's latest creation as if in a dream.

"I have some important papers I want you to sign," he said kindly.

"Oh?" she said, stalling for time, remembering her father's advice.

"Here," said Kurt gently. "Here, sign."

She stared up at him from hollowed eyes. "Must I?"

"Don't I look after your best interests, darling?" he said silkily.

"Yes."

"Then just sign here, darling."

"Shouldn't I read this first?" she inquired. Perspiration stood out on her pale brow.

"Why tax yourself?"

She attempted to concentrate on the papers in front of her, but nothing made any sense to her. She clenched her fists. Then, with a gesture of despair, she placed her signature as he directed. Despite a feeling of dread, she dashed off her extravagant signature with a self-confident flourish.

Barbara Hutton had made many mistakes, but this would be the worst one of her life.

CHAPTER 25

COUNTESS BARBARA RENOUNCES U.S. CITIZENSHIP

WOOLWORTH GIRLS STRIKE IN TWO STORES:
SIT-DOWNERS IN 14TH STREET NEW YORK CITY
BRANCH RECEIVE FOOD AND BEDDING FOR
ALL-NIGHT PROTEST. WORKERS ASK FORMER
BARBARA HUTTON (COUNTESS
HAUGWITZ-REVENTLOW) TO INTERVENE

The Woolworth strikers sent a cablegram to Countess Barbara Hutton von Haugwitz-Reventlow today. Her fortune is based on the store chain. They declared: Hunger strikers in New York store ask her intervention for a living wage.

The former Miss Hutton's name figures also in an earlier demonstration by the strikers in which placards were carried about the store with lettering to the effect: MISS HUTTON COUNTS MILLIONS WHILE 5 AND 10 GIRLS COUNT TEN- AND TWELVE-DOLLAR SALARIES.

COUNTESS BARBARA ARRIVES IN NEW YORK

The former Miss Hutton was mobbed when her boat docked. People carrying placards pressed around her as she went through Customs and later stepped into her limousine. As crowds grew violent, police were summoned. "What have I done?" she asked. "I sold my Woolworth stock long ago."

As her town car drew up before the awning of the Pierre Hotel, ten Woolworth workers chanted in loud voices:

> Barbara Hutton has the dough, *parlez-vous*
> Where she got it we sure know! *parlez-vous*
> We slave at Woolworth's five and dime.
> The pay we get is sure a crime.
> Hinkey-dinkey *parlez-vous*.

A little later, London, Paris, and Rome newspapers banner-lined additional details of the shaky Reventlow marriage:

SPLIT FOR COUNT AND COUNTESS. TOO MANY
DIFFERENCES SAYS BABS
COUNTESS EXPLAINS RENUNCIATION
COUNTESS CLAIMS SHE GAVE UP CITIZENSHIP BE-
CAUSE OF TAXATION
COUNT PLANNING TO GIVE BABS FIVE YEARS OF HELL

In her stately red brick mansion, Winfield House, Barbara was pacing up and down the celebrated Savonnerie carpet. She was chain-smoking, and her long red-lacquered fingertips kept tossing one Marlboro after another into the sculptured marble fireplace. Her vermilion lips were stretched into a taut line. Her silver gilt hair was upswept into several Tootsie-Roll curls—the vogue of the time. She had never appeared more distinguished, the way her snobbish Kurt preferred her to look in public.

Barbara was waiting for Elsa Maxwell to arrive. Barbara was nervous about this meeting because Elsa had telephoned her to say she could arrange a reconciliation. Elsa Maxwell was nervous, too. She hoped to bring Barbara and Kurt back together again and she hoped to get handsomely rewarded for this service from both parties.

On this chilly autumn day in November 1938, a fire burned warmly in the hearth. There was a pleasing fragrance of wood smoke in the room, mixed with the Countess's flowering perfume and cinnamon-scented candles. The stately rooms of Winfield House always smelled fresh. Perfumed candles burned every day throughout the house. Jean, an English parlormaid, whose sole job was to see that fresh flowers were put in every room every day, was now arranging white snapdragons and white lilacs in vases.

The whole house today was in shipshape order. The housekeeper had put on white gloves and run her finger over all the furniture, and woe to the maids if there was any sign of dust! Kurt had a mania for cleanliness and formality: two footmen stood at attention behind the double doors of the drawing room where Barbara sat, waiting. Her sleek and contented dachshunds dozed by the tapestry firescreens, a striking counterpoint to their mistress's agitation.

Abruptly, the solemn butler announced Miss Elsa Maxwell, and the famous columnist and party-giver lumbered into the drawing room. Elsa was always wheedling clothes, jewels, and money from her girlfriends. It was a cold day, and she hoped to get a silver-fox cape from Barbara, as well as a lot of cash to stuff into her lizard handbag. Janet Flanner had written: "Elsa was built for crowds. She has never come any closer to life than the dinner table."

"Well, my beauty, I'm here to help you out on this momentous reconciliation day," boomed Elsa. Happily, her vast arms encircled the frail figure of the Countess, and she planted a long, lingering kiss on Barbara's sculptured face.

"Elsa, dear, I'm so grateful for your giving me moral support at this difficult time."

Elsa flung herself into an antique chair, which creaked ominously under her bulk. Her fat hands reached for a bowl of nuts and she asked: "Have you got any caviar, my pretty puss?"

"Yes," said Barbara, "the Aga Khan sent me truckloads after my recent party for him, and I can't eat a bit of it since it's so fattening."

Barbara eyed the butler, and presently a liveried footman returned with a crystal bowl filled with a pound of caviar in shaved ice. "Have a great appetite," cried Elsa as she shoveled one large spoonful after another into her mouth. "Of course I have enormous vitality and food fuels my energy. Barbara, you exude enormous amounts of energy. I don't know how you manage without food."

"Genes. I come from good farm stock."

Elsa looked up to her with worshiping eyes. "I've never seen you look more lovely, Barbara. Truly, you can say what you want about Kurt Reventlow, but he's given you an air of great style and allure. I don't know any woman living who has your allure." Elsa's eyes lingered on Barbara's extraordinary pearls and diamond earrings.

Elsa's remarks filled Barbara with a sense of irony. Barbara was amused to think that her artificial facade managed to conceal her inner turmoil. "You're very sweet, Elsa." Her words had an ambivalent quality that made Elsa sit up and eye her hostess with fresh interest. She realized Barbara had grown up. Barbara obviously had learned a lot about the world. Elsa wondered what advice she could give to benefit herself. Kurt was staying at Claridge's and had contacted Elsa with some gripping news. He was willing to give Elsa $50,000 if she could stage a reconciliation between the warring husband and wife.

Kurt had told Elsa he wanted five million from Barbara and that she'd be more pliable if they lived together.

"Barbara, dear, I really think Kurt has a genuine affection for you. And such affection is very rare in the world we live in, as you know. I mean, can you count three people who would really care if you lived or died? I can't!"

Barbara had often reflected on the sincerity of her circle. Her eyes seemed to grow more heavy-lidded, giving her a weary, sophisticated look. Her cheeks were hollow, her long neck set well on her shoulders, and she was fast becoming a lady of the world. "It's an odious thought," reflected Barbara with a half smile.

"Of course Kurt isn't popular in London; but you are, my darling," boomed Elsa truthfully. "Why you've become a personage of the world, my siren; that's what everyone likes about you. Naturally, you're the dream of every shop girl because they'd all love to be in your shoes. Oh, Barbara, I'd give my eyeteeth to be you!"

Barbara regarded the fat woman cynically. She lit a cigarette and said: "I hate this house. I hate all the pomp and ceremony that makes me a prisoner here!"

"Oh, I'd give my soul to be a prisoner here," said Elsa as she gobbled up more caviar.

"I've decided I'm not going to live here another minute," cried Barbara.

"You'd better stay here," warned Elsa, "or you'll lose your son."

"Kurt Reventlow's not getting my son," said Barbara with a surprising determination. Her jawline stood out in her pale oval face.

"Remember, my dear," said Elsa ominously, "you're a Dane now and you're completely in Kurt's power."

"I'm certainly not in his power!"

"You and Kurt both need each other. So why not go along with the marriage? Most of my friends' marriages are miserable, but they've merely settled for companionship."

"I don't want Kurt's companionship," said Barbara, her eyes flashing dangerously.

"You can have lovers," suggested Elsa slyly.

"Don't be vile!"

"Every married woman we know has lovers, Barbara," purred Elsa.

"Don't remind me."

"At least you don't have to pay lovers so much, my dear. Your

Aunt Jessie told me you're tearing through your fortune and the shape that the world's in today—I'd be very careful. It wouldn't suit you to be poor, Barbara. You're used to holding all the aces in your hand. When you snap your fingers, people dance. Remember what Vincent Astor said, my puss. 'Every dollar saved makes your army even more powerful.' And you want power, don't you, Barbara?''

Barbara leaned gracefully back on the marble mantelpiece, flanked by rare Chinese porcelain Temple vases. "I'm a very feminine woman, Elsa."

"Did I say you weren't?" asked Elsa silkily.

"A woman having as much money as I is put in a rather embarrassing situation as far as a man's concerned," Barbara began quietly. She resembled the musing, full-length Duchess of Gainsborough hanging brilliantly across the room.

"Both your husbands have resented you for holding the trump cards."

"And how do you think women feel about me?" asked Barbara, running swiftly from the above-mentioned subject.

"They think your money gives you an unfair advantage over them. And it does."

The front door slammed and Barbara gave a start. From the hall came sounds of two-and-a-half-year-old Lance. The pretty, little, round-faced cherub trotted into the room. Barbara forgot her misery at the sight of him and knelt down to take him in her arms. What an angel he was, and how she loved him. His nursemaid, who was called Sister Latimer, watched mother and son with an affectionate smile.

"Lance," she reprimanded, "you'll ruin your mother's coiffure."

"It doesn't matter," said Barbara softly. As she felt his warmth and smelled his sweetness, she suddenly recalled that terrible day when she ran into the drawing room and found her mother lying dead on the floor. Suddenly the room became misty. She thought the lights had dimmed. She often had these attacks of disorientation, which disturbed her a good deal.

Barbara's hands began to grow moist and she put the little boy down. Lance loved to play with his mother's collection of gold snuffboxes so he went over to a black lacquer Chinese-decorated commode and began moving these boxes about.

Elsa watched the touching domestic scene with an envious smile. Barbara saw Maxwell's expression and shivered. Another wolf around her.

"Elsa, is something the matter?" She suddenly wondered how much this visit was going to cost her.

"God has denied me the most important things in the world— love and family. Why? I keep asking myself but then, of course, I loathe self-pity. It's almost as bad as envy. Where are your wonderful pearls, Barbara?"

Barbara was suddenly glad to smile. "The goose has them," she said.

"The goose?" questioned Elsa, astonished.

"Mr. Cartier told me," explained Barbara, "that if the goose swallowed my pearls they would come out with a brighter luster."

Elsa's bulk shook with mirth. "Now I've heard everything, dear Barbara. Now you've inspired me to write a brilliant column about you in the *Journal-American.*"

"Please don't," said Barbara, making a traffic-halting gesture. "The press is really taking me over the coals these days."

"And how do you feel about being a Danish citizen?" Elsa inquired with a roguish expression.

"I'm ashamed, of course," Barbara replied, smoothing one perfectly arched brow with her long, delicate fingers. "Father wrote me the most devastating letter. I shall never forget it. Nor forgive him."

"Well," said Elsa, "you can scarcely blame the man. He told me last night he's going to fix you."

"Fix me?"

"Yes, that's what he said. Scout's honor."

"Father's here in London?"

"Didn't you know? Why, he was dining with Kurt last night."

"Oh my God!" The tension pains became so great that Barbara felt faint.

Elsa moved over to Barbara and tried to reassure her.

"I'll rescue you from the press, my captivating Countess."

"I'll be eternally grateful." The two women exchanged understanding looks.

"I'll rescue you from that devil Kurt, too," said Elsa.

"Can you?" said Barbara with deep concern.

"He's a gentleman, after all," cried Elsa.

"Yes, and a gentleman is what Barbara Hutton needs, doesn't she?" The look of anger was so fierce in Barbara's eyes that Elsa saw a glimpse of what Barbara could be if she lost control.

"You mustn't be angry, Barbara," said Elsa. "Anger and guilt are the two things that carry us over the brink."

"Father and Kurt together—I just can't believe it," cried Barbara furiously. She made a fist and shook it. "They just can't do this to me!"

The two women stood in the grand entrance flanked by two towering marble columns and a malachite vase from a St. Petersburg palace. The staircase had been ripped from a French château piecemeal. Now Barbara took a cigarette from her Fabergé case designed for Franz Joseph, the last Emperor of Austria. It was eighteen-karat gold, decorated with sapphire blue enamel and a medallion of diamonds in the center.

"What a lovely thing!" Maxwell commented.

"Take it," said Barbara.

"Thank you," said Elsa, putting it into her purse, and reflecting that she could get $25,000 for it right away.

"Don't thank me, thank Grandpa Woolworth," said Barbara dryly. How often would I and her friends hear this from her.

Elsa gave Barbara a grateful kiss and then without another word the butler bowed her out of the door. Barbara went to the window and watched Elsa depart. A tan Duesenberg town car that Barbara had given Kurt as a present last year drew up before the entrance, and the strong-featured Count himself stepped out. With fascination, Barbara watched Elsa and Kurt carry on a conversation, a surreptitious one, it seemed to Barbara. The two nodded their heads, Kurt's features became even more hawklike, and Elsa's lips curved into a greedy line. Then Kurt helped her into the car and the elegant equipage vanished down the drive. Barbara moved back to the drawing room with a resigned air. She felt fatalistic about Kurt. "I loathe him," she once said, "but I thought I might as well return to him. Besides, there was nothing I could do about it, was there?" Yes, she could face the rage that she felt inside, but it disturbed her too much to reflect on her anger. Accepting the knowledge of further self-destruction and suffering, she prepared herself to meet her husband. The anxiety became so great that a chilled perspiration broke out and she felt drops of sweat trickle down her blouse. In a moment, the poker-faced butler announced that Count Reventlow had arrived.

CHAPTER 26

In the drawing room Kurt asked his son, "How would you like to go to Denmark for Christmas with me, Lance?"

The boy sat on his father's lap as Kurt made a great fuss over him.

"My son is not going to Denmark," announced Barbara coldly.

"Have you any better ideas?" said Kurt in the same tone.

"Yes, he's coming to America with me," Barbara informed him.

"Can't we compromise?" asked Kurt.

It saddened Barbara to look at her son and to think he was unaware of the drama being enacted around him. Barbara had so often been a pawn in her childhood. History had an unpleasant way of repeating itself. She suddenly had a premonition of what the future would hold for Lance.

"What is it going to cost me?" she asked.

"You've become hard, Barbara."

"You've made me so," she replied with loathing.

"You've become worldly."

"It's essential to deal with you and your kind."

"Why do we have to keep wounding ourselves with harsh words?" said Kurt with a smile. When he smiled he was particularly handsome, and Barbara felt a faint attraction for him.

"What do you suggest we do, Kurt?"

"Go to Saint-Moritz for Christmas festivities and have a second honeymoon," he replied. He gazed at her with such longing that she found herself falling under his spell. No matter what, handsome men always had this effect on her. The feeling that made her hate herself even more.

"Why don't we go to Switzerland in a few days?" pursued Kurt.

"As you like," said Barbara, almost hypnotized by his eyes.

"Why don't we celebrate and give a few parties here?" Kurt suggested with unaccustomed enthusiasm.

"All right," she agreed, eager to escape her own dark train of thought. She pressed a royal-blue enamel bell and her social secretary, Miss Livingstone, appeared. Barbara gave instructions to alert all her friends for a big black-tie dinner.

That evening the reunited Reventlows had a cozy, candlelit dinner in the informal upstairs sitting room. A little later they turned on the Victrola and danced to "Night and Day." Kurt was an excellent dancer and she'd always admired the graceful and masterful way he moved. He even smiled once or twice. A real treat. She'd just seen Cary Grant in *Bringing Up Baby*. She indulged herself in a delicious fantasy in which she was flirting with the silver screen's most sexy leading man—as Anita Loos had told her Mr. Grant was.

"You're in a very good mood tonight, Barbara," Kurt said.

"Yes, I'm in a very good mood," she said, her Grant fantasy lingering. She wondered why were men so insensitive.

They retired to their dressing rooms and prepared for bed. Barbara swallowed some Seconal, flung her head back, and washed them down with champagne. In her trailing satin and maribou she made her way to her luxurious bed. Lying against the pillows, she felt a pleasant detachment. She felt immune to pain. Nothing seemed to matter.

She was about to swallow more pills when Kurt emerged naked from the dressing room. He took her hand and gave her a meaningful stare. The Danish warrior made a great show of love-making. The reunited ones slept in each other's arms.

The next morning they awakened early; nine was dawn for Barbara.

"Let's breakfast downstairs," suggested Barbara in a capricious mood.

In the formal Adam dining room downstairs, butlers and footmen stood at attention. Barbara wanted to laugh. She didn't dare because Kurt took all the ceremony very seriously. This morning he was unusually pleased with himself, and even smiled at her across the length of the polished mahogany table. Between the Count and Countess were enough ornaments to make a sale at Christie's: eighteenth-century candelabra, etched Venetian crystal goblets, bouquets of pink carnations and Siberian blue iris in the apple-green Meissen bowls, a truckload of vermeil.

"Why can't I ride with you this morning?" said Barbara, her Cary Grant fantasy still lingering in her mind.

"You may," said the Count formally.

Hand in hand they went to the stables. Some grooms assisted her onto the glossy chestnut. Barbara said good morning to the groom and Kurt glared at her. "Really, my dear," he said cuttingly, "my wife must never speak to a servant."

"Oh, Kurt, how absurd you sound in 1938."

"Formalities must be observed," he reminded her coldly.

To divert him from his eternal obsession with protocol she suggested a race.

"I'll beat you," he challenged.

"No," laughed Barbara, "I'll win."

They galloped wildly through the park and even down to the main thoroughfare. Londoners were intrigued to see the much-photographed Count and his famous wife in smart tweed riding clothes and hats.

They galloped back to Winfield House. Barbara's sleek mare

was about to leap over a wall when she lost her balance and fell to one side, throwing Barbara with a resounding thud onto the ground. Kurt dismounted and gathered Barbara into his arms.

"Are you all right, darling?" he asked gently.

"I'm seeing a lot of stars," she laughed.

"I'll take you home," he said with a meaningful look. She was pleased with his concern and was quite looking forward to a noontime embrace.

Kurt helped his limping wife back to the house. She hung on to his arm in a girlish fashion, more frail and helpless than ever.

The butler opened the front door. "Señor Cesar is in the drawing room, m'lord," he said disapprovingly.

"A common dancing man in our drawing room?" snapped Kurt.

"He insisted, m'lord."

"How amusing," Barbara said, exchanging a humorous look with the butler.

"Very bad form," Kurt sniffed.

"Yes, sir," replied the butler. "By the way, your ladyship, the Duke and Duchess of Sutherland are detained in Paris, so they won't be able to make your dinner tonight."

"I hope the South American band wasn't detained in Paris?" said Barbara with a smile.

"No, m'lady. They just telephoned and said they would be here sharply at eight."

A warm throaty voice came from the drawing room.

"Countess, Countess, we must practice our rumba."

"Thank God you're here, dear Cesar," said Barbara, running toward her dancing master.

South American music had suddenly become the rage in London, and Cesar, a muscular young Argentine opportunist, was giving lessons to all the grand, titled ladies. He was a sleek man on the order of Cesar Romero, with patent-leather hair and a flashing smile. After kissing Barbara's hand and giving her an insinuating smile, he turned on the Victrola and led her into the exciting and rather erotic rhythm of the rumba. He was well built and liked to titillate the ladies. This morning he was being unusually suggestive.

"You should flirt with me tonight, fair Countess, when we put on our exhibition. Ah, we shall show Their Royal Highnesses how Latins make love to music."

"I'll try," she said, with a nifty shake of her slender hips.

"And please, Countess, wear something vivid tonight. Something daring that reveals, not conceals, your elegant figure. Your breasts are like Gothic madonnas, flawless and beautifully sculptured."

"Cesar, truly, you mustn't hold me so close."

"Why not, Countess? You know, I'm insane for you. . . ."

Like every other con man in Europe, he'd heard of Barbara's incredible generosity; he wanted some of this largesse for himself.

Some ladies she knew could and would flirt with Cesar, but not Barbara Hutton. The promiscuous road was not for her. Despite everything, she felt her sense of morality, code of honor, or what have you, saved her from being carried downstream. . . . There was enough self-loathing in her already to prevent her from further humiliating herself with baser and baser acts.

CHAPTER 27

That evening at eight, a long line of Rolls-Royces unloaded before the stately portals of Winfield House. A six-piece red-coated orchestra was playing in the hallway. The guests, of which a King would be proud, were ushered upstairs by a fleet of footmen. A pompous butler stood at the doorway and announced the greatest names in Europe:

"Prince Thurn und Taxis."

"Prince de Rohan."

"Prince and Princess Ruspoli."

"His Excellency, Herr von Ribbentrop."

"Countess di Frasso . . . Sir Charles and Lady Mendl."

Count and Countess Reventlow received in the drawing room, standing by the magnificent sculptured fireplace. The room was fragrant with white tuberoses and fresia. It was a beautiful cream-colored room with gold scrolling on the ceiling and walls. Six crystal chandeliers of amazing brilliance, dating from the eighteenth century, were reflected in the tall gilt-wood mirrors standing over gilt-wood console tables, all made by Mr. Chippendale himself.

Barbara looked incredibly striking in a black lace, off-the-shoulder evening dress that was flounced all around like Empress Eugénie's in the Winterhalter portrait. She wore a magnificent diamond tiara and diamond pendant earrings. A bowknot was on her bosom—made of *tremblant* diamonds. She curtsied in her graceful, fragile manner when the royalties arrived.

"I can hardly wait to see you do the rumba, Barbara," said the Duchess of Kent. Like most of the other women present, she was in silver lamé—stiff with jewels and coronets.

Everyone, in truth, looked a bit stiff and long-necked this evening. The now confident and relaxed Barbara put them all at ease. After years of living in Europe, she had perfected a certain line of small talk—dealing with current events, movies, books, and the theater—that rippled effortlessly from her tongue. Barbara had at last arrived. The Farmington girls would have been impressed.

After dinner, the imported South American band played in the downstairs drawing room. Barbara and Cesar did a reckless samba which caused a ripple of amusement among the guests. The dazzling pair bumped about to the torrid Latin rhythm—his husky Latin swarthiness a strong contrast to her porcelain figurine appearance. Barbara was a great dancer and she executed the complicated steps on her fragile high heels with a perfection that would have delighted Fred Astaire.

On the paneled walls the panoramic Canalettos of Venice looked down at them from heavy gilt frames. Everybody got into the mood and eventually all the guests were exuberantly trying to copy the steps of Cesar and Barbara. Trays of champagne were passed about continually and the hundred guests went home saying that Barbara really knew how to give a good party.

By the age of twenty-six, she had evolved from a lonely, unsophisticated, chubby girl to a slender, worldly hostess, one of the most celebrated in England. No one could understand why such a sweet and natural woman had married that severe and pompous

Dane. It didn't help matters that Kurt had fought in the German Army in the First World War, especially now when Hitler and his Nazis were on the verge of overthrowing Europe.

The next day the Count and Countess Reventlow left on the evening train for Saint-Moritz. They traveled with his valet and her personal maid, her social secretary, his butler, and two bodyguards. Four bodyguards were left to guard Lance at Winfield House, for fear of kidnapping. Also accompanying them were sixteen wardrobe trunks, twenty-eight suitcases, hat boxes, jewel cases, dressing cases, Barbara's sixteen fur coats, and two dogs. Barbara often complained that you had to change your clothes six times a day at the Palace Hotel.

Next evening, Barbara trailed into the huge dining room and was greeted by dozens of friends. She was wearing delicate lilac chiffon that was pleated and draped like a Grecian tunic. Her remarkable jewelry made her the focus of attention. At one table she noticed people whispering about her and felt their hostility. Later at the bar, the American author and Pulitzer Prize winner Louis Bromfield attacked her viciously. In the twenties, Louis had chased all the Duchesses in Paris, London, and Rome, but now in the late thirties, after many years in India, his values had altered drastically and spirituality had come forward. He was noted for his vision, and what he saw ahead for Europe was fearful. The vulgar Hutton woman represented everything that once had been glamorous to him. Looking at her lovely face and fragile figure, he hated her for her seeming lack of concern. In Spain and Austria hundreds of thousands of people were dying this very minute, and soon Hitler would smash through Europe with his panzer troops and shrieking Stuka dive-bombers.

After his third brandy stinger, Louis turned savagely toward the elegant Countess. "You pass yourself off as a lady, Barbara Hutton," he shouted. "Don't you know a lady is never conspicuous! You imbecile, the holocaust is coming and your London palace will be bombed to smithereens! Christ, you're a stupid woman. It makes me sick to think that you're an American. Oh, but I forgot, you aren't. . . ."

CHAPTER 28

Snow was falling thickly, in great wet flakes, outside her sitting room window at the Palace Hotel. Barbara gazed out the frosted windows, listening to the tinkling bells on horse-drawn sleighs and the happy cries of the skaters from the rink below. Standing there in her warm sitting room with a log-fire burning, she smiled wistfully, remembering that lonely girl at Farmington, who watched her classmates go home for Christmas vacation. At least, she thought, things had changed. They certainly wouldn't be snobbish to her today—but then she wondered, reflecting on that Bromfield man's words.

Barbara was being gripped by a growing state of paranoia. She felt that people were taking sides against her. She could see that people were critical of her, and she could never bear people's criticism. Bromfield had upset her. She longed to pack up and leave immediately.

The phone rang shrilly on the French marquetry commode. Like everything in the room, it was of the Louis XV period, formal and grand as Kurt insisted. "It's long distance, madame," said Madeleine, the French maid. "From your father."

Barbara smiled grimly.

"Bring me a glass of champagne, dear, would you?" She always needed to be fortified with a drink when dealing with her father.

Frank Hutton never gave his daughter any sort of greeting; today he didn't even wish her a Merry Christmas. "Do you know, Barbara," Frank began in his loud voice, "that that bastard husband that you're married to doesn't even pay for your hotel bills! That Danish bounder didn't even pay your Hotel Ritz bill when you were staying there last year."

"Didn't he?" asked Barbara indifferently.

"Jesus, woman," he shouted, "why do you have to pay for the whole show all the time? That con man has two million of his own now, which you unwisely settled on him in the first blush of nauseating passion."

"Merry Christmas, Father dear," said Barbara.

"When are you coming to your senses about that German swine?"

"Swine?" Barbara intoned. "People have informed me that you two have become thick as thieves. And isn't that an appropriate expression for the two of you?"

Hutton continued in his harsh manner. The tone of his voice was so unpleasant that Barbara gave a shudder and removed the receiver from her ear.

"Are you listening, you imbecile?"

Madeleine brought her a glass of chilled Lanson, Barbara took a sip, and said, "Yes, I'm listening." She exchanged a mock martyred look with her maid.

"What are you drinking?" came Frank Hutton's voice. "Don't tell me I'm going to have an alcoholic for a daughter!"

"It's what you'd like, isn't it?" snapped Barbara. "I mean, it's what you expect."

"Yes, it's what I expect," he grunted.

"I suppose you're calling me because you want some more money," she drawled.

"Why shouldn't I take money from my own daughter? It's my own money. After all, I made it, didn't I?"

"We've been through this before, Father," said Barbara wearily. She glanced down at the skaters in the rink. In the distance rose the snow-covered mountaintops of the Engadine. Suddenly the wintry landscape seemed threatening. The sun had just gone down and the clouds were a hostile gray color. All at once the cries of the happy crowds outside her window seemed ugly—an intrusion on her privacy.

"I'll bet that Danish husband of yours never even gives you a bouquet of flowers, does he?" came Frank Hutton's angry voice over the wire.

"Did you ever give my mother any flowers?" said Barbara.

"How can you expect me to remember such things?" he exploded.

"I'd remember such things," said Barbara wistfully.

"I only remember that I'm coming to London to yank you out of your fool's paradise. I'm not letting that punk get his mitts on any more of your stocks and bonds. . . . I suppose you've fallen in love with a handsome new con man by now?"

"Kurt and I are quite happy," replied Barbara. Certainly she couldn't say she was unhappy with Kurt, though because of the terrible citizenship scandal she knew she could not trust the man. Once again she glanced out the window. The gray clouds were shot with mauve, and the darkness was rapidly falling. The old fears that always came with the evening took hold of her. She felt lost and frightened. Talking with her father inevitably increased her sense of isolation.

She became conscious of her father's voice again. "I'll bet that Danish scoundrel wouldn't even buy you a caviar sandwich."

The door opened and Kurt Reventlow strode in. He was smartly attired in ski clothes and his cheeks were ruddy from the cold air.

"Would you buy me a caviar sandwich, Kurt?" said Barbara with a strange smile.

"Can't you order it from room service?" said Kurt with a rather disagreeable frown.

"No," she said. "I want you to go to the village and buy me some."

"My valet is drawing my bath," said Kurt.

"*What did the bastard say?*" came Frank Hutton's voice.

"He says the valet is drawing his bath," explained Barbara.

"Who's paying for the valet?"

"Oh, Father, aren't you ever in the Christmas spirit?"

"Give your father my best, and a Merry Christmas," said Kurt, striding into his bedroom.

"Kurt sent you his best, Father, and Merry Christmas," said Barbara sweetly.

"Keep your head in the sand, you ostrich," Hutton's fierce voice crackled over the wire and Barbara again held the receiver away from her ear. Barbara realized it would be a long diatribe so she moved over to the table and began to talk to Lady Mendl, who was on another line.

"I hope you're coming tonight, Elsie, dear," she said sweetly, "and I must confess I need someone to cheer me up. The holiday season is always particularly trying for me. I'm conscious of my failures."

"I have a divine new face for you that will cheer you up," said old white-haired Elsie Mendl with a wicked laugh.

"Not that naughty Roman Prince who chased me on the ski slopes yesterday?"

"No, darling," said the elegant matchmaker. "It's a wonderfully wholesome American specimen. He's fallen in love with your pictures and he's asking me all sorts of delicious questions about you. Do you flirt, Barbara?"

"Better not," said Barbara, laughing grimly.

"Americans are the only thing nowadays. Why all of us American expatriates are returning home now. Consuelo Marlborough and Bessie Drexel and Audrey and Millicent are all gone. My Rollses are all packed and ready in Paris in case that devil Hitler tries any more of his monkey business. And I've made great friends with the pilot of the Lisbon Clipper, just in case."

"Is this divine stranger the pilot, by any chance?"

"He's a golfer," said Lady Mendl. "And watching his muscles ripple as he's hitting the ball is something to drive you out of your mind."

"That's all I need now," said Barbara, "and probably my husband is listening on the other extension."

"Darling Barbara," said the greatest decorator in Europe, "please do not seat me next to that horrible Hoare Belisha. Churchill I will take, but these politicians today are so depressing I could scream. By the way, ducks, I hope you have all your money invested in America. . . ."

Laughing to herself, Barbara picked up her father's receiver. He was ranting and raving now about Roosevelt, and the terrible taxes that the traitor-to-his-class was inflicting on us poor rich people. "God damn it, I think you should come back to America, Barbara, for better or worse. It's the only safe place left in the whole crazy world. *Am I getting through to you?!*"

"All right," she said thoughtfully. She bit her nail for a moment. "I'll come to America.'

"With your *child,*" he shouted.

"Yes, you're so right," she said with an anxious frown. She heard a click on the extension and knew Kurt was listening in the bedroom.

"Are you there?" shouted Frank Hutton.

"I feel I'm in a trap here, Father, and I wish you'd come and help me."

"I plan to come to London as soon as the market shows some improvement. Now in the meantime, Barbara, don't give him anything; he's a dangerous man. . . ."

Abruptly the phone went dead and Barbara cried, "Father, Father, don't hang up. I need you. . . ."

Kurt entered in the dressing gown she'd given him for his last birthday, his forty-first. The robe was gray moiré with peak gold satin lapels. It brought out the color of his eyes. Now looking at them, she felt frightened.

"You don't need your father, darling," Kurt said fawningly.

"Your bath is waiting, Kurt."

Husband and wife took each other's measure for a moment.

"God, you're stupid, Barbara Reventlow," Kurt shouted.

"Let's hope I won't be Barbara Reventlow much longer," she snapped.

"You cheap, common American fool!"

Her head felt as if it would explode.

"How dare you call me common and cheap, you parasite!"

"You'll be sorry," he yelled.

Then he turned on his heel and started furiously out of the room. The door banged shut. For good measure, she flung a lamp at her husband's retreating figure. The anger she felt frightened her because it was so overwhelming. She flung herself on the sofa and began to cry.

CHAPTER 29

Barbara could not control the anger welling up in her. She could not swallow the old resentments and hurts as she usually did. At nine she was still furious and shaking all over from her father's and her husband's insults.

"I refuse to put up with their horrible behavior anymore," she told herself. Then she became conscious of talking out loud and wondered if she was losing her mind. She was dressed in Monsieur Balenciaga's elaborate black taffeta, but gazing at her reflection, she decided it was too formal, too sedate.

Angrily she jerked at the bow on her shoulder and ripped it off. Savagely she tore off the dress and trampled it under her high heels, then kicked it under the dressing table. She raced through her closets, decided that red would express her fury best. The evening dress she selected was scarlet crêpe de chine, cut low unlike her other clothes. That would show Kurt!

The vast corridors downstairs were chilly and Barbara was grateful for the sable jacket about her shoulders. There were dozens of little tables set up in the hall and now people turned and looked at her as she fluttered by in her conspicuous dress and blazing rubies. She felt their criticism, and thought, "To hell with them!" Defiantly, head high, she moved toward the best tables at the front of the hall.

Barbara was a great favorite with all the captains, concierges, ski instructors, bartenders, waiters, and bellboys. Now, it rather amused her to listen to their "Good evening, Countess," "How are you this evening, Countess?" "You look so lovely, Countess," "Your party's going to be a great success, Countess," "Is there anything we can *do*, Countess?"

With a dry smile, she pulled out a cigarette from an eighteenth-century gold box, and the hands of five men hastened to light it for her. As usual!

"Will you dance with me later?" said a stocky young Austrian Prince with blond hair and red cheeks.

"Perhaps."

"You dance so beautifully, Countess," remarked an Italian Count, ardently kissing her hand.

"How kind you are."

"Can I help you in any way?" asked a French Viscount who worked at Cartier.

"Yes. Help me arrange the flowers at the dinner table."

A shadow seemed to fall over her and she felt threatened. Instinctively she turned and found the cold gray eyes of Louis Bromfield watching her. "What do you want?" she asked coldly. "Haven't you said enough unattractive things to me already?"

"No, I haven't even begun to tell you the truth about you, Miss Hutton."

"I'm not Miss Hutton," she replied distinctly. "My name is Countess Reventlow."

"You'll always be Miss Hutton to me," said Bromfield with an ugly expression.

"I don'*t* know why you choose to persecute me."

"Because you're such a spectacle, Miss Hutton. You wore emeralds last night. I suppose you're going to wear sapphires tomorrow?"

Barbara sensed that he had an effeminate streak in him and now she said, "Are you envious?"

No man likes to be hit where his masculinity is concerned and Louis was no exception. He was married, had three daughters, and liked to think of himself as a conservative man. Only his family circle knew about his secretary, George, and even they didn't know what transpired between Louis and George. Now he had an uncomfortable feeling that this Hutton woman saw through his façade, and saw him for what he was. A fair man, he felt a vague tingling of admiration for this hateful playgirl. Suddenly he saw a bejeweled and handsome Countess di Frasso bearing down on them—chattering away gaily to Lady Mendl and a whole crowd of merrymakers. The sight of these other American heiresses proved too much for him to take.

Bromfield said spitefully: "I daresay next year you'll be entertaining Herr Hitler in your London palace. Perhaps Goering would be a suitable new husband for you, Miss Hutton? He's handsome as hell and loves display and ostentation. But your friend the Duchess of Windsor must have told you about him. . . ."

There had been ugly talk about the Duke and Duchess of Windsor when they toured through Nazi Germany the previous year. The Duchess herself was said to have many German admirers, including Herr von Ribbentrop. The Duke was often heard to remark he had more German blood in him than English.

The courageous and effervescent Dorothy di Frasso warmly embraced Barbara and remarked on the beauty of the table settings.

"You always do flowers so beautifully," said Countess di Frasso, whose Villa Madama in Rome was one of the showplaces of the Eternal City. She'd often entertained Barbara there and the two had become fast friends.

Barbara made an elegant gesture to indicate the author standing next to her. "Mr. Bromfield tells me that next year I'll probably have swastikas decorating the table. And that Herr Goering might be my new consort. What do you think about that, Dorothy?"

Dorothy di Frasso laughed in her good-natured way. "Oh,

Louis is like all writers when he gets a few drinks in him. He likes to dramatize things, make a big production out of it.'' She waved her diamond-braceleted arm. ''And talk about productions, darling, you should have seen Bromfield when he was in Hollywood working for Sam Goldwyn; Sam always called him Mr. Bloomberg. And Jesus, Louis, I hope those Nazis don't pick up on the 'berg' because we wouldn't like to see you incarcerated in a concentration camp.''

''You'll all be in concentration camps unless you get out of Europe right away,'' said Bromfield.

''They wouldn't dare,'' drawled Lady Mendl haughtily. ''Why think of the important people that we all know.''

''Those Nazi gangsters have you all on their kidnap list,'' said Bromfield. ''Why, those hoodlums will have you all rounded up like cattle.

''And talking about cattle,'' Louis continued dramatically, ''there's a Czech patriot who told me about being thrown in a cattle car full of lime. Do you know what lime does to your pretty flesh, Miss Hutton?''

Barbara shrank back in horror. ''Dorothy, could it be possible?''

Motherly Countess di Frasso put her arm around Barbara's waist. ''This headline is joining me in Hollywood next year, Louis. Didn't you know that, Barbara?''

''No, I didn't,'' said Barbara, feeling a trifle better.

''Hollywood's the only place to be these days,'' said Dorothy in her robust way. ''And darling, Cary Grant's told me he's dying to meet you.''

''Don't tease me, Dorothy,'' said Barbara, warming by the minute.

''And here's another dark-haired charmer who's much taken with you,'' Dorothy continued. A vigorous dark-haired man stepped forward and grinned at Barbara, and Dorothy looked up at him affectionately. ''You know Bobby Sweeney, don't you?''

''I've heard of him, of course,'' said Barbara. ''Who hasn't?''

The two beautiful young people smiled at each other and the

older ones watched them enviously. Countess di Frasso watched Barbara's expression in a knowing way. "Isn't Bobby one of the most attractive men you've ever seen, Barbara?"

"Rather," said Barbara, smiling into Sweeney's twinkling blue eyes.

"What wouldn't I give to be twenty years younger and twenty pounds lighter," chuckled Dorothy. "Don't you agree, Elsie dear?"

"I'd give my best signed Louis Quinze commode to have Mr. Sweeney look at me that way." They all laughed except Louis Bromfield, who glared at the couple.

"Make hay while the sun shines," he said nastily.

Louis strode off angrily and Barbara smiled gratefully at Dorothy di Frasso. In her impulsive way she kissed her friend, who was a surrogate mother to her. Barbara always felt a rapport with some women—even more than she did with men. Dorothy and Elsie were among her favorites; she felt they wouldn't sell her down the river like Elsa Maxwell and her gang of cutthroats.

Kurt Reventlow was striding cockily down the lobby and Dorothy warned Barbara with a high heel on her friend's instep.

Kurt bent low and kissed Barbara's hand. "Good evening, my dear," he said in his formal manner.

"Good evening, my dear," said Barbara, making fun of his tone.

"You seem in splendid form tonight, Barbara," remarked Kurt, staring coldly at the young American.

"I *am* enjoying myself, thank you very much."

At nine thirty the party moved into the dining room. During dinner, Barbara danced with Bobby Sweeney. They moved so beautifully together she began to think he was the solution to all her problems. And he was an American. The young man spoke now of Palm Beach and the friends they had in common. He was becoming more and more appealing to Barbara. Even her father couldn't object to Palm Beach and Sweeney. He and his brother Charlie had the right credentials: they chummed around with the right crowd in London. Charlie Sweeney was married to the most

beautiful woman in English society, Margaret Whigham
. . . later the Duchess of Argyle. Barbara didn't know Americans like this existed. He was certainly the antithesis of the crass
American businessman that she associated with her father.

"Will you take lunch with me tomorrow, Countess?" came
the voice of Bobby Sweeney breaking into her reverie.

"Do you think it's possible?"

"Why not?" he replied.

With Kurt glaring at them, Barbara felt uncomfortable. Kurt
finished his brandy and ordered another as he watched them. He
was smoldering while Barbara humiliated him publicly with this
youthful American. He wondered how to further punish her.

CHAPTER 30

When they returned to their suite of rooms, the fire was burning brightly in the grate and the fragrance of the white fresia was heavy in the warm air. Kurt's valet and Barbara's personal maid came out of the bedroom. They'd been listening to the radio and their faces were strained. Kurt's valet, a Pole, had just received a letter from his mother in Danzig.

"Bad news, Stanislaus?" asked Barbara with concern.

"Mr. William Shirer reported that 1939 will be the year of destiny for Hitler. What does that mean, Countess?"

"That Hitler's certainly not coming to Paris," cried Madeleine hotly.

"Nor Warsaw," said Stanislaus with equal vehemence.

"What on earth would we do without you?" said the ever-dependent Barbara. She knew that the servants would now take their leave and wished passionately that they would stay. Once alone with Kurt she knew the axe would fall.

"Shall I stay, Comtesse?" asked the intuitive Madeleine in French. Like all the servants, she hated Kurt and resented his patronizing manner.

"Our cavalry will save the day," said Stanislaus, lighting the Count's cigarette.

"Thank you, my good man. You may go now. Good night."

Young Stanislaus started toward the door but Madeleine loyally remained. She sensed that her mistress needed her and she wanted to protect the Countess from that coldhearted brute.

"Comtesse, I shall take your jewelry downstairs," she suggested as she began to help Barbara disrobe.

"The hotel is safe, Madeleine," said Kurt coldly. "You may go now."

The two women exchanged glances.

"Could you get me a brandy, Madeleine? I feel all of a sudden a little chill."

"You've had enough brandy, Barbara," said the humiliated husband. He spoke so severely that Barbara shrank. She wished the floor would swallow her. She said goodnight to Madeleine and the maid vanished.

Barbara sat down at her dressing table and began to unscrew her ruby and diamond ear clips. From the corner of her eye she saw Kurt glaring at her and cracking his knuckles. Aloud, with false brightness, Barbara said, "Kurt, dear, don't you think we're safe in London?"

"Not with Hitler's air force, you imbecile."

"Is it so large, then?"

"Don't you read the newspapers?" he shouted.

"No, I don't," she said.

"You should."

"There's quite enough ugliness in the world and I see no need to brood about it the way you all do."

He crossed over the large, thickly carpeted room and rested his strong hands on his wife's naked shoulder. "You know, Barbara, sometimes I think you're playing games with me. You're not half so vague as you pretend to be."

"I'm not?" she asked, stalling for time.

"There's no need to lie and pretend with me," he said. "I know how your clever little female mind works."

"You do?"

"I do."

His grip tightened around her neck and Barbara managed to say lightly, "If you're going to strangle me, Kurt dear, please get it over with quickly. You know I can't abide pain of any sort."

"You're going to have much more pain if you don't listen to me," he said distinctly.

"Meaning?"

"Meaning that you'd better come to your senses and wake up to your present situation."

"And would you enlighten me about my present situation, Kurt dear?" she asked in honeyed tones.

"We're a happily married couple," he said sarcastically, "with a beautiful little son and heir who is the apple of our eye."

"You're quite right about Lance."

"You know I'm devoted to you, Barbara darling," he said, bending down to kiss her neck. "You cannot imagine how much I think about you and Lance."

There was a double meaning that was not lost on her. "What do you intend to do with us, Kurt? I'm sure you have a lovely scheme hatched up, don't you?"

He drew up a chair and sat down next to his wife. "Next year we shall return to my properties in Denmark and sit out the war. Bromfield is right. There is a war coming. Any minute."

"Really?" said Barbara, her heart sinking.

"Of course. You are quite welcome in my Copenhagen house, Barbara dear," Kurt offered nonchalantly as he puffed on his cigarette holder.

"You're so kind," she said.

"However, dear spouse, your social life will be restricted somewhat."

Husband and wife looked at each other in a tense moment.

"And what plans do you have for us in the New Year?" asked Barbara with chilling politeness.

"We shall return to London tomorrow and dismantle Winfield House."

"We will?"

"We will," he said in a threatening tone. "Now get into bed

and behave like a loving wife. You know, Barbara, I do love you in a way.'' He began to fondle her arm and she wrinkled her nose in distaste. ''Am I so unattractive to you?'' he added.

Barbara's reply was to stand up and move to her dressing room. She stepped into her peignoir of satin and lace and swallowed a double amount of sleeping medicine.

Barbara's beds were always a thing of beauty, and Madeleine had taken special pains to make this one alluring. The linen was cool and soft and smelled of fresh ironing and verbena sachets. The blankets were the softest baby blue cashmere bordered with satin. The coverlet was an extraordinary work of art; it had once covered the banquet table of Princess Massimo in the eighteenth century. The lace was so delicately worked it took four women three hours a day to launder it. The half-dozen bed pillows were plump and downy—made from the finest Norwegian goose feathers.

Now husband and wife lay together on this magnificent bed with no love in their hearts. Both were smoking cigarettes and both were scheming.

''Wouldn't it be safer, Kurt dear, to return to New York?'' ventured Barbara gently.

''No,'' he replied disagreeably.

''But Father just told me that America is the only safe place left in the world.''

''I don't like America,'' said Kurt Reventlow.

''Why not?''

''Americans don't know their place.''

Barbara had heard this many times and could never think of any words to combat Kurt's absurd snobbery. She decided to appeal to him, and try a different course. ''Don't you think Lance would be better off in America?''

''How many times must I tell you that America to me is revolting?'' cried Kurt angrily.

''It must be revolting for you, then, to live on American money.''

He turned on the pillow and looked at his wife. ''That remark's not worthy of you, Barbara.''

"But Kurt dear, I must make you see reason."

"Our son is a Danish subject," said Kurt evenly.

"I'm aware of that fact," she replied through tight lips.

"And you, too, are a Danish subject, Barbara Reventlow."

"That wasn't worthy of you, Kurt."

An uncomfortable silence fell between the warring parties.

Presently, she said: "It was bad of you, Kurt, to make me sign away my American citizenship."

"You fill me with bad thoughts, Barbara."

"Am I so bad, then?" she asked.

"Yes, Barbara. You fill me with bad thoughts, and I resent you for that. . . ."

In a moment Kurt was sleeping soundly on his side of the bed. Barbara lay there for a moment in silence puffing on her cigarette and watching the glowing coals in the fireplace.

At daybreak Kurt was awakened by the village church bells. He had slept fitfully and did not feel rested at all.

Conscious of his wife lying beside him, painfully aware of the flowery perfume she always wore, he decided for certain he must kidnap the boy and hold him in Denmark until an appropriate ransom was forthcoming. Kurt didn't like the idea of Mr. Hutton coming over to help his daughter. He knew he had to work fast. Kurt had enough good instincts in him to feel bad about the evil thoughts going through his head. However, he wanted to win, the same way that Hitler wanted to win. If the poor woman beside him had to be sacrificed, then so be it. Besides, Barbara had been a pawn right from the beginning. It was Barbara Hutton's fate to be used. She was born to be a victim of men.

At ten the Reventlows were taking their breakfast in the sitting room. The wintry sunlight fell through the tall windows and lit up the carpeting in bright yellow patches. Barbara gazed at the yellowness and passionately wished the grayness inside her would fade. The grayness she saw all around her was only an illusion, of course, born of her confusion and despair.

"You look tired, Barbara," observed Kurt, not unkindly.

"I didn't sleep."

"Something on your mind?"

"Christmas always fills me with despair."

"Why?" he asked, staring at her.

"Christmas is a family time," she reflected, staring into the fire. "My failure to create a happy family is brought home to me with terrible force during the holidays."

He was struck by the bitterness of her words and felt momentarily ashamed of his kidnapping schemes.

"So you feel you have failed, Barbara?"

"Haven't we failed?" she echoed dully, not raising her eyes.

"It will be good to see Lance tonight," said Kurt, "and I'm sure he's missed you. In any case, I'm sure I can give him a good life in Denmark."

She looked up from the fire and studied her husband thoughtfully. "So you intend to take him now?"

"Von Ribbentrop told me that they intend to invade Czechoslovakia next year. England and France won't lift a finger and Hitler will plunder the whole of Europe."

"Then it's hardly logical to remain in Europe, is it?" she questioned sharply.

"I'd rather have my wife and child in Europe than in America with that terrible Roosevelt and all that phony democracy. You've told me a million times yourself, Barbara, that you prefer the life here on the Continent."

"But all my friends like Elsie Mendl and Bessie Drexel are returning to America. Millicent Rogers even married an American and Audrey Emery wrote me she was buying a plantation in Tidewater, Virginia."

"Is that what you're contemplating?" he quipped sardonically.

Barbara felt the color redden her cheeks. Under his hard eyes she became suddenly fearful and apprehensive again. Gazing at him, she knew he had something terrible in store for her . . . which was indeed close to the truth.

CHAPTER 31

On that morning in July 1939 when her father was to arrive, Barbara awakened in a panic at Winfield House. All of her friends had gone to Ascot for the day. She hadn't dared to attend the races because she feared leaving Lance alone in the house. There was no telling what underhanded maneuvers Kurt was capable of inflicting on her. She and Kurt had separated again, but she'd been told that he was in London, which increased her state of anxiety. The child's nurse, Sister Latimer, was a devoted soul and sympathetic to her cause, but Barbara had no way of knowing what Kurt would offer her. He'd already bribed the butler and one of the footmen to spy on her. The awful knowledge that Kurt would surrender all claims to the child if enough money changed hands haunted Barbara.

As she worried about her estranged husband and his schemes, the phone buzzed by her side and Madeleine announced that Mr. Sweeney was on the wire.

"Good morning, darling," he said radiantly.

"Good morning."

"What's the matter with you? You sound a stranger."

"I'm a stranger to myself." She gave an uneasy laugh.

"A stranger to yourself. What does that mean?" he asked tenderly.

"I'm all confused," she said frowning. "I have no control over my emotions anymore."

Changing the subject, she said, "I thought you were going to Ascot, Bobby."

"I can't very well go to Ascot and leave you in this peculiar state of mind. What is the matter, darling? You can certainly tell me, of all people."

"In case you've forgotten, Father's arriving today." She couldn't keep the harshness from her voice.

"That should rather please you, shouldn't it?" asked Bobby gently.

She shook her blond head, her red lips a taut line.

"Very little about my father pleases me."

"But your father's going to help you now, against Kurt."

She sneered. "You're more of a dreamer than I am, Bobby Sweeney."

"Now, Barbara, your suspicions are really making you demented."

"If you had a father like mine, you'd be demented, too. He's up to something. He's up to something. He's up to something with Kurt! I tell you, it's true!"

"I'll come right over," reassured her anxious friend.

"You are not to come over here, Bobby Sweeney!"

"Barbara, I don't know what's come over you. Recently you're so high strung and nervous that you're going to drive yourself into a clinic. . . ."

Ticki stood by the window and made an alarming gesture.

"Your father has arrived and he seems in a terrible mood. He's looking at the house now and shaking his head."

Barbara extricated herself from her admirer's concerned attention. "Better quickly get dressed," said Barbara, flinging back the covers and running toward her boudoir. "I'll wear the new black Schiaparelli—the one I wore to the Duke of Wellington's funeral."

Ticki flung up her hands in a humorous fashion.

"Do you think such a funereal costume is appropriate, Barbara?"

"That's the only thing that *is* appropriate."

An upstairs maid drew Barbara's bath and liberally sprinkled it with gardenia bath oil. Barbara tossed off her bed jacket and stepped into the warm water. "Let's hope it won't be my funeral," she said with playful grimness. The thought of her father being in her house filled her with dread. She was about to reach over and take some Seconal pills, but then Ticki, who had found out about the sleeping medicine, entered the room.

"Poor Barbara is getting that look in her eye again," said Ticki, watching her anxiously. "Your father is going to make you very unhappy, I'm afraid." But somehow, talking about her father made Barbara less afraid. She knew it wouldn't be good to greet him with her tail between her legs.

"Don't worry, Barbara," said Ticki, "I shall take care of everything."

"You're an angel, Ticki," she said with affection. "Now steer Mr. Sourpuss into the dining room and fatten him up with some juicy tidbits. He's very greedy, you know."

"He's not the only one who's greedy," said Ticki.

"Oh? . . . ." said Barbara, distracted and unable to follow two trains of thought at once.

"Yes, I've been meaning to tell you about the way the cook and kitchen help pad all the bills downstairs."

"That's the least of my problems," said Barbara. "Now, I must go downstairs and receive my father properly. . . ."

Half an hour later, the head butler, Henry, announced Mr. Hutton. Barbara was severely dressed in her mourning costume. Her silver-gilt hair was swept up from her temples and brushed high off her forehead; her maid had arranged it in pretty curls on top of her head. A superb marquise-shaped diamond flashed vividly on one of her long, exquisite fingers and Marie Antoinette's pearls were about her neck.

Mr. Hutton looked at his daughter with pride. She was the finished product. The greatest jewelers, dressmakers, coiffeurs, and skin specialists had transformed his daughter, and only child, into a work of art. He felt almost a peasant's awe at this dazzling creature and the splendor that surrounded her. Nevertheless, he felt the old hatred and resentment building.

Father and daughter greeted each other with courtly manners, but there was no warmth or feeling in their meeting. Each one had scores to settle. Barbara tried with difficulty to keep her expression sweet.

"You certainly live well, Barbara," he remarked, glancing around. His sharp eyes behind the pince-nez were cunning and avaricious. His thin lips drooped at the corners. To Barbara, he seemed to have shrunk. His neck had disappeared into his shoulders, increasing his squat and forbidding appearance. He hadn't aged well as did his brother, Ed Hutton.

"I try to live well, Father," she replied.

"It seems you've raided the biggest shops and galleries in Europe."

"I have."

"How many rooms have you here?"

"Forty—give or take."

"How many servants?"

"Thirty-one, I believe, with my six bodyguards."

"Quite Marie Antoinette you are, my dear Countess."

"Let's hope I don't lose my head."

He gave her a long, shrewd look. "You will if you don't listen to me."

She ground out her cigarette and lit another. It was strange not to have half-a-dozen hands spring forward and light it for her. "I intend to listen to you, Father, really I do."

His lips twisted. "You never listen to anyone, you willful creature."

Thunder rumbled in the great park outside; lightning flashed in the stately trees, formal gardens, and Italianate statues of the Four Seasons. A bolt of white light flashed into the vast room, and Barbara sprang to her feet. Her dogs began to bark ferociously.

"Has the war started?" Barbara said in an attempt at humor.

"I wouldn't make fun of it," snapped Hutton. "It's as serious as your impending divorce."

Barbara arched her thick black brows. "Am I to divorce, then?"

"You imbecile!" He flung a dozen newspapers onto the floor by her feet. Barbara knew she was supposed to bend down and read the newspapers, but she didn't move.

"Read them!" he commanded.

"I can see what's written in those headlines," said Barbara distinctly.

"How did all this talk of you and Sweeney become public knowledge?" shouted the furious father.

"We go around a great deal together."

"A married woman behaving so conspicuously with a young man?"

"Bobby and I are very much in love," Barbara said defiantly.

Frank Hutton began to shake with laughter, and the sound of it was ugly. "Who is this Sweeney and what does he do?"

"He's a golfer," Barbara said in a quiet voice that further infuriated the old man.

"A golfer?" sneered Hutton. "Do you mean to tell me he supports himself by playing golf? That's not a profession for a man."

"Oh, Father, Alex and Kurt had no profession either. But Bobby's a darling and you'll adore him. He has such a sweet temperament. . . ."

Frank Hutton's eyes were so stony that Barbara froze.

"I have no wish to hear about your latest lover," he said slowly and maliciously.

"As you like," she cried, tossing her elegant head.

"I just had a long conversation with your husband at Claridge's."

"Oh?" said Barbara, gulping.

"Yes," replied Frank Hutton, his small eyes never leaving his daughter's face. "Yes, your ears should be burning, Barbara Hutton."

"I daresay you talked lovingly about me, you two. Devoted as you are to me."

"Yes, the conversation concerned you and your willful behavior and neurotic extravagance. And your life here at Winfield House. Wouldn't it be easier for you to let those photographers just take pictures of you and Sweeney naked in bed?" He indicated the newspapers on the floor, which were full of her romantic interludes with Mr. Sweeney.

"I forbid you to talk to me in such a manner, Father."

"You forbid?" he sneered. "Who do you think you're talking to in that high-and-mighty tone? By the time Kurt and I are finished with you, you'll be singing a different tune."

She clenched her fists to control herself. "So you've taken his side against mine, is that it?" she said tensely.

"I haven't taken Kurt's side," said Hutton, observing the perspiration on her forehead and thoroughly enjoying watching her. "You know I never take anyone's side, Barbara dear."

"Oh," she flung back, "you're too clever for that."

"I'm glad you recognize I'm clever, Barbara," he said smoothly. "It's a pity you didn't inherit any of my cleverness. You're a sick woman, my dear. And Kurt and I are very worried about you."

"Sick, am I?" said Barbara, and the words seemed to catch in her throat.

"Sick," repeated Hutton, shaking his head, his cold eyes never leaving her face. "It's not prudent that a little boy remain with such a sick mother. A sick woman who throws all conventions to the winds. And spends twenty million dollars of her capital in less than ten years—on wine, jewels, parties, yachts, palaces, and men. . . ." $20,000,000! It couldn't be true!

Not able to believe what she had just heard, she said, "Father, you can't be serious about you and Kurt."

"I am," he replied ominously.

"You mean you'd sell me down the river for financial reward?"

"Money is money," said Hutton.

"So you think that if you take Kurt's side, you can brand me an unfit mother and get control of my fortune, is that it?"

"You're not so dumb after all," chuckled Hutton.

"I'm going to fight," said Barbara. "I'm going to fight both of you. Fight you as of this moment!"

"People like you can't fight."

"Perhaps I'll surprise you, Father. In any case, you have a fight on your hands, and a big fight at that, I promise you!"

"That's all right with me," said Hutton. He stood up and flung his cigar into the grate. Without another word he turned on his heels, walked down the length of the great room, and opened the door. Just before he passed through the door he turned and gave his daughter a malevolent look. She didn't flinch but she met his flinty eyes with stony composure.

When the front door slammed and she heard the heavy Rolls vanish down the drive, she sprang to her feet with such vehemence that a priceless little table overturned, and a Chinese porcelain bowl smashed noisily onto the floor. The sound was magnified in a fearful way in her agitated mind. Blindly she ran across the palatial room, stumbling and whimpering.

A moment later the servants were surprised by the sight of Countess Reventlow running like a mad thing up the grand staircase . . . sometimes taking two steps at a time. The usually majestic ladyship was sobbing uncontrollably, her hair in disarray.

Ticki found her in the nursery clutching little Lance to her side. "No, no darling," she was saying softly. "No, my dearest, they won't have you. I shall never let you go. You want to be with Mummy, don't you, angel?"

Outside the raindrops were streaming down the windowpanes.

A high wind had come up and the heavy curtains were ballooning wildly into the room. Ticki closed the window. Barbara didn't even seem aware of her presence. Without a word Ticki closed the door and left mother and son alone.

CHAPTER 32

The impression of Barbara and Lance made an indelible mark on Ticki's heart. Much later when the whole household was asleep she saw a ray of yellow light in the Countess's great rooms below. The poor, tormented woman was awake like herself, probably pacing the floor and chain-smoking. Impulsively, Ticki put a robe on and started quickly downstairs. Faint music from the radio came from Barbara's door.

Ticki stayed by the door until she fell asleep. When she returned to her room, the light in the sky was a tender gray and the birds were beginning to sing. Halfway between sleep and consciousness, she became aware of the stableboys' laughter in the gardens below. They were always the first to move about at Winfield House. As they looked up at Barbara's windows and pitied her (they'd just read the morning papers and the latest developments of the poor American woman's marital trials), in their hearts they envied her.

"No doubt about it," one of the youths said. "That Count of ours is a rotter."

"Yes, indeed, feel sorry for her ladyship. She deserves better."

"They're all a mystery to me. They're worlds apart from the likes of you and me. Imagine her own father saying things like that about his daughter."

"Well, they have their morality and we have ours. I wonder what the Countess would have been like if she'd been born normal run-of-the-mill like us, Gus? . . ."

And Barbara, at her window ledge, heard the youth's words and felt more alone than ever.

CHAPTER 33

The next morning found Barbara and three-and-a-half-year-old Lance sitting on the canary-yellow sofa in the pearl-gray drawing room, the scene of her grim meeting with her father. Barbara was painstakingly doing some needlepoint by the window. Jean, the maid who arranged fresh flowers every day, was putting the finishing touches to a bowl of white hyacinths. Outside, the trees were still dripping from yesterday's storm, but it was a miraculously lovely summer day. The sky was as clear as the vivid light in her Canalettos.

The child was lying on Barbara's lap with his arm around her waist, and Ticki read aloud the ghastly newspaper reports. Barbara smiled with irony to think that Lance's father had promised her five years of hell in the headlines if she didn't submit to his wishes.

Barbara put down the needlepoint and nervously began to play with a golden snuffbox which had belonged to the Duc de Choiseul, who'd given the beautiful object to the mistress of Louis

XV. The greedy woman had returned to Paris to retrieve her jewelry and been beheaded by the revolutionary mob. Now in her mind she relived the execution scene, wondered how she herself would behave.

Lance stared up at his mother and frowned, not pleased that she was distracted. "Mummy, when is that nice Mr. Sweeney coming to take us to see the horse show? I like horses, Mummy, don't you?"

"Yes," replied the mother vaguely, "I do."

"Mummy, can't we take a trip? I don't like London."

She glanced down at the boy. "Why on earth don't you like London?"

"I like the beach at Monte Carlo," the boy said, reaching up to play with her pearls.

"Well, in that case let's go to Monte Carlo," said Barbara, smiling down at him.

"I like the beach at Venice even better," the boy said dreamily.

"In that case, my cherub," said Barbara playfully, "let's go to delicious old *Venezia*."

"Venice is so beautiful, Mummy," he whispered, his eye resting on her sculptured face.

"Do you like beauty, Lance?" she asked tenderly.

"You're the beauty queen of the whole world, Mummy."

The phone rang and the footman announced that Count Reventlow was on the wire. She picked up the receiver and said, "Yes?"

"Is that you, Barbara?" came Kurt's voice. "You sound different."

"I am different," she said meaningfully.

"Your father and I want to come over and take the boy for a drive."

She laughed harshly. "You must think me an awful fool, Kurt."

"You mean you refuse to allow the boy's father and grandfather to see him?" he asked with false surprise.

A shrewd look passed over Barbara's taut features. She had something of her father in her after all. The amazingly long scarlet nails began to drum on the black lacquer table. Her mind raced.

"All right," she said sweetly. "Come around three. Lance has his rest after lunch and Sister and I will have him all ready by then."

"I love you when you're like this, Barbara," Kurt said affectionately.

"Yes, isn't it wonderful? . . ." She hung up the receiver and glanced at Ticki. "Dear, let's quickly pack some things. We'll get the one o'clock flight to Venice."

A moment later the drawing room was a hubbub of activity. Miss Livingstone, the Countess's secretary, was in a state of shock over the sudden news. She liked to take weeks planning trips. Sitting at the George III writing table, she glared at the Countess and thought what a capricious creature she was.

Miss Livingstone dialed British Airways and began to talk to the reservation clerk. "I want space for three on the one o'clock flight to Venice today, please. This is the Countess Reventlow's secretary speaking. You can't? You won't? But my dear chap, the Countess will be *most* annoyed."

"Hire a private plane," tossed Barbara.

"The Countess wants a private plane," echoed Miss Livingstone into the mouthpiece. "How much did you say? Oh, that's exorbitant!"

"My dears," said Barbara with a careless laugh, "have I ever quibbled about the cost of things? . . ."

"You'll be a pauper someday, poor Barbara," said Ticki woefully.

It was a pretty twin-engined silver plane. The pilot was ruggedly handsome and most solicitous. Barbara's high spirits became almost manic. For once in her life, she quite liked herself.

By her side, Ticki was poring through a pile of newspapers. "That Hitler and that Mussolini are up to no good," Ticki was saying anxiously. "Do you think Mussolini might try to kidnap you?"

"Nonsense," Barbara replied incredulously.

"They say that German troops are massing on the Polish border," Ticki persisted.

"Rubbish. Isn't it rubbish, Lance?" Barbara said, squeezing the boy to her tightly. "Don't you think it's rubbish, Lance?"

"Rubbish, rubbish, Mummy," agreed Lance. "Oh, Mummy, will Mr. Sweeney join us in Venice?"

"I'll call him the moment we arrive," said his mother. "And isn't it nice that we think about the same things, Lance?"

"I like Mr. Sweeney better than Daddy," said Lance, and the two women exchanged amused looks over his head.

A moment later the sleek aircraft began to descend slowly. They could see the sparkling Adriatic below, and the curving Italian landscape. At the Venice airport the swarthy Italian police officers regarded Barbara's figure sullenly. She was in summery white silk and a white Panama hat. The *carabinieri* knew that the cost of the diamond flashing on Barbara's hand would have supported them and their village for a lifetime.

"You'll have to go through Customs, Contessa," said an amazingly insolent brute.

"I don't feel like going through Customs," replied Barbara coldly, staring him in the eye.

The three men exchanged a look and the older one commanded, "Open your suitcase, Contessa."

"I won't," cried Barbara and passed swiftly from the terminal and out into the bright sunshine. Beside the pier, her enormous black motorboat lay waiting.

Three boatmen in her canary yellow and blue livery stepped forward to greet her.

"Ah, Contessa, welcome, welcome. How we've missed you. The Lido beach is waiting for you eagerly. Elsa Maxwell is giving a big party for you tonight and the Duc de Aosta wishes you to lunch with him tomorrow."

The police shrugged helplessly. Scowling, they watched the

Countess and her entourage being helped into the massive launch. They knew the Duc de Aosta was the cousin of their King.

As they arrived at the familiar Excelsior Beach Hotel on the Lido, the orchestra was playing tea music on the terrace, and a man was singing "Our Love Is Here to Stay." The usual fleet of reporters and photographers rushed up to her. But even they didn't bother her.

"Will your husband join you, Contessa?" one of them asked.

"Why not?" said Barbara.

"Is everything settled?"

"Our love is here to stay."

A group of handsome friends fell all over her on the beach. "Poor Barbara," cried Anna Maria Cicogna, "poor Barbara, how you suffer!" The rest of the women echoed this sympathy. Barbara's image was always poor-Barbara-born-to-suffer, and the attention she received was gratifying. Now especially after her father's harsh words, Barbara was pleased by all the "poor Barbaras." Indeed, she liked women to feel sorry for her. Better pity than hostility.

"Remember," said Countess Cicogna, "Reventlow holds all the aces in his hand."

"Don't pay that bastard off," advised Lady Sylvia Ashley, who had just married Douglas Fairbanks, Sr. Sylvia looked wonderfully glamorous in polka-dot silk pajamas, with her blond hair falling over her forehead and over one eye, well before Veronica Lake made this style her trademark.

"Poor Barbara," said Dorothy di Frasso, "men are vile. My goodness, these Europeans are greedy."

All her friends counseled her to try to patch things up with Kurt. It was true, he did hold all the aces in his hand. What could she do but make the best of a bad situation?

Reventlow flew in a few days later. Barbara didn't trust her emotions to see him alone, so husband and wife had a talk in the huge marble lobby of the Excelsior with its doors opening onto the sea. Reporters, photographers, and curiosity seekers of all nationalities immediately surrounded the pair. Kurt was nasty as ever, and she noticed what a cruel face he had. She wondered what she had ever seen in him. At the end of the conference, he delivered an ultimatum to her.

"It's five million or else, Miss Woolworth."

"You'll never get it."

"Then I'll get Lance," he replied.

"Dreamer!"

CHAPTER 34

The summer passed with more ghastly war bulletins and more threats from Kurt. The only bright spot was the new dance craze called the Lambeth Walk and Barbara's brief little infatuation with an Italian Prince. The press hounded her everywhere. Every move she made was avidly reported, and the French reporters were particularly persistent. It was worse than the old days of her debut in New York. Meanwhile, hostile letters were arriving from America. One letter was addressed: "Barbara Hutton, Venice, Italy." It came from a woman in Passaic, New Jersey, who said she had seen pictures of Barbara with sixteen different fur coats. Could Babs send her an old one?

"I get these letters all the time," commiserated Sylvia Ashley Fairbanks.

"And what do you do?" asked Barbara.

"I still remember what it's like to be poor," replied Sylvia, a former chorus girl from the slums of London who hooked a Lord and a rich one too. "So I often send them some of my old pelts;

of course, my personal maid takes all my last year's clothes—doesn't yours, Barbara?''

"Yes," replied Barbara.

"Listen, Barbara," cried Sylvia in her vital fashion. "Join me on the night train to Paris tomorrow evening, and I'll wise you up about these tough guys. You're just too kindhearted. Why, people tell me you're a soft touch to every hard-luck story, and now I hear even old Elsa's bleeding you white. Of course, Elsa's good value and she does help rich girls with their problems. . . ."

Two days later Barbara was in her apartment in the Paris Ritz, the grand rooms that she kept all year round. Lady Mendl gave a big party at Versailles that night at her celebrated Villa Trianon. By a cascading fountain, Barbara and Elsa had a talk in the garden. Every three minutes, fresh rockets were sent up into the sky and exploded into a rainbow burst of color.

"Well," said Elsa in her booming voice, "well, my fragile seashell, I'd give my heart and soul to be you, Barbara Hutton. Some people think it's good for the soul to be poor, but I can tell you the only thing good for the soul is to be rich—rich, rich, rich!''

"You wouldn't like to be stuck with Kurt Reventlow," Barbara sighed, glancing up at the fireworks display.

"Remember, darling," commented Elsa sagely, "there are plenty of fish in the ocean, especially in the Mediterranean, ha, ha, ha. Listen, beauty, let's hit Monte Carlo tomorrow and we'll find you a new fish."

"Why not?" said Barbara, exchanging looks with a handsome young English Marquis who had been her dinner partner.

"Somerset Maugham is aching to immortalize you in print," said Elsa, putting an arm around Barbara. "I'll get him to give a dinner party in your honor, and we'll meet Berenson and all the intelligentsia. Why don't you try a literary marriage this time, Barbara? Those writers could do something exciting to your head."

Barbara perked up. "Oh Elsa, how thrilling. Mr. Maugham is one of my favorite authors, and it would be diverting to have a platonic marriage."

"And Maugham is rich, too," said Elsa. "Think of all those Gauguins and Renoirs you'd have. Why haven't you collected any, by the way?"

"Father tells me I've spent too much money," replied Barbara, still shuddering from the memory of his recent words.

"I'll find you a rich man who'll give you some Impressionists," cried Elsa emphatically.

Baron Rothschild came up and kissed Barbara's hand, remarked that he'd never seen a more elegantly dressed woman, then he vanished into the coolness of the garden.

"I'll get you somebody like him," cried Elsa. "Wouldn't it be nice to have your coffers filled with fresh money for a change?"

"Oh Elsa, do let's give lots and lots of parties at Monte Carlo, and only have the most beautiful, seductive and wicked people. I just want to be happy and enjoy myself and treat every day like a holiday, the way Alexis Mdivani used to do."

In such an elated state, Barbara and her usual entourage joined Elsa on the Blue Train. Dinner time found them drinking champagne cocktails spiced with brandy and bitters. Barbara got high as a kite and loved it. Early the next morning she pulled up the blinds in her compartment. White sailing yachts sparkled on the turquoise sea. Pink geraniums cascaded over balustraded terraces. Pretty orange-tile-roofed villas set in mournful cypress trees went by. From a rumble seat of a Ford convertible, some children waved at her. White gulls flapped their wings.

Elsa burst into the compartment with her usual aura of enthusiasm. "Isn't it always thrilling to arrive in Monte Carlo at daybreak, my beauty? I've been to dear old Monte for twenty-five years, and I should be used to it, but I shiver all over when I see the Beach Hotel and the gambling casinos, and those royal palm trees enveloped in their purple mist. And there's no more beautiful sight than the great sailing yachts of the Vanderbilts and Westminsters in full sail."

"Oh, Elsa, you're a poet."

"Talking of poetry, Barbara dear, did I tell you that Lawrence Tibbett and Grace Moore want to sing some of your rhymes?"

"No!"

"Yes!" continued Elsa eagerly. "They were completely won over by the beauty of your poems, so I set them to music and the results were breathtaking. Alas," Elsa added, her voice dropping, "the Depression crowds at home would have none of Maxwell and Hutton."

"Do people at home think me merely a playgirl?" said Barbara in her innocent way.

"I'm afraid so," replied Elsa. "I'm one of the few people who knows that you're an artistic person with a strong creative drive. If you didn't have money, Barbara, I think you could make it on your own talent. You'd be a perfect actress, and think of the joy of having Garbo's salary!"

Barbara laughed. "Yes, that would be a novel experience."

Traveling with Elsa was a superlative experience. She enjoyed picking up strangers, only if they were rich and attractive, of course. All sorts of amusing adventures ensued and Barbara's spirits were kept buoyant. At the Monte Carlo station Elsa singled out a good-looking Brazilian. After a few words, he was only too delighted to share his Mercedes with the two ladies. He was divinely sleek and racé like a wolfhound. If the two women were charmed by him, he felt the same. By the time they arrived at the Hôtel de Paris, the sleek stranger was telling them that he was going to have a dinner party for them that evening.

"Is a hundred too many," asked Elsa, "for us to ask?"

"The more the merrier," laughed the South American good-naturedly.

An army of bellboys streamed out of the creamy Edwardian facade of the famous hotel and gave the celebrated Countess the royal treatment. Barbara was incredibly well thought of at all the watering spas. She never made scenes like so many rich spoiled women, treated all the help with kindness and concern, even liked to listen to their problems.

Elsa always tried to make Barbara see her situation in a different light. As Elsa lumbered through the great marble-columned lobby with its stained-glass ceilings and fountains and dozens of fashionable people sitting about in graceful Louis XV chairs and sofas, she lectured Barbara: "Have you ever read *Tobacco Road* or *The Grapes of Wrath?*"

"Yes, my heart went out to those poor people."

"Well, fair Countess," Elsa continued, "ninety-nine percent of the world's women spend every hour in the kitchen and every other hour cleaning and making beds all day.

"They do?"

"Just think how lucky we are to have adventurous careers, Barbara, with every day a holiday and every evening a celebration."

"Yes, I'm very grateful," said Barbara smiling.

"I was born poor, you know," Elsa continued, "but I was determined to have a colorful life surrounded by clever rich people. Anyone can have the life they want, if they just set their mind to it."

"Do you think so?"

"The only thing is that I wish I could be thin and graceful and lovely like you, and have men drooling over me like that divine South American. Think of all the wonderful things he'll do to you tonight at our dinner gala."

"I can hardly wait!"

Grand titled ladies and best-dressed ladies made a great fuss over Elsa. After exchanging a few words, Elsa and Barbara moved to the concierge's desk.

"Here are all the names that you see in the fashion and society pages," cried Elsa angrily, "and they're all nitwits."

"Really?" replied Barbara, astounded.

"Half the women we know here are just grand horizontals who made it on their backs. They couldn't make it in the cinema or the literary world. They expect recognition for hooking a rich man. Recognition and publicity is all these lovely, narcissistic ladies want, and I dish it out to them," cried Elsa.

An elegant woman who now called herself Princess de ———fell over Elsa with delighted cries. Elsa viewed her with a fish eye. When the Princess had vanished, Elsa continued her explanation about publicity seekers. "Why, that one's a famous tart."

"Is she?" said Barbara, astonished. "But she's so grand."

"Money's the only thing that makes you grand. Why, if most of these Duchesses and Princesses didn't have a dime, they'd be shuffling along sniveling and begging in the Bowery. As for you, Miss Barbara Hutton, I'd like to see *you* behave like a tart and get some presents from these rich gents."

"But what would I do?" asked Barbara, smiling.

"Just do what you're doing, darling. Why, I'd make you a bet that you could be old Joe Kennedy's mistress in a minute if you wanted him. He gave Gloria Swanson beautiful presents. You've got to change your pattern, Barbara, and think positively. . . ."

Barbara stared out the window that evening and watched the daylight fade on the sea. Cary Grant was singing on a record on her Gramophone from a movie he made with Jean Harlow. A night maid came in and began to tell Barbara about her boyfriend who owned a bar, but they couldn't get married and have children until they had more money. "How many years have you known him?" asked Barbara.

"Twelve," the girl replied, "and I've never looked at anyone else."

Later, when she was alone, Barbara reflected how incredible it was that people should love each other for twelve years. She never thought that love would last for her for more than three or four at the most. Then her French maid brought in her diamond necklace and diamond bracelet in their black velvet boxes. As Barbara put them on, she reflected that she might have missed a good many things that the average person takes for granted, but she did have excitement, glamour, and beauty. Her pink-and-blue drawing room was filled with fragrant tuberoses from the South American gentleman. Somerset Maugham had just called. The Duke of Westminster asked her out on his yacht the next day to have a picnic lunch at Saint-Tropez. Outside her french windows were the lights twinkling for miles up and down the coastline, twinkling as brightly as the necklace about her throat.

She went down the red-carpeted staircase at nine and almost immediately was surrounded by hand-kissing, titled men and tycoons.

CHAPTER 35

That evening dinner was served on a promontory overlooking the Mediterranean. People whirled about gracefully to the music of the dance band between courses. In Paris, Barbara had ordered forty models from Chanel, Molyneux, and Schiaparelli. She wore a wonderful violet crêpe, with dozens of pleats, that was light as air and seemed to float about her. She was greeted with the usual oohs and ahs and attracted the attention of all the photographers.

Like so many lonely, rich women with no sense of belonging anywhere, Barbara focused her energies on being a fashion plate. Wallis Windsor, the ideal for the women of the late 1930s, was really quite a plain woman. Yet through dieting, clothes, hairdresser, jewelry, discipline, and terrific concentration, she had transformed herself into an artfully striking woman. Everyone in Barbara's set worshiped the Duchess. Barbara herself kept all the Duchess's letters in a secret place in her writing table, tied with a little pink ribbon.

All the women in this international set were spoiled, luxurious creatures. They had no responsibilities, no realistic cares or problems. Their children were looked after by nannies, their household chores attended to by secretaries, footmen, butlers, and the inevitable French chef. These women had never set foot in a kitchen, never boiled water for coffee or an egg, and rarely even entered the nursery. Most of their mornings were spent lying in their beds or on a chaise longue, telephoning, and most of their afternoons were spent shopping, sometimes flirting, and then getting ready for the evening ahead.

It took a great deal of effort and time to look as the Duchess of Windsor or Barbara Hutton or Mrs. Harrison Williams. To be a queen of fashion took endless amounts of energy and money. Eventually, intelligent women got out of the fashion trap, but many of these peacocks surrendered completely to this narcissistic régime, content to be highly publicized for their style. In truth, Barbara herself began to get a bit tired of this dressing and undressing. Her hair took two hours to fix in elaborate coils. The color had to be applied every three days so the roots didn't show.

Basically, men were the ultimate reward for all those boring hours of grooming. That night, Barbara attracted Freddie McEvoy, a muscular, mustached gentleman, who'd upset her earlier by his intense stares. He had curly brown hair, a tall and muscular figure. He was dashingly dressed in a double-breasted white dinner jacket. He sported cabochon sapphires down his shirt front. His full sensual lips and a long suggestive nose gave him a satyr look. Dorothy di Frasso had warned Barbara about this famous adventurer. She said he was a rotter with some integrity, which appealed to Barbara.

Freddie McEvoy spent his summers in the south of France and his winters in Saint-Moritz, where he behaved so recklessly on the bobsled that he was nicknamed Suicide Freddie. Dorothy di Frasso said he was a gigolo, a black marketeer, and once had even killed a man in a drunken brawl in Marseilles. ''He's absolutely wild at l'amour and he's unequaled in the feathers, darling,'' Dorothy had concluded, which was always nice to hear about a prospective beau. No other type could appeal more to self-destructive Barbara Hutton than Suicide Freddie. He'd help block out her father's hateful words.

A dozen men cut in on Barbara and led her smoothly around the floor. They bore the greatest names in Europe, but most of them literally didn't know where their next meal was coming from. They were handsome, they had sex appeal, and they knew how to pour on the charm.

Freddie McEvoy lounged by a balustrade with a glass of champagne in his hand. He kept watching Barbara with a cynical smile. She couldn't take her eyes off him. She knew he was trouble, but he had more style than anybody in the whole room. She heard that he'd won a $10,000 bet that he could race from Paris to Cannes in less than nine hours. He'd also won $18,000 playing backgammon and Barbara, who was fond of the game, was dying to take him on.

Suddenly, Freddie stood before her and the ardent South American who was dancing with her sullenly vanished.

While the orchestra played "Dancing in the Dark," a round yellow moon came up over the delicate fronds of the palm trees. Intoxicating jasmine permeated the air. The twinkling stars were as bright as the lights of Monte Carlo. Freddie wanted to take her to Portofino in his Maserati. His offer excited her, but Daisy Fellowes had asked Barbara to go off on her yacht for lunch. Elsa had also arranged for Somerset Maugham to have a cocktail party for them. A handsome French Prince was giving her quite a lot of attention, too.

She and Freddie returned to the Hôtel de Paris at daybreak, as yellow and pink streaks appeared through the gray sky.

Presently Barbara jumped out of the car and said, "I'll just change to another dress."

"I'll be waiting," he told her, behind the wheel.

"Do I need any money?" said Barbara, who never carried any.

"I've got everything you need right here, baby," he told her.

Her exhilaration was shattered when she returned to her pastel-and-gilt drawing room.

Ticki rushed toward her. "Oh, Barbara, the American Ambassador, Mr. Kennedy, has telephoned three times already," she cried urgently. "Whatever could he want?"

"The war has probably started," Barbara said with a little shrug.

The phone rang shrilly on the vermilion-lacquered writing table. Ticki announced that His Excellency, Ambassador Joseph Kennedy, was on the line from London.

"Yes, this is Countess Reventlow speaking," Barbara began. "To what do I owe this honor?"

"I'm telephoning all the important Americans I know to tell them to return home as quickly as possible. I've hired a private plane for you, Countess, tomorrow afternoon. You and I will talk in my office the following day."

Barbara returned to the Maserati and told Freddie the bad news.

"Come here," he said roughly. He gave her a kiss she never forgot. She didn't see him again for eight years, but she never forgot the kiss.

CHAPTER 36

Barbara had met the Joseph Kennedys often in various London drawing rooms. She thought Rose Kennedy a charming and lovely person and liked the Ambassador's disciplined vitality. She also liked their nine children. Kathleen, a pretty young lady of eighteen, was rumored to be engaged to the Duke of Devonshire's son and heir.

Although Barbara, in fact, did not think about money, and was not impressed by it, she did admire the tremendous fortune that Joseph Kennedy had built up. Aunt Marjorie Hutton, now married to Joseph E. Davies, the U.S. Ambassador to the U.S.S.R., had put her stamp of approval on the Kennedys and advised Barbara to make friends with them—in case something dire happened.

"Joe Kennedy's richer than I am," said Aunt Marjorie, "and that's saying something."

Barbara and her aunt were fond of each other and were often in communication. In her latest letter, Mrs. Davies scolded Barbara about her marital failures with her usual wit. "If you're contemplating marriage again, Barbara dear, just remember to rotate your hips. It makes things more pleasant for the man."

Every time Barbara had met Kennedy, he was most polite and attentive to her. They often discussed her extravagant Aunt Marjorie's rather ludicrous position in poor and Communistic Moscow. Aunt Marjorie had her great white sailing yacht, *The Sea Cloud*, cruise into the Bosporus, complete with crew of sixty. She had bought up all the available Fabergé in Moscow.

Barbara's stately Daimler carried her to Grosvenor Square and the American Embassy, a palatial thirty-six-room house almost as big as Barbara's, the gift of J. P. Morgan. Her heart was beating excitedly at the prospect of her meeting with the famed womanizer, Kennedy.

As the bodyguards helped Barbara out of the car, a crowd quickly formed around the beautiful Countess. Like her friend the Duchess of Kent, she favored daytime costumes made by Capt. Edward Molyneux. Molyneux adored pearl-gray cut in severe lines. Barbara wore a classic gray-flannel suit, her marvelous pearls, and a dashing small hat quivering with egret feathers set over her forehead. Forever photographed in the local newspapers and magazines, Barbara had the aura of a monarch to the London populace. She didn't appear on balconies in a blaze of diamonds and ribbons, but the parties at Winfield House were almost as grand as those at Buckingham Palace.

Barbara's high-heeled pumps resounded on the marble floor as she was ushered into the Ambassador's Georgian paneled library. He was formally dressed, but his long legs were propped up on an antique mahogany table desk. Barbara liked the air of health about him, particularly his high color. The lusty ladies' man, Joseph P. Kennedy, regarded her with ardent admiration. From behind his spectacles she saw a pair of appealing blue eyes. She thanked him for the plane.

"It's lovely to see you safe here in London, Countess," said the Ambassador, kissing her hand.

"Do you really want me to return to America right away?"

"Yes," nodded the Ambassador in his vital manner. "Yes, I've warned all the nine thousand American residents here in England to leave the country quickly."

"Then the war is coming?"

"Definitely."

"The Duke and Duchess of Windsor don't seem too concerned," said Barbara. "He told me he's not leaving Paris."

"He's not exactly famous for his gray matter, Countess. Now let's sit down here and have a cozy talk. I've always wanted to get to know you a little better."

Barbara leaned back in the rather stiff Georgian chair covered in tapestry. She loosened the pair of sublime and bushy platinum foxes that encircled her neck and pulled off her gloves. A thirty-carat sapphire on her finger caught the light and she noticed the Ambassador staring at it. He was also staring at her trim legs and the outline of her breasts. She glanced rather nervously toward the door but no footman was standing there. She was alone in the room with the vigorous womanizer! She'd heard that Gloria Swanson had been his mistress. Barbara wondered what it would be like to bed down with a man of fifty.

"Would you care for a cocktail?" the Ambassador asked.

"I rarely imbibe," she replied coyly. She pulled her skirt down below her knees and crossed her legs.

"Can't I give you anything?"

"Just advice, my dear Ambassador."

"I'd love to give you that," he said warmly. He stood up and moved over to her side. "You need somebody to look after you, you know."

"I do?"

"Yes, you need a strong and powerful man."

"Perhaps," she said, giving the man some hope.

"I think all your follies have been made because of your choosing the wrong man."

She lifted up her veil and those extraordinary eyes gazed up at him. "And you're the right man, Ambassador Kennedy?" she whispered, deciding to go along with him. She remembered Elsa's words and wondered if she should be a tart.

"You couldn't find anybody better to suit your needs," he replied. "I'd like to satisfy your needs, Countess."

Their eyes met and she nervously recrossed her legs.

"You would?" she asked, pouting.

"I must tell you, you're a very desirable woman. You don't mind my telling you that, do you? Does Mr. Sweeney make you happy, Countess?" he asked with a lusty expression.

"He's sweet," smiled Barbara.

"Well, I'm not sweet, Countess, but I know how to make a woman happy. And I like to give a beautiful woman presents."

Joseph Kennedy had struck a responsive chord. Barbara loved the idea of having a man give her costly presents instead of paying for them herself. She was tired of paying for all her jewelry herself. She thought it would be wonderful to have this attractive older man pay for it.

Joe Kennedy knew his women well and he said, studying her, "I'll bet you're thinking now of a present you'd like me to give you, aren't you, Countess?"

"You mind reader," she giggled.

"There's a necklace of black pearls that I hear the Duke of Westminster wants to sell. Do you like black pearls, Countess?"

"They're awfully expensive. Can you afford them, Mr. Ambassador?"

"Call me Joe," he muttered, and pounced on her.

Barbara managed to elude his strong hands but as she ran away from him her platinum foxes fell onto the floor. She wanted to retrieve them but thought, Oh, the hell with them, and rushed out the door.

As the great car carried her back to Regent's Park, Barbara carried on a frantic conversation with bodyguard and chauffeur. What was she to do? And where to go?

"The *Athenia* is leaving day after tomorrow, Madame. You'd better be on it, Your Ladyship," warned the bodyguard.

"The *Aquitania* would suit you better," suggested the chauffeur.

"Oh, my dears, what's going to happen to me?" cried Barbara.

"You'll return to New York, m'lady, and we'll go into the army. My dad was killed in the first one—at the Marne it was, a real slaughter—"

The hall of Winfield House resembled the preparation stage for an auction at Christie's. Maids and footmen were packing away porcelain, crystal, and silver into great cases. The Boucher tapestries had been taken off the walls and some footmen were on stepladders dismantling the Waterford chandeliers. The famous Savonnerie was rolled up.

"I gave orders to have everything packed, Barbara," cried a frantic Ticki.

"They say Hitler's Air Force is going to bomb London any minute," shrieked Madeleine. "Oh, madame, it's a catastrophe!"

"Telephone my father in New York," commanded the Countess.

"We've tried," replied Ticki, "but the lines are all tied up."

"Get Lance and pack his things," said Barbara, "and call the curator of the National Gallery and tell them to take away my Canalettos for safekeeping."

The two servants hesitated, and Barbara cried somewhat sharply, "Don't just stand there looking at each other. There's not a moment to be lost. And Miss Livingstone, make a reservation for us all on the *Aquitania*."

Miss Livingstone was coming down the stairs with a carton of rare Chinese porcelain and jade. She was so nervous about the state of affairs that, hearing Barbara mention her son, she dropped the carton. The priceless objects smashed all over the floor.

"What is the matter with all of you?" asked Barbara in her most high-strung state.

No one dared tell her about Lance. Presently, Miss Livingstone took a deep breath and gathered sufficient courage to say, "M'lady, be prepared for bad news."

"Bad news! Isn't there quite enough bad news already?"

"Count Reventlow has kidnapped little Lance, and we don't know where he's taken him. . . ."

CHAPTER 37

All over London newsboys were shouting: "GERMAN TROOPS STREAM INTO POLAND. WAR IMMINENT. WARSAW BOMBED. HITLER'S TANKS CANNOT BE STOPPED." On all the street corners, silent, stunned crowds were forming. Barbara's bodyguards, footmen, butlers, and grooms were all conscripted.

The war news was bad enough, but then there was little Lance to think about. For the next two days—the eleventh hour before the lights of Europe were to black out for six years—the telephone lines were burning between New York and London, London and Paris, Paris and Denmark. Barbara didn't see a soul and didn't sleep at all.

Finally, Frank Hutton's rough voice came over the line on September 3, the fatal day when England, then France, declared a state of war with Nazi Germany.

"Where have you been?" cried Barbara. "I've been trying frantically to get you in your New York office!"

"I'm living quietly in an old plantation outside of Charleston," he said glumly. "Afraid the end is near."

She disregarded his self-pitying tone.

"Have you discovered anything about Lance?"

"My network of spies," said Frank Hutton, "tell me your son is safe and sound in Biarritz with his father."

Barbara took a deep breath. "Oh, thank God!" Then added, "I suppose it's going to cost me plenty?"

"Plenty," he replied sourly. "But you're used to that."

"Yes, I'm used to that," and always hoping to please him she added softly, with charm, "It's going to be nice to live in America again, Father. Perhaps we can become close now and I can become the daughter you've always wanted."

"You can never be my daughter," he said.

"Oh?"

"The person who holds the purse strings is always the man."

"You're not implying I'm masculine, are you?"

"Your money puts you in the driver's seat, Barbara," he replied gruffly.

"I'm sick and tired of hearing that!"

"That's why Kurt grew disenchanted with you."

"That man only wanted my money," cried Barbara angrily.

"All of us love you, Barbara," said Frank Hutton reflectively, "but it's your fate to have us envy and resent your great wealth." The line buzzed and Hutton's voice became harsh again. "Now rush down to Biarritz, Marie Antoinette. If you need any help, call your Aunt Marjorie in Moscow. And Joe Kennedy's a regular fellow and will look after you. Call me as soon as you get back to New York."

"But how am I going to get back to New York?" she replied furiously.

"Get yourself space on the *Lisbon Clipper*."

"I can't," said Barbara. "It's all booked."

"You've been a worry to me all my life," he said disagreeably. "Now you're worrying me when I'm at the grave. Typical selfish, thoughtless, irresponsible Barbara Hutton." The phone went dead and Barbara slammed the receiver down in a rage. How dare he call her irresponsible! Had he ever been responsible for her? Hadn't he killed her mother and sent Barbara herself off to those hostile boarding schools. It was due to his stupidity that all the ruinous publicity had started.

The housekeeper announced that Mr. Churchill was on the telephone. "Pack everything, my lovely girl," he told her. "Nothing's safe from that terrible monster, Hitler. And be careful of kidnapping. The Nazis might try to get a big ransom for Lance."

The next days were a nightmare for Barbara. Packing and moving had always unbalanced her, especially now on the eve of this terrible war. One of her sanity supports was Winfield House, that solid rock of red brick and cream marble that she had built herself. Its forty rooms represented the only real home she'd ever had. Ironically, she hardly ever spent any time in this beautiful house, and most of the moments there had been unhappy. She felt a wild desire to stay in London, but, of course, Ticki talked her out of it and the servants continued their packing.

Barbara's two dozen servants crated all the treasures of Winfield House. Marie Antoinette's Savonnerie rug, her gold plate, her suite of Louis XV furniture, her priceless Coromandel screens were all sent to a warehouse in the country. Only her $4,000,000 jewelry collection remained. Her father had warned her of the possibility of a robbery. One morning an armored car came to the Georgian mansion and took Barbara's collection of emeralds, rubies, sapphires, and diamonds back to the vaults of Coots Bank.

Air-raid sirens shrieked. People on the street wore gas masks. London schoolchildren were packed up and sent to the country. The lunchrooms of the Ritz and Claridge's were no longer lively and glittering, but forlorn. London at war was a very different town from a London at peacetime. Barbara moved about forlornly among the once-magnificent rooms of Winfield House, denuded and stripped of their brocade and damask curtains, crystal wall lights and crystal chandeliers, tapestries, and palace furniture.

Only the magnificent staircase, which had been ripped out of a seventeenth-century French château, remained in all its glory. Sadly, Barbara moved out the french doors into the formal lawn and garden at the rear of the house. A warm September mist lingered in the leaves; the foliage was just beginning to turn. The orange marigolds and box hedge exuded an autumn scent.

On September 4, the liner *Athenia* was torpedoed, and twenty-two Americans perished. Ambassador Kennedy warned Americans not to board the *Aquitania*, a great Cunard liner which was one of Barbara's favorites and which resembled the ill-fated *Titanic* with its four towering red smokestacks. Ambassador Kennedy promised her a motorcycle escort from London to Southampton. "Then you're on your own," he told her, "but I'll have the French officials look after you."

"We're leaving for Biarritz tomorrow morning," Barbara announced to her household.

A caravan departed from Winfield House the next day. Two policemen on motorcycles led the way and acted as interference. Two armed detectives, Ticki, and Madeleine rode in Barbara's car. Behind this imperial Rolls-Royce were two station wagons filled with suitcases and Vuitton trunks. Sirens wailing, the motorcade proceeded down the long drive and out the gates. Barbara stared tearfully at the stately Georgian mansion with its towering chimneys.

"Don't look back, dear Barbara," said Ticki, patting her hand. "A new life awaits you in America."

"I'll probably never see the house again," said Barbara wistfully. She never did. During the war, she gave the house to the American government and, subsequently, American Ambassadors have used it as their residence. For a moment, watching the sprawling red-brick mansion vanish from sight, she thought of all the money spent on this house. A heavy sense of futility settled over her. She dreaded another hostile greeting in New York.

In Le Havre, Premier Deladier gave Countess Reventlow another police escort, and she proceeded down to Biarritz. On the way, they read all the newspaper reports. She was horrified to learn of the destruction of Warsaw and the speed with which Hitler's powerful tanks were racing over the Polish countryside. Hitler was shrieking on the radio: "I shall build U-boats, U-boats, U-boats! I shall build airplanes, airplanes, airplanes!" The fury in his voice astounded Barbara and she remarked, "He sounds like a madman!"

Everyone seemed in a daze in Biarritz. In that ornate nineteenth-century structure, the Hôtel du Palais, built by Napoleon III for the beautiful Empress Eugénie, which had been the scene of happy days with Alexis Mdivani, the Reventlows had a tense reunion. Little Lance ran into her arms and she held him close. Later, in a grandiose, raspberry-and-gilt apartment, where Eugenie and Napoleon had quarreled, the Reventlows exchanged dire words. Finally, Kurt agreed to let Barbara take Lance off to America.

"For half a million," he said.

"All right," Barbara replied wearily. "And what about a divorce, Kurt?"

"That'll cost you much more."

The divorce didn't become final until three years later, at which time Kurt raked in another $1.5 million.

That evening, Frank Hutton called his daughter to warn her that the Nazis were planning to kidnap her son. "I'd advise you to go to Monte Carlo immediately and then cross the Italian frontier. Proceed to Naples, where I've made reservations for you on the steamship *Conte di Savoia*."

"But Mussolini's on Hitler's side, isn't he?" asked Barbara anxiously.

"Not yet he isn't," replied Frank Hutton. "And be sure you have a police escort all the way in to Naples. You never can tell what those Nazi cutthroats are capable of. . . ."

Two days later, in great secrecy, the Reventlows' caravan pulled out of the Hôtel de Paris in Monte Carlo. As they were racing toward the Italian frontier, along that mountain road known as the Grande Corniche, Barbara noticed with horror that two beetlelike Citröen cars were following them.

"I don't like the looks of those gangster faces behind the wheel," cried Barbara in alarm.

"We'll be safe when we get into Italy," said Ticki soothingly.

As soon as the frontier closed behind them, Barbara's police escort left them and they were on their own. The swarthy Italian officials had been most disagreeable to her despite the two American flags flying on either side of the motor. With a sense of foreboding, Barbara drew her little son closer to her. Somewhere between Genoa and Naples, Barbara and her station wagons were separated. With terror she realized that her great Rolls was alone on the road and the two beetlelike cars were in hot pursuit.

Barbara rolled down the glass partition that separated her from the chauffeur and bodyguard. "You'll have to drive faster, George!"

"The accelerator's right on the floor, Your Ladyship," said the chauffeur tensely.

The heavy car careened through the dusty streets of Naples, scattering hens and dogs and people alike. They swiftly checked into the Excelsior Hotel and telephoned the American Legation there. Italian police guarded their suite until they boarded the Italian liner, the streamlined *Conte di Savoia*. At the time of departure, the smokestacks let out the mournful wail that Barbara knew so well, and then the proud ship glided over the Mediterranean and out the Straits of Gibraltar. There was much talk of torpedoing by U-boats, and Lance was in an excited state of expectation.

At twilight, Barbara and Lance stood on the promenade deck and watched the outline of Europe vanish behind them. Certainly, Barbara Hutton's good times in Europe were finished forever. When she returned eight years later, she was a tired, sick woman, old before her time.

CHAPTER 38

The hostile reporters who greeted her in New York were bad enough, but as her limousine drew up before the Hotel Pierre at 61st Street and Fifth Avenue, a dozen Woolworth workers shouted at her. They held picket signs, which glared at her: BARBARA HUTTON! IS EIGHTEEN DOLLARS A WEEK TOO MUCH?

Another one read: BABS! WOOLWORTH AGREED TO ARBITRATE YET REFUSED TO ABIDE BY THE AWARD WHEN IT LOST. IS THAT THE AMERICAN WAY?

Another one: BABS HUTTON FLEES EUROPE'S WAR. SEEKS PEACE. BUT HOW ABOUT PEACE WITH THE UNION?

BARBARA HUTTON! WHY DOESN'T WOOLWORTH DEAL WITH US?

Reporters questioned her endlessly, and she replied, "Do people realize I have no more to do with running the Woolworth stores than I have with the running of the British Empire?"

247

The police were summoned and Barbara was led through the revolving doors. The experience was shattering for her. The angry voices haunted her for weeks afterward. There was no place she could go for refuge.

That evening she had dinner with her Aunt Jessie, but Mrs. Donahue wasn't overly sympathetic to her niece. "You've got to stop all this gadding about," said Mrs. Donahue severely. "Why can't you settle down here and marry an American?"

"I am in love with an American," said Barbara softly.

"What's this Sweeney like?" asked Mrs. Donahue coldly.

"Little Lance adores him," said Barbara. "He has a very kind heart."

"I only had one man in my life," lectured Mrs. Donahue, "and one man was quite enough, thank you. You've already had two, Barbara Hutton, and three is out of the question. . . ."

Aunt and niece were sitting in the sumptuous drawing room of Mrs. Donahue's duplex at 834 Fifth Avenue, which was overdecorated, giving the feeling of a museum rather than a home. There were splendid Chippendale and Queen Anne pieces, all heavy and ornate. From the paneled walls hung stiff oil portraits by Romney, Gainsborough, and Sir William Beechey, lit by the inevitable portrait lights. Heavy damask curtains, quivering with ball fringe and tassels, were drawn over the immense windows to give the rooms that look of fashionable gloom. Barbara always had a strong urge to rip the curtains down and let in some air. She never could understand why her aunt kept these heavy draperies drawn both morning and night, when the glorious view of Central Park was spread out before them.

Served by silent, poker-faced butlers, the two Woolworth women dined alone in the formal English dining room, with more Chippendale and more portraits. It was about as cheerful as a morgue. Barbara went home with a heavy heart.

Bobby Sweeney had given her a little black curly-haired poodle. Her happiest moment since her return to America came when she entered the Pierre apartment and the darling jumped all over her and licked her face. For fear of the press, she and Bobby lived in different hotels. The next day she had a lunch engagement with him at the Colony Restaurant, which was just a block away on Madison Avenue. Wearily, she slipped into bed and drew the satin coverlet over her. The dog lay beside her on the pillows and was a great comfort to her. She took up a volume of Tagore's poetry, which she found soothing. She had spent many winters in India, where she discovered this Indian poet. At three o'clock in the morning, when Ticki came in to see how her poor Barbara was, she found the Countess lying there still reading the book of poetry. It was nice to see her looking at peace.

A memorable incident took place at the Colony Restaurant the next day. Always punctual, indeed, usually a minute ahead of an appointment, Barbara was sitting in the vestibule waiting for Bobby. She was glancing through *Vogue* magazine listlessly and smiling at various acquaintances who passed by on the way to the bar or the dining room. She was seated thus in her platinum foxes and Paris-tailored suit when two of her bitterest enemies from Farmington came in. They stared at Barbara with surprise. At that moment, Mr. Rockefeller, a banking friend of her father's, came up and sat down next to her. Her Farmington enemies were astounded and impressed. Revenge was even sweeter when Errol Flynn came in and exchanged some flirtatious words with Barbara. It was good to settle some old scores. In contrast to her plain and dowdy former classmates, Barbara felt proud of her sleek, elegant silhouette.

When Bobby joined her, they moved into the dining room where they sat on the little cozy red banquette to the right of the door. Many old friends approached to greet her warmly throughout the meal, among them Jimmy Donahue, who suggested they spend Christmas in Palm Beach. Lance and his nanny popped in, and then all of them rode out to the World's Fair. Having a lovely time, Barbara and Lance rode the merry-go-round. Bobbing up and down on the wooden horse with the little boy in her arms, Barbara thought America wouldn't be so bad after all.

One evening, Barbara bumped into Doris Duke at ElMorocco. Doris's marriage to handsome Jimmy Cromwell was breaking up, and the two girls commiserated.

Doris announced her intentions to move to Hollywood.

The two women, who were labeled the richest girls in the world, wittily discussed the problems that their money caused in their marriages.

Next morning, Dorothy di Frasso telephoned: "Angel face, I'm having a party tonight. Hurry down and meet divine Cary Grant. He's standing here next to me now and I can hardly bear to be so close to all that charm and muscle. He's positively drooling to meet you, sweetheart. . . ."

Barbara was so excited getting dressed that evening that she spilled half a bottle of perfume all over herself. Her hairdresser was taking hours with her curls, until finally she could stand it no longer. "Dear," she said, "please hurry, because I'm going to meet a wonderful man."

Cary Grant was wonderful, all right. A man was singing the lyrics of Cole Porter's song "I've Got You Under My Skin" when Barbara met the famous actor.

Responding to the lyrics, Barbara thought grimly that this was one time she was going to win. And she was definitely going to wake up to reality. And most definitely Cary Grant could help her—could save her! He held her hand tenderly and his warm, compassionate eyes told her he cared for her.

In a moment they were sitting in a corner, and so it all began. Right away, listening to him, watching him, she realized he was different from the others. This man was something special, and she'd have to go slowly with him. Intuitively, she felt he was sincere and had a good heart, and she was right on that score. There was the added attraction that he worked for a living. What's more, he was successful at it.

She was excited to discover that Cary Grant was attracted to her as much as she was to him. She had a wild hope that he really could save her from herself. He was a positive, constructive man with a goal and a purpose. She was convinced he could conquer all of her negative thoughts and evil patterns.

They talked a moment and then he suggested they take a trip to Mexico.

As his handsome eyes watched her, Barbara thought she would faint with joy. She could not believe her ears. Was this a proposal? All of a sudden, her worst instincts came to the front. She doubted that such a good-looking and famous man could care for her.

Dorothy di Frasso had been watching them and couldn't bear the suspense. When she saw Grant leaving her party, she rushed over to Barbara. "Darling, how did the meeting go? Are you mad for him?"

"Mad!"

"What are you going to do about it?"

"I'd better think about it now," said Barbara seriously. "A third marriage better be the last marriage."

"What will you do with Sweeney?" asked Dorothy.

"I don't know. He'll be furious," said Barbara. Never courageous in matters of the heart, she wondered what on earth to tell him.

Barbara rented the luxurious Palm Beach villa from her old friend Mrs. Harrison Williams for Christmas and New Year's of 1940. She and Bobby attended the usual polo and tennis matches, lunches at the Bath and Tennis Club, and dinner at the peerless old Everglades Club. They were happy enough, although she kept a lively correspondence going with the fascinating Mr. Grant on the side. Life was more exciting with these little intrigues. Mary and Laddie Sanford urged her to pursue the famed actor.

Though she and Cary Grant did not meet again in 1940, she did see his movie, *The Philadelphia Story,* and thought it was one of his best films. Watching him make love to Katharine Hepburn, a willful heiress who was similar to Barbara in temperament and style, made her realize that Cary Grant was the man for her. She believed that he could *truly* save her.

At the same time, she had no idea of what to do about Bobby Sweeney. She had grown fond of him; in fact, dependent on him. She wasn't the type to toss someone aside lightly. It took a good deal of her considerable charm to ease Bobby out of her life and to convince him that she wasn't the right woman for him. So they parted.

In 1941 Barbara spent every available moment with Cary

Grant. She rented Buster Keaton's old house in Beverly Hills. They often traveled throughout Mexico, where she took a great fancy to Cuernavaca and Taxco. Much later she built a Japanese-style house outside of Cuernavaca. Jimmy Donahue, thrilled by Cary, said he was the nicest guy he'd ever met. Ticki approved heartily, too. Of course, six-year-old Lance's opinion was the most important of all.

"He's the nicest friend you've ever had, Mummy," he told her.

"What would you think if I married him, dear?"

"Oh Mummy, I'd like nothing better," said the boy, wrapping his arms around her. "And Hollywood is so much nicer than Europe. . . . I'd like to live in Hollywood always. . . ." And he did until the day he died some thirty-one years later.

CHAPTER 39

With predictable venom, the press labeled them "Cash n' Cary." There were headlines saying that Hollywood's biggest box-office star had merged with the world's richest woman. They were married on July 8, 1942 at Lake Arrowhead, a popular place to elope in those days. Barbara would remember the perfect summer day till she died. The blue skies were cloudless and warm sunlight shone on the serene waters of the lake. With Cary gazing at her lovingly, Barbara finally felt at peace from her torments. Since she had his good values to sustain her, she believed her self-destructive spiral was halted for a time.

Barbara was at the height of her loveliness, looking fragile, wistful, and feminine in a severely tailored suit and a little lace blouse. Her eyes were radiant and her lips, which tended to droop at the corners, were turned upward. The groom lived up to his reputation of being the most handsome and charming man in Hollywood. Barbara always loved to give her husbands presents. On their wedding day, Cary wore a large pearl stickpin from Cartier.

They posed graciously for the photographers for an hour. People from all over America sent her letters and telegrams wishing her happiness. A nice change!

Much later, she used to tell me, "I loved Cary the most, he was so sweet, so gentle. It didn't work out, but I loved him."

In the beginning the marriage worked well. She tried hard to defeat her old self-destructive habits, tried to alter her image. She instantly gave a few million dollars for the British War Relief to equip twenty-four ambulances and went as far as to become a nurses' aide. Making certain that Lance had the proper love and attention, she was pleased that he was a happy, outgoing child. She found she enjoyed supervising the children's parties. She even knitted a pair of argyles for Cary. She tried to avoid the party set from her European playgirl days, knowing that Cary would not feel at home with their frivolity. Her marriage to Cary Grant had changed Barbara Hutton.

"For a long time I protected myself from my friends," Barbara used to tell me. "But then finally Hollywood was too tough a place, I didn't feel I belonged there. It's part of the disease of the outcast, you know, to feel you never belong to any place or to anyone. I'm the original wayfarer. For a time it gave me infinite solace and strength to belong to Cary. I prayed my feelings for him would endure forever. But you know 'forever' is hardly in my vocabulary."

By the middle of 1943, Barbara found herself slipping back into her old habits. Cary was busy at the studio most of the day. She felt out of things, on the shelf, as it were. She began to seek her gay companions once again: Dorothy di Frasso, Elsie Mendl, Baron Eric Rothschild, Baroness Renée de Becker, and, of course, vigorous Elsa Maxwell. Elsa threw many wartime galas, under the pretext of bond drives or victory celebrations. Frances and Sam Goldwyn threw a big party for Barbara's old friend Leslie Hoare Belisha. Ann and Jack Warner gave a dazzling dinner for Lady Diana and Lord Alfred Duff Cooper, and Lady Diana had visited Barbara in Palm Beach a few seasons back. Doris and Jules Stein of M.C.A. were great hosts, too. The Steins' and

Warners' daughters played with Lance. Hollywood's elite made an enormous fuss over Barbara. Born people-pleaser that she was, she could never resist people who so obviously liked her.

The movie capital under the palm trees and tropical sun brought back memories of Monte Carlo and Venice to Barbara. Try as she might, she could not get interested in those Hollywood parties where everyone discussed their latest films and the box-office receipts. Those gatherings were almost as dull as the old days when her father and his cronies talked endlessly about stocks, bonds, inflation, dividends, and yields. In Hollywood, one could forget there was a war going on, although uniformed soldiers and sailors were in the studio lots and at fancy nightclubs like Mocambo and Ciro's, where Barbara used to see Rita Hayworth dance to the South American strains of the samba Brazil.

Cary, who liked order and routine, rarely went out. He would get up at dawn, return from the studio at six, and have a cocktail with Barbara, followed by a quiet dinner. He wasn't too talkative during the evening. He liked to settle down in a comfortable chair and memorize his lines for the shooting the next day. He relaxed from the studio pressures by listening to the radio or pasting clippings into his album. He began to yawn about ten, when they'd wander upstairs to the bedroom. Lights usually were turned out by eleven, the latest.

"A working actor is very different from an actor on holiday," Barbara used to tell me sadly. "And Cary was extremely different from his screen image—you know, the way he was in *The Philadelphia Story:* fun, laughing, and naughty all the time." He was really a serious man.

Elsa Maxwell was staying with Evelyn Walsh McLean, who Barbara remembered from her Palm Beach days with Aunt Marjorie. Mrs. McLean always wore the enormous Hope Diamond, which had inspired Barbara so many years before. Barbara would often discuss the history of her jewels with Mrs. McLean.

She told Mrs. McLean one evening that she was wearing Marie Antoinette's pearls, and Mrs. McLean said, "You'll have bad luck in spades, the way I have. Be careful, Barbara, you've got yourself a great man and stay away from the destructive party set and all its promiscuities and booze.''

Her words could not have been more appropriate. After thirty, Barbara began to discover that liquor gave her comfort. She found a few gin cocktails conquered that feeling of disappointment that often arose at five o'clock in the afternoon.

By early 1944 Barbara was beginning to feel tired. She lost interest in things and liked to stay in bed, daydreaming. She suffered from severe stomach cramps. Often at night she'd awaken in such pain that she would have to have a drink. She was still on that ruinous coffee and RyKrisp diet. One day she described her condition to Dorothy di Frasso, who made an appointment for her to go to see her doctor.

"You must eat more, Mrs. Grant," the doctor advised.

"Silly man," she said.

"Why 'silly,' Mrs. Grant?" he said gravely.

"Everyone's always telling me to eat more," replied Barbara lightly, "but I'm strong as a horse, truly I am."

His probing eyes never left her face.

"You don't feel strong as a horse now, do you, Mrs. Grant?" he asked.

Barbara hated to admit she was sick.

"What if I don't?" she flung back defiantly.

"Can't you be honest with your own doctor, Mrs. Grant?" A distinguished, gray-haired man around sixty, the doctor represented a father figure to Barbara. She fell into her little-girl role, as she often did with authority figures. "I do feel weak and dizzy all the time, I must confess, Doctor. And I have sharp pains in my stomach, which keep me awake at night."

"How long have you had these sharp pains?"

"A year or so," she replied airily, but she felt a growing fear inside of her.

"I want you to come in and have some tests, Mrs. Grant," the doctor told her.

"I loathe tests. I suppose you even want me to go into the hospital!" she responded spiritedly.

"It would be easier to do them there," he said gently.

She was wearing a black-and-white flowered silk print, a large black cartwheel hat, and white gloves. Now she lowered the veil and said, as she moved toward the door, "Perhaps I'll be back."

"It would be prudent if you returned, Mrs. Grant, for those tests." The significant tone of the doctor's voice made her stop, turn around, and give him another look. He told her not to smoke, so she puffed on a cigarette, and slammed out the door.

"Sweetest Philip, such a good audience you are! Forgive me if I've upset you."

"It's a fascinating story," I replied, "and I'm fascinated by you, Barbara."

She squeezed my hand and gazed toward the stately windows.

Outside in the Place Vendôme a melancholy mauve light had turned the gray buildings to a deep purple. Lights were beginning to gleam across the magnificent square.

Presently the woman in bed sighed, and turned her beautiful blue eyes on me.

"You aren't tired of my story after all these months here at the Ritz?" The timbre of her voice moved me and now I squeezed her hand.

"Please go on," I said warmly.

"The rest of my history is sad," she said with becoming gravity. "Perhaps I should end here and start tomorrow?"

"I couldn't bear the suspense!"

"Remember, it isn't a happy ending."

"Perhaps it will be, after all. . . ."

"No," she said, shaking her head, "no, there are no happy endings for Barbara Hutton."

I put a lot of enthusiasm into my voice and eagerly leaned forward in my chair.

"I'll make you a bet!"

It warmed my heart to see the frail woman smile.

"Now you sound like Cary. . . ." The mood of failure fell over her. Lost in a long-ago reverie, she began to play with the collection of jewelry spread over the antique lace coverlet of the great bed.

Her personal maid entered, and moved across the vast room silently to draw the heavy curtains and to light some lamps. She was richly dressed in black, a hand-me-down from Barbara, and a sprinkling of fine pearls and diamonds. A duchess would have been pleased to look like her.

Barbara and the maid exchanged some pleasantries, then Barbara said: "Has my husband returned?"

"The Baron von Cramm is dressing to go out for dinner, Madame."

"Is he?"

The maid withdrew across the heavy carpeting and Barbara flung me a mocking look.

"Now back to dear Cary," she smiled. "He was certainly thoughtful. He always gave a good deal of himself although he claimed he didn't."

"You loved him the most, didn't you?" I asked.

She swallowed and her red lips trembled. "Yes" she whispered.

"Did you go back to the doctor for tests, Barbara?"

"By now you must know, sweetheart, how little Barbara pays attention to advice given!"

"Willful as ever," I returned with a smile.

"Little did I know that my life was over at that point. . . ." Again her thin lips trembled at the corners, she seemed on the verge of tears. Sometimes silence is the best audience so I sat quietly stroking her hand and gazing with love at her.

Abruptly Barbara held up a gold mirror and gazed critically at her reflection, smoothing the flesh about her neck and cheeks.

"Do I look horribly old, Philip?"

"An ogre!"

She smiled. "Fourteen years ago I was beautiful like you, and Cary loved me deeply but we had bad luck."

"Tell me . . ."

"I wanted so much to have a baby with him. . . ." Again the tears seemed to choke her.

"Yes? . . ."

"I tried three times, had three miscarriages . . . but failed. Typical Barbara." A bitter sound came from her.

To steer her into different water, I asked, "Did you make many friends with the Hollywood actors and actresses?"

"Yes," she nodded, "but I was most unreasonably jealous of all those pretty girls who threw themselves on Cary. I was often in despair, beloved!"

"I suppose many of his leading ladies fell for him!" I said encouragingly.

"Ginger Rogers made a movie with him and people told me they had flirted. I don't know about Laraine Day and the others. In any case, every time we went out to a premiere or a dinner those sirens stuck to Cary like glue . . . all under the pretext of discussing their roles and directors. You know! . . . women are very sly and cunning, Philip dear, and love to have what someone else has . . . especially someone they envy . . . and they envied me!" she added grimly.

"Perhaps you should have become an actress, Barbara?"

"I should have had a baby!" she flung back and her eyes dilated with anger.

"Cary loved children very much. He was wonderful with Lance as I've told you." She smiled nostalgically at the memory. "Cary made me a bet he'd be a happy father by the end of the war. . . ."

A knock on the door interrupted us. Then a formal voice said, "Barbara? . . ."

"Do come in, Gottfried," said Barbara flashing me a significant look.

Across the vast, tall-ceilinged room came a tall, athletic man most beautifully dressed and groomed. Gottfried von Cramm dutifully presented himself by the bedside, clicked his heels and kissed his wife's hand. Barbara gazed up at him with that hopeful way she adopted with all good-looking men.

"What are you doing tonight, my dear?" she inquired.

"Dining with friends."

"Anyone I know?"

"No, they're Germans . . ."

"Oh? . . ."

A coolness passed between husband and wife. Never had I seen a more mismatched pair.

The Baron's taut lips became tauter.

"Now I must go, Barbara," he said.

"I'm not detaining you."

"Goodnight."

"Goodnight."

Again there was the clicking of the heels and the kissing of the hands, then a most formal exit.

"Charming fellow," I remarked sarcastically.

"He WAS charming," Barbara replied, her mouth drooping savagely, "until he received his settlement. Money's all they ever wanted . . . except for Cary. . . . He loved me for my-self . . . yes he did . . ." Her voice faded and she began to talk as if to herself.

I stood up and moved to the windows. I parted the heavy drap-eries and stared out into the chill November evening.

"What do you see, Philip, dear?"

"A beautiful star . . ."

"What else?"

"A gorgeous woman in a sari and incredibly large pearls is stepping into a white Rolls-Royce."

"That's the Maharanee of Baroda, she's dining with the Ar-turo Lopezes tonight at Maxims, they wanted me to go . . ."

"Oh, Barbara, why didn't you?" I scolded.

"I wanted to be here with you and finish my story."

I was touched, returned to the bed and kissed her.

She took me in her arms.

"Would you like to go to Maxims, dear?"

"Oh, yes!"

"Well, then, tomorrow evening I'll get together a little party and ask the Baroda and other colorful types . . . would that make you happy?"

"Yes!"

She smoothed my hair tenderly.

"A young man like yourself likes to go to parties and see people. I used to. I was called the most famous playgirl of all times. In any case, dear, you've made me very happy.''

I sat up and gazed at her intently.

"Barbara you've made me feel so much better, truly.''

"You have the same effect on me, too, sweetheart. I think we need each other.''

"That's just what I wanted to hear, Barbara!'' I said joyfully. I stood up and laughed.

"I wish I were your age and had your high spirits.''

"You will soon, Baroness!''

"Telling my story always makes me feel better, too,'' Barbara continued gravely, her eyes never leaving mine.

"It helps you to understand yourself better.''

"Indeed it does, Philip, and I'm so grateful to you for sitting here these past months. It couldn't have been too amusing for you. In fact, sometimes I think I'm a depressing and corrupting influence.''

"What a thing to say, Barbara Hutton!''

"It's true, isn't it?'' she replied with a challenging air.

"Tomorrow evening we're going to Maxims in a white Rolls-Royce and I'm going to dress you in a black lace from M. Balenciaga and your famous pearls and . . .''

"And emeralds and diamonds . . . !''

"And rubies and sapphires, and we'll dance and dance to marvelous waltzes and pretend we're in the Belle Époque like Lillie Langtry and Edward the Seventh!''

And so I left Barbara in a contented state of mind, as I always did. Or attempted to do.

The following rainy day at noon I returned to the bedside. I handed her a bouquet of Parma violets I'd bought in the damp arcades of the Rue de Rivoli.

"It's the first time anyone's brought me flowers in ages,'' Barbara said in childish delight. She made such a fuss over them and me that I felt nice and manly. A true prince consort. Indeed she began to call me Prince Philip after that day.

Presently as was my custom I sat by the bedside, took her

hand, turned my eyes on hers and the old story began once more. The crystal wall lights and chandeliers seemed to dim, the music faded, there was only Barbara and I sitting there together. No one ever entered the room, the telephone never rang. We were in our own special private world. If it was comforting for her it was comforting for me as well.

The old give and take, the warm currents passed between us and Barbara was saying, "Today is the last day of my story, sweetest Philip."

"No, no, it must go on forever!"

"Well, where was I yesterday?" she said in a bewildered manner.

"Yesterday we left off with you and Cary in Hollywood in the Forties . . . fourteen years ago . . . and lots of pretty girls were chasing Cary and lots of handsome men were chasing my heroine . . . I'm sure! . . . Come on, Barbara, admit it! . . ."

Barbara smiled and collected herself.

"Elsa was always introducing me to handsome new faces . . ."

CHAPTER 40

To stir up some activity and publicity, Elsa Maxwell threw a gala garden party to celebrate the liberation of Paris in the summer of 1944. Elsa was in great form this evening because victory was in sight and soon all her gay, fun group could return to Europe and play in those divine palaces. All the screen magazines and newspaper photographers converged on the Cary Grants when they arrived at the party. Cary was in black tie and a sleek satin-lapeled dinner jacket. Barbara wore her famous Chanel evening dress that had caused such a sensation when it appeared in *Vogue* a few years earlier. The gown was of sumptuous heavy satin embroidered with silver leaves from the bodice curving around to the hem. With it she wore diamond and ruby ear clips, a ruby and diamond bracelet, and a collar of rubies and diamonds. Anita Loos wrote that Barbara looked like a silvery wraith in her favorite party dress.

In the many pictures of her taken that evening, she looks weary and disappointed with an air of remoteness that was creeping over her features. She was smoking a cigarette to control her nerves. Her illness was giving her many bad moments at this point. This was definitely a gray day for Barbara. She'd had a few gin cocktails at home, but she couldn't get out of herself and into that state of euphoria. Even Elsa, pushing the new rage, Frank Sinatra, at her, did not break through her mental anguish. Sinatra was definitely not her type!

Elsa, as usual, saw the handwriting on the wall where the Grants were concerned. "You're dying to get back to Europe now that the war is over, aren't you, Barbara?" Elsa boomed.

"I do miss Paris and London," she sighed. The headache behind her eyes was deepening.

"I'm going back to Paris soon," cried Elsa. "I wish you'd join me, darling."

"I don't think Cary would like it," Barbara whispered.

"Do you care what Cary thinks?" asked Elsa.

"Of course I do," said Barbara loyally.

"Level with me," said Elsa sharply. "It's all finished between you, isn't it?"

"I suppose," she replied faintly.

"There's a divine Russian Prince who's been writing me letters about you."

"Dear Elsa, I've had enough Russians."

"This one's very different," said Elsa seductively. "He's not only athletic and a bicycle champion, but he's a great gentleman. He's never been married, which is an A-plus for his character."

"How old is he?" Barbara asked, her interest aroused.

"Your age," replied Elsa. "Of course, he's a great ladies' man and every girlfriend I have is chasing him and wants to marry him. And you've got everything to get him, Barbara. You're still a lovely creature."

"Am I?" said Barbara with total lack of self-confidence.

"A little too thin and drawn, my dear," replied Elsa, "but that's fashionable. Dear Barbara, aren't you getting tired of those third-class Hollywood vulgarians? I mean, all they do is work,

work, work, and a girl has to play once in a while, don't you think? Barbara Hutton, you belong in Europe.''

"I don't belong anywhere," said Barbara with a dull expression.

"A romantic girl like you needs Europe, needs the history and the past of Europe, the great palaces and aristocrats and the sumptuous parties in the Venice palazzos. It's not your fate, Barbara, to be with breadwinners. You're more at home with the aristocracy. I mean Jack Warner and David Selznick are workers, and not in the same league as the Duke de Richlieu and Prince Furstenberg.''

"I daresay you're right," said Barbara. The pains in her stomach were so sharp that she bit her lip. All the blood seemed to drain from her face.

Elsa was startled by the pain on Barbara's face.

"Is there anything I can do, Barbara? You look terrible.''

Barbara clung on to Elsa's arm.

"Could you take me inside the house, Elsa?" whispered Barbara. "And please call my doctor. . . .''

The Grants were separated twice, but their friends always got them back together again. Rosalind Russell, who adored both Barbara and Cary, invited them to her house for a reconciliation. The next morning her husband came into their bedroom and found Barbara sound asleep in bed and Cary was sound asleep in the bathtub. Roz was so enamored of Barbara that she even named her son Lance. Barbara's extreme generosity overwhelmed her, as it did so many people. Barbara sent her a $75,000 diamond bracelet to go with her meager wedding ring. When Roz protested that she couldn't keep it, Barbara remarked, "But this is just a trifle, a little souvenir. And what are gifts when one gives love?" Cary himself had been the recipient of magnificent gifts, too. A Boudin painting and an Utrillo were among the presents with which Barbara rewarded him for giving her his love.

However, the Grants just couldn't patch up their differences;

their friends and life-styles were just too different. Barbara in truth was only happy with a man that she could buy, and she couldn't buy a number-one box-office attraction who was making $500,000 a year.

On August 30, 1945 Barbara and Cary Grant divorced on the grounds of mental cruelty. Cary was the only husband who didn't receive a penny of alimony.

"I shall never remarry again," Barbara told the press in New York.

The following year, Barbara bought the twenty-room palace in the Casbah in Tangier, Morocco. She enjoyed being back in her old apartment at the Ritz overlooking the Place Vendôme. All of her old Louis Vuitton trunks were brought up from the basement. Ticki was with her. She was dining at Maxim's with good-looking and vigorous Prince Igor Troubetzkoy. Elsa told her that he was a descendant of a Lithuanian royal family—whatever that meant!

Her tall stately rooms were flooded with white and pink and red peonies, and all of her European entourage loyally gathered around her. How they'd missed their golden goose. These friends showered her with love and attention, and, of course, they were rewarded handsomely. The Duke and Duchess of Windsor, Mrs. Harrison Williams, the Arturo Lopezes were all united at the dining room at Maxim's. The doctors were after Barbara to go into the hospital, but she refused. She went to Monte Carlo instead, with dear Igor. "Typical willful Barbara behavior," she told me, chuckling.

CHAPTER 41

Barbara always said that the reason her marriage to Igor Troubetzkoy didn't work out was because of ill health and three major operations. "A man can't feel very romantic when you're always in the emergency room," Barbara said sadly.

In any case Igor proved to be a delightful companion for a while. He was a good friend of dashing Errol Flynn and great lover, Rubirosa. On his own, he didn't have the money to play in the international set, but he did after he married Barbara. Igor was thirty-eight years old, tall, blond, muscular, and still a bachelor, which was rather surprising since so many women had thrown themselves at him. Like all of Barbara's husbands he was vigorous. In fact, he was bicycle champion of France. He courted her in a romantic way, sending her books of poetry and bouquets of flowers and tender messages of love. He kissed her hand often and whispered heavenly things in her ear.

On February 28, 1947 they were married in Saint-Moritz, Switzerland, the scene of many of Barbara's escapades with Mdivani and Reventlow. When they returned to Paris, she gave an elaborate party at the Ritz and had the usual five-piece string orchestra. She also had the same menu that she'd had on her famous twenty-second birthday party thirteen years before. There was melon, caviar and blinis, cold salmon with sauce tartare, breast of chicken *sous cloche,* white asparagus with hollandaise sauce, fresh raspberries with ice cream, and liqueurs. Part of Barbara's tragedy was her inability to change old patterns. Now ill and tired most of the time, she fell into a rut and never managed to get out of it.

Her ability to cope with what was in store for her was shaky. Barbara had seen Porfirio Rubirosa, the Dominican playboy-diplomat, many times here and there in Paris. He'd been married to her good friend Doris Duke, who spoke glowingly of him. Daniele Darrieux, called the most beautiful woman in the world, had been his bride before Doris. One day, Barbara was sitting in the grandstand at Deauville watching the polo matches. Life at the lovely old-fashioned resort by the English Channel was led at a stately but exciting pace reminiscent of Biarritz. She had divorced Igor the year before and had reached the amazing age of forty. Reaching this momentous age was really a milestone for self-destructive Barbara, who had no faith at all in the future.

"Doesn't Rubi remind you of Alexis?" cried Elsa Maxwell, sitting by Barbara's side. "The same joie de vivre, the same muscles, the same sweat. Oh, l'amour! They say a woman isn't the same after a night with Rubi."

"Really?" said Barbara, who was dying for a change.

"Look at him," cried Elsa. "He's so healthy, so vigorous. Why, darling, he'll make you well again."

Barbara directed her binoculars onto the muscular figure of Rubirosa on his polo pony.

"Yes," said Barbara hopefully. "I think he could get me well. Spirit is what I need now."

Barbara became Madame Rubirosa on December 30, 1953. She was all done up in black by M. Balenciaga. Friends said she appeared to be going to a funeral, which the marriage turned out to be. Rubi was so passionate on the wedding night at the Pierre Hotel that Barbara ran into the bathroom to escape him. She suffered a broken ankle and reported that the sight of Rubirosa naked was appalling. The bridegroom, the newspapers reported, went out to celebrate. Rubi was also having a flamboyant affair with Zsa Zsa Gabor. Miss Gabor gave even more press conferences than Barbara about her feelings for the divine Rubi. "Rubi loves me, I love Rubi, but who loves Barbara?"

The Rubirosas were separated seventy-three days later, and Barbara was some $2,000,000 poorer. They were divorced in 1955. Once again, Barbara said she'd never remarry. She also swore that she was never going to drink champagne before a wedding ceremony, since it fuddled her brain and made her even more confused. As for Rubi himself, this charming and colorful playboy gambled his ill-gotten gains away on the stock market and the gambling tables of Monte Carlo. He died in an automobile accident in 1965. He was having money problems. A poor, old playboy is hardly welcome on the international scene.

Barbara Hutton, however, was always welcome on the international scene. Sick and old, tired and disillusioned, Barbara was always warmly accepted by the aristocracy of Europe. Despite her suffering, the numerous operations on her stomach, she was always sweet, always thoughtful, and always generous. And generosity was the paramount thing money-hungry aristocrats with no desire to work admired.

One of the many good-looking aristocrats who were attracted by her generosity was the dashing blond athlete, Gottfried von Cramm, a Baron who was most graceful on the tennis courts. Barbara herself was too weak to play tennis, but there was nothing she liked better than watching the game itself. Barbara felt a foreboding when Gottfried began courting her. This hard, Germanic man rather reminded her of Kurt Reventlow. The mere thought of Reventlow made her have a drink and a Seconal. Barbara was still on those blessed barbiturates and champagne that would keep her in that pink cloud that was essential in her ivory tower.

"I'm mad for you, darling Barbara," Gottfried kept telling her. He was so virile, so masculine. She found it difficult to resist him.

"You absolutely cannot get married a sixth time," wrote Aunt Jessie Donahue.

"He's just like Kurt," telegraphed Jimmy.

Willfully, Barbara became Madame la Baronne von Cramm in a romantic wedding ceremony in Versailles, in the shadow of the palace where Marie Antoinette used to live. Barbara promptly settled $2,000,000 on him. She was rather astonished when the athletic bridegroom asked for a million more to restore his mother's and brothers' castles in Germany.

"The roofs are very bad," said Gottfried, "and the rain comes in."

"Dear me," replied Barbara dryly. "We mustn't have that."

She visited Germany and reported that Gottfried's mother and brothers treated her like a leper. The memory of the war and their defeat was still fresh, and they hated this notorious American heiress of a five-and-ten-cent-store fortune. They were barely civil to her. As it was, they spoke German all the time in front of her. She felt as bad as those old days in Farmington when those nasty little girls shunned her. However, born people-pleaser that she was, she paid for everything. Her relationship with von Cramm was never the same. They lived very separate lives for years and divorced finally in 1961.

I met the frail and ailing Barbara during this period of disenchantment. The first thing I did when I arrived in Venice that memorable August evening was to go to Harry's Bar and rub shoulders with Afdera and Henry Fonda, and Consuelo and Rudi Crespi, two of the most glamorous couples I've ever seen. There was glamor everywhere in Venice that year of 1957 and, more than anything, I wanted glamor and excitement! I was highly imitative in finding myself and discovering what was important to me. So, wide-eyed, downing one champagne and peach juice after another, I listened, listened, listened. There were enough stories in Venice that year to write several scandalous books. Maria

Callas and Onassis were beginning their greatly publicized passion. Ari's wife, Tina, was seething. Elsa Maxwell was promoting Callas and even gave a stupendous Headress Ball on the rooftop of the Danielle Hotel in her honor.

What appealed most to my romantic imagination was Barbara Hutton and the greedy hangers-on that formed a phalanx around her whenever she stepped out of the Grand Hotel. Harry's Bar was buzzing with stories of the rapacious ways of the Hutton courtiers and her *dame de compagnie,* not to mention the cold and ruthless von Cramm, who ignored his wife completely now that he had his settlement and his castles restored.

The next morning I saw Barbara arriving at the dock of the Excelsior Hotel at the Lido Beach. Her entrance was reminiscent of Cleopatra, however Gottfried von Cramm was certainly no Marc Antony. She was surrounded by hand-kissing courtiers who often reaped their rewards. Barbara gave one courtier a $100,000 Paris apartment while a female hanger-on received half-million-dollar dowries for her children.

Barbara was dressed in scarlet Chinese beach pajamas with frogs running down the blouse. She wore her famous pearls and her tiny feet appeared like sculpture in her gold sandals. She looked incredibly pale and vulnerable. The five courtiers and prince consort–husband formed a protective circle around her and made their triumphant way to their cabana on the hot yellow sands. Later, as I was walking by her cabana, her huge eyes caught mine and they seemed to plea for help.

The unsurpassed brilliance of the Venetian season began. Its glitter and grandeur still lingers in my mind, every detail etched clearly in my memory. At the magnificent Renaissance palace of Charlie Beistigui, Barbara and I exchanged a few words while her retinue glared like fierce tigers. We managed some more conversation at the grandiose palace of Countess Lily Volpi. The next evening at the Palazzo Papadopoli, Barbara and I talked beneath a ceiling by Tiepolo. The following evening, at the gorgeous gothic palace of Count and Countess Brando Brandolini, my host and hostess for many summers, Barbara and I stood, holding hands, on a marble balcony on the Grand Canal and talked intimately. The fragrance of tuberoses was heavy in the summer evening air and candles flicked in the stately rooms with their frescoed ceilings and thick golden brocade walls. What a romantic scene it was, with the moon rising over the palaces across the water and gondoliers serenading on the canal.

"Come to Paris, Philip sweetheart," Barbara was saying.

"I will."

"I'm so lonely and frightened."

"I'll help you."

"You can save me!" she whispered.

And so my friendship began with my old childhood idol, Barbara Hutton. We spent the whole autumn together in Paris and arrived in New York on November 14, which happened to be Barbara's forty-fifth birthday. We promptly went to stay with Jimmy Donahue in his house, Broad Hollow, the great Georgian manor house in Old Brookville, Long Island, that he bought from Alfred Gwynne Vanderbilt. Here Jimmy played the country squire in a house designed for the English country gentleman by Billy Baldwin.

Jimmy and I became friends. He'd been friends with my mother before the war and he understood. He realized that I loved Barbara and had her best interests at heart. Jimmy used to go into New York nearly every night, and he'd come home at five o'clock in the morning, invariably high.

One early morning before Christmas, he woke me up and we drank by the fire downstairs. "I guess you think Barbara and I are just a couple of fools. Yes, you might call us the biggest misfits in the world."

"But you can change, can't you?" I said innocently.

"Rich people like Barbara and me don't have to change," replied Jimmy angrily.

"Why not?" I asked.

"Because there'll always be people like you who will put up with us, because we're so sweet and charming and lovable."

"Yes, you are that," I replied thoughtfully.

"Say what you want about inherited wealth," said Jimmy. "It's kept me and Barbara from hitting bottom. Mother was always there to pick up the pieces. Whenever I get into any scandal, she merely writes out a check. Do you understand?"

"Then you don't ever want to pull yourself together, do you, Jimmy?" I asked.

"Rich people like me and Barbara don't have to pull ourselves together," replied Jimmy.

"That's too bad," I said.

"Too bad!" He gave a raucous laugh. "Why, we've always lived in an ivory tower, existing in a divine state of euphoria created by manic spending orgies. Have you ever known anyone to spend like Barbara?"

"No," I replied, feeling slightly depressed.

"Cardinal Spellman tells me I shouldn't talk like this," continued Jimmy drunkenly. "He says I should have faith in the future, faith in tomorrow. But can you imagine me or Barbara changing our tomorrows?"

"I guess not," I replied sadly.

"People are stuck with us for better or worse," laughed Jimmy loudly. He raised his glass gaily. "If they don't like it, they can go to hell!" He smashed his glass against the fireplace. Whenever Jimmy drank a lot of whiskey, he had a Jekyll and Hyde personality change. He became mean, and frankly he was a bad drunk.

His roommate Joey saved the day. He was a puffy-faced man with red veins in his nose, but he had charm and obviously adored Jimmy. "Come on, old boy," he said, taking Jimmy's arm. "I'll take you up to bed."

Jimmy reeled out of the room leaning on Joey Mitchell.

"You see, Philip, there's always somebody to pick up the pieces. Who's going to pick up your pieces?"

"Am I such a mess?" I asked.

"Not yet you aren't, but you stay with Barbara and you will be. And frankly, Philip, don't you want to get out and make a life of your own? Oh, I know you think of Barbara as a mother and you miss your mother, but take it from one who knows, forget your mother and go forward. You've got the guts and character to make it on your own."

"I do?"

This scene made quite an imprint on me. And I hated being dependent.

Early in January, Barbara and I flew off to Mexico City. Jimmy Douglas was part of the entourage now.

Barbara and I said goodbye one afternoon in Acapulco a month later. Fortunately, I'd always had a wholesome strain and I knew for my survival's sake that I must leave Barbara. Jimmy Donahue's words still rang in my ears. I had to make a life of my own. I was twenty-nine. It was time for me to grow up. For better or worse I must try it on my own.

It was an emotional moment for me, because I was not only saying farewell to Barbara but to my mother as well. I bent down and kissed her. "Goodbye, Barbara," I said, and the tears streamed unchecked down my face the way they had ten years before when I saw my mother lying in the coffin.

"Goodbye, Philip dear," she said. She gazed up at me from those enormous blue eyes fringed with long black lashes. "Remember, sweetheart, you'll never meet a woman again such as Barbara."

I never did.

Jimmy Douglas was Barbara's constant companion for two years. They traveled all around the world together. They visited India, Hawaii, China, Siam, Austria, and Egypt. All the places that Barbara had visited with Alexis and Kurt and Igor and Gottfried.

Lloyd Franklin was a brawny young Englishman who came into Barbara's life in 1960. Lloyd was twenty years old and described as a Greek god. He was wonderfully wholesome and fresh-looking. Barbara was almost fifty at the time, but she hungered for this boy as she'd never hungered for anyone. She met him one night in a bar in Tangier. He was playing the guitar and singing in a pleasant deep voice. His shirt was open to the waist and his powerful chest reminded her of Alexis's.

She stayed at the nightclub until five o'clock in the morning, listening to Lloyd sing and play. She sent one of her courtiers over to him and he joined her for a drink. They talked a moment in the candlelight, and then he said, "I'd love to see your palace in the Casbah."

She stood up and took his arm.

"Then come," she said. . . .

Barbara and Lloyd vanished into the Casbah and weren't seen for a month. When he emerged, he was no longer a hippie but an English Lord. Saville Row clothes, Cartier watch, and a new sophisticated hairdo completed the picture. He also began to play polo. In the springtime, they went to Paris and London, in the summers they went to Tangier. In the fall they went to Venice. A few weeks in Paris followed, and then the inevitable visit to Jimmy Donahue and Aunt Jessie in New York. After a month in Mexico the happy pair went on to Hollywood and Honolulu.

And so life continued for Barbara Hutton. The same old circle, the same old routine. Yes, it was Barbara's fate that she could never change.

In early 1964, Barbara learned that her Lloyd was having a big love affair with an Indian maharanee in Deauville, where he was playing polo. Barbara thought her heart would break when she heard the news. A few weeks later, when Lloyd returned, she told the servants not to allow him into the house. From a Persian window, she watched his husky figure depart with a sorrowful air. He kept looking back, but once you've crossed Barbara, you're through forever. Her pride couldn't allow her to be made a fool of by a twenty-four-year-old. After all, she was Barbara Hutton.

To get revenge on Lloyd, she married an artist that she'd seen around the Casbah. He was handsome and robust like all of her admirers. His origins were obscure, so she had him elevated to the title of Prince Doan Vinh Na Champassak. Barbara became Princess Doan in a civil ceremony by the pool of her exotic Japanese-style palace in Cuernavaca, Mexico. The groom was three years younger than Barbara. Lance was by her side as he always was at the weddings.

They separated in 1966. The prince said nobly, "She gave me more than four million. She gave me love."

Barbara said she would never marry again. This time, her words were truthful. Barbara Hutton was finished with marriage. The next thirteen years of her life were sad ones.

CHAPTER 42

Barbara staggered under a series of cruel blows. The first tragedy was Jimmy Donahue's death at the age of fifty-one in 1966. She never quite recovered from this blow. The year after Jimmy's terrible death came Lloyd Franklin's demise. Lloyd was only twenty-six years old. Like Alexis Mdivani, he was decapitated in his car. He was passing a car on a road outside of Tangier when a truck abruptly appeared and smashed into him.

The long procession to the graveyard had begun. Ticki told her that she was going to die. Barbara's reaction was, "Ticki, you can't leave me! I forbid it!"

Like her grandfather, Barbara became grandiose at the end of her life. The grandiosity had always been there, lurking under the surface, but it became more apparent in old age, as these character defects do.

The cruelest blow of all was the death of Lance. Mother and son had become closer and had a real rapport. They began to understand and accept each other. He was killed in a plane crash in

1972 at age thirty-seven. He had been married to and divorced from Jill St. John, the actress, and Cheryl Holdridge, a former Walt Disney Mousketeer. Lance had been intimate friends with Cary Grant throughout his life, telephoning Cary whenever he needed advice. Lance felt nothing but contempt for his father, especially since Count Kurt passed himself off as a pillar of the community in Newport, Rhode Island. He was very much the grand gentleman, a model of propriety and morality. He hotly denied that he ever received any money from Barbara. "He enjoyed the good life on Barbara's money," Jimmy Donahue often said.

A few months later, Aunt Jessie Donahue died. For a long time she had been slipping into senility, and at the end was rather like Barbara's grandmother, poor Jennie Creighton Woolworth, who spent the last years of her life rocking on the porch of the great sixty-room house in Glen Cove, Long Island. Mrs. Donahue rocked away in her luxurious twenty-eight-room duplex. In the daytime, the curtains were always drawn, all the heavy green jade lamps were burning feebly, and someone's noble ancestors were staring down at her.

Barbara became close to Woolworth Donahue, Jimmy's brother, toward the end of his life. She spent many enjoyable weeks in Palm Beach with Wooly and his good-looking blonde wife, Mary. Cielito Lindo, the enormous old house that Jessie Donahue had built in the twenties, had been torn down, but Wooly lived comfortably in a rambling twenty-room hacienda surrounded by a high wall and barking dogs. Whenever Barbara visited, there was a cordon of policemen guarding the gates.

The last time Barbara stayed with Wooly in 1973, he was dying of cancer. There is a telling picture of the two cousins together. Barbara is more frail than ever, her face is a mask. A stony remoteness seemed to have hardened her features. Her expression seemed to say, "Nothing can hurt me anymore." With Wooly's death, her last Donahue relative was gone. Barbara suddenly realized she was totally alone, without a relative in the world.

By the mid-1970s, Barbara had gone into a decline. Her doctors told her she could travel no more, so she holed up at the Beverly Wilshire Hotel in Hollywood. She had broken her hip, her teeth and gums had given out, and her eyesight was troubling her. Toward the end, light bothered her so that she kept the lights dimmed with pink Kleenex tissues over the light bulbs.

The world for the most part had forgotten Barbara Hutton, but now and then her name cropped up in the newspapers. In the spring of 1978, a book titled *Heiress* about Barbara's aunt, Marjorie Post Hutton Davies, the General Foods queen, was published. In one section, Marjorie's granddaughter Marwee rambled on:

> Then I got tied up with Barbara Hutton. Dina [Merrill] put me onto that problem. She has been living out here—first at the Beverly Hills Hotel, now at the Beverly Wilshire. She's in a pretty bad way . . . and broke, too. It's no surprise, the way she was giving away those hundred-thousand-dollar bracelets to maids and nurses.

Even the staid old *New York Times* stated in July 1978:

> Barbara Hutton, the Woolworth heiress who lives in seclusion in the Beverly Wilshire Hotel in Los Angeles, was ordered by a court there to pay Thomas Creech, her former chauffeur, $12,000 in wages she has owed him since 1976. Mr. Creech contended in a suit that in the six years he worked for Miss Hutton he was obliged to perform many chores that had nothing to do with driving, such as lining the windows of her suite with aluminum foil to keep out the sunlight, keeping lamp shades covered with pink napkins and insuring that the 65-year-old Miss Hutton was served only round ice cubes, as she dislikes square ones.

Jimmy Douglas, still amazingly youthful despite his fifty years, was a yearly visitor. He reported to friends in his native Paris that Barbara was still lovely-looking and that there were times when she was gay and full of fun as in the old days. However, he continued, Barbara had good days and then she had bad days. The world press printed that Barbara had lived on Coca-Cola, that she traveled with dozens of cases of Coca-Cola everywhere she went. Jimmy reported, nevertheless, that Barbara drank a potion, a mysterious elixir concocted by her health doctors, which was noncaloric and yet filled with all the essential vitamins one needed to survive.

Jimmy also told me that Barbara no longer drank alcohol, that she had even given up Seconal. Having been addicted to barbiturates for years, she showed real strength of character by ridding herself of this compulsion. Jimmy went on to say that it was Barbara herself who had spread the rumor that she was broke. She didn't want to be an easy prey to all the nurses, doctors, and chauffeurs who came and went in her hotel suite. Even this showed a progression in Barbara's character.

Barbara told her visitors: "The biggest worry in a woman's life when she becomes sick and old and infirm is not loneliness. That's bad enough, God knows. The most pressing worry is lawyers. Lawyers suddenly don't want just a piece of cake, but the whole cake. Yes, they're far more lethal than those greedy husbands I had."

Barbara's fears became paranoid. She told her visitors that she was kept a prisoner in the hotel, that all her mail was opened, and telephones tapped. She complained that none of her old friends could get in contact with her because of this. She told Jimmy that her money had been mismanaged, but at least she had her jewelry left.

Even though she had rid herself of the Seconal and alcohol, the old terrors were still with her. When the blue light would descend and darkness settle over the purple hills of Los Angeles, the old phantoms gathered around her. Her father, jeering at her, the Farmington girls glaring at her spitefully, Alexis's decapitated body in the car accident, all flashed before her mind. And then there was the cruel death of Lloyd and darling Lance. There was no one close to her heart anymore, like Jimmy Donahue, whom she could telephone.

Barbara had often told the press: "Nothing infuriates me more than rich people who keep saying they're unhappy because they have wealth. I always tell them they should go down on their knees and thank God they have money."

But would Barbara Hutton be comforted by her money in her final destination? It seemed there was nothing or no one to fall back on now.

CHAPTER 43

One rainy afternoon at the Ritz Hôtel in Paris, Barbara was telling me about her life in Hollywood in the 1940s when illness struck her.

"And then what happened after Cary Grant?" I asked.

"It was all over," she said.

"All over?"

"My life was finished," she said sadly.

"Nothing happened after Cary Grant?" I pursued.

"My life ended when I became ill in 1945. I was only thirty-three, but my life was finished."

"How so?"

"After my divorce from Cary, there was an endless period of emergency rooms and operations. Many times the doctors said I would die. When you lose your health, your whole personality changes and you become self-absorbed and remote. The magic spark that makes life such an exciting thing is snuffed out and only a shell remains."

I was moved to tears. "Oh, Barbara," I said, "what an awful thing to say."

"It would have been better if my life had ended back in 1945," she intoned tragically. "Soldiers die when they're eighteen. They say the good die young. What do you think?" She watched me, then added, "Frankly, I no longer ask myself these questions, because I'll never know the answers. In any case, I'm grateful for each new day I'm alive, even if I am in a kind of a prison here." She gave an empty laugh. "There are no bars on the windows here, no locks on the doors, no armed guards to restrain me. But I'm frightened, frightened of everything . . . frightened to go out on the streets . . . frightened of anxiety attacks and frightened of feelings of disorientation."

Years later I was to feel these mental tortures myself and often reflected that I could have helped Barbara if I'd understood the nature of her illness. You only understand this hell if you've been through it yourself.

Barbara Hutton died of a heart attack in her rooms at the Beverly Wilshire in Beverly Hills, California, on Friday, May 11, 1979. She was sixty-six years old, almost the same age as her Grandfather Woolworth when he died. Ironically, it was the hundredth anniversary of the opening of the Woolworth stores. Even though Barbara was forgotten for the most part, her obituary was on the front page of the *New York Times*. Many other newspapers compared her life-style with Howard Hughes'. At the mortuary where her body was taken, the attendants said they had no idea that Barbara Doan was the famed Woolworth heiress, Barbara Hutton. Her lawyer telephoned to say the body would be flown to New York on Monday. All of Barbara's many friends tried to find out where the funeral was. Too late, we all learned that there was a memorial service at Woodlawn Cemetery in the Bronx, in the Woolworth mausoleum. Only ten people were there at the service, Barbara's first cousin, Dina Merrill, and her husband Cliff Robertson among the group. Dina Merrill is the former Nadenia Hutton, the daughter of Barbara's Aunt Marjorie and Uncle Ed Hutton.

Now, thinking of Barbara's life, I am reminded of a poem she read me from her book, *The Wayfarer,* those long-ago autumn days at the Paris Ritz:

Can it all be in vain?
The hopes and sorrow;
The laughter and tears;
And dreams of tomorrow?